DEEP
TRUTH

Other Hay House Products by Gregg Braden

Books

The Divine Matrix

Fractal Time

The God Code

Secrets of the Lost Mode of Prayer

The Spontaneous Healing of Belief

CD Programs

An Ancient Magical Prayer (with Deepak Chopra)

Awakening the Power of a Modern God

Deep Truth (abridged audio book)

The Divine Matrix (abridged audio book)

The Divine Name (with Jonathan Goldman)

Fractal Time (abridged audio book)

Speaking the Lost Language of God

The Spontaneous Healing of Belief

Unleashing the Power of the God Code

All of the above are available at your local bookstore, or may be ordered by visiting:

Hay House USA: **www.hayhouse.com**®
Hay House Australia: **www.hayhouse.com.au**
Hay House UK: **www.hayhouse.co.uk**
Hay House South Africa: **www.hayhouse.co.za**
Hay House India: **www.hayhouse.co.in**

DEEP TRUTH

Igniting
the Memory of
Our Origin, History,
Destiny, and Fate

GREGG BRADEN

HAY HOUSE, INC.
Carlsbad, California • New York City
London • Sydney • Johannesburg
Vancouver • Hong Kong • New Delhi

Published and distributed in the United States by: Hay House, Inc.: www
.hayhouse.com • *Published and distributed in Australia by:* Hay House Australia Pty. Ltd.: www.hayhouse.com.au • *Published and distributed in the
United Kingdom by:* Hay House UK, Ltd.: www.hayhouse.co.uk • *Published and
distributed in the Republic of South Africa by:* Hay House SA (Pty), Ltd.: www
.hayhouse.co.za • *Distributed in Canada by:* Raincoast: www.raincoast.com •
Published in India by: Hay House Publishers India: www.hayhouse.co.in

Editorial consultation: Stephanie Gunning • *Editorial supervision:* Jill Kramer
Cover design: Charles McStravick • *Interior design:* Pam Homan

The two photographs of Göbekli Tepe by Berthold Steinhilber originally appeared
in *Smithsonian* magazine in November 2008.

Library of Congress Cataloging-in-Publication Data

Braden, Gregg.
  Deep truth : igniting the memory of our origin, history, destiny, and fate / Gregg
Braden. -- 1st ed.
     p. cm.
  ISBN 978-1-4019-2919-0 (hbk. : alk. paper) 1. Civilization--Philosophy. 2. Civ-
ilization--History. 3. Civilization, Modern. 4. Philosophical anthropology. I.
Title.
  CB19.B66 2011
  909.8--dc23
                                          2011017202

Tradepaper ISBN: 978-1-4019-2922-0
Digital ISBN: 978-1-4019-2920-6

15 14 13 12   6 5 4 3
1st edition, October 2011
3rd edition, October 2012

Printed in the United States of America

CONTENTS

*"It is the hallmark of any deep truth
that its negation is also a deep truth."*
— NIELS BOHR (1885–1962),
NOBEL PRIZE–WINNING PHYSICIST

A new world is emerging before our eyes. At the same time, the unsustainable world of the past struggles to continue. Both worlds reflect the beliefs that made them possible. Both worlds still exist—but only for now.

From the global crises of terrorism, collapsing economies, and war; to the deeply personal beliefs surrounding abortion, relationships, and family, the issues that divide us are clear reflections of the way we think about ourselves and our world. The fierce nature of our divsions is also a clear indication that we need new ways to think of our most cherished relationships.

New discoveries regarding our origin, our past, and the most deeply held ideas about our existence give us reasons to rethink the traditional beliefs that define our world and our lives—beliefs that stem from the false assumptions of an incomplete and outdated science. When we do, the solutions to life's challenges become obvious, and the choices become clear.

This book is dedicated to revealing the deepest truths of human life by sharing scientific discoveries that have yet to show up in our textbooks and classrooms; and nevertheless hold the key to the way we think of our world, one another, and ourselves.

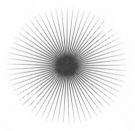

INTRODUCTION

There is a single question that lurks at the very core of our existence.

It's the unspoken question lying beneath every choice we'll ever make. It lives within every challenge that will ever test us, and it's the foundation for every decision we'll ever face. If God had a cosmic question "counter" to track the things we humans wonder about most, then I have no doubt that this device would have maxed out and returned to zero so often in registering this one question alone that even *God* would have lost count of how many times it's been asked!

The question at the root of all questions—one that has been asked countless times by countless individuals during the estimated 200,000 years or so that we've been on Earth—is simply this: *Who are we?*

While the question itself appears simple and brief, the way in which we answer it has implications that we simply cannot escape. It tears directly into the heart of each moment of our lives, and forms the lens that defines the way we see ourselves in the world and the choices we make. The meaning we give to these three words permeates the fabric of our society. It shows up in everything we do, from the way we choose the food that nourishes our bodies . . . to how we care for ourselves, our young children, and our aging parents.

Our answer to who we are underlies the core principles of civilization itself: it influences how we share resources such as food, water, medicine, and other necessities of life; when and why we go to war; and what our economy is based upon. What we believe about our past, our origins, our destiny, and our fate even justifies our thinking regarding when we choose to save a human life, and when we choose to end it.

In what may be the greatest irony of our existence, at the dawn of the 21st century, following more than 5,000 years of recorded history, we have still not clearly answered this most basic question about ourselves. And while at *any* time discovering the truth of our existence would be worth the time, energy, and resources needed to do so, as we currently face the greatest crises affecting life and survival in the memory of our species, it's especially critical for *our* time, here, now.

The Clear and Present Danger

One good reason for us to know who we are stands above all others. Maybe it's no coincidence that today, after three centuries of using the scientific method to answer the most basic question about ourselves, we also find ourselves in deep trouble here on planet Earth. It's not just any old run-of-the-mill trouble we're in. It's the kind of trouble of which dramatic novels and science-fiction blockbusters are made.

Just to be absolutely clear: It's not Earth that's in trouble. It's us, the people who *live* here on Earth. I can say with a high degree of confidence that our planet will still be here 50 years from now, and 500 years from now. No matter what choices we make during that time period—no matter how many wars we wage, and how many political revolutions we begin or how badly we pollute our air and oceans—the world that our ancestors called the "garden" will still be here making the same 365.256-day journey around the sun each year, just as it has for the past 4.55 billion years or so.

The question is not about Earth; it's about whether or not we will be *on* Earth to enjoy it. Will *we* still be here to enjoy the sunsets and sensual mysteries of nature? Will *we* witness the beauty of the seasons with our families and other loved ones? As I'll explore in a subsequent chapter, unless something changes soon, the experts are betting against us.

The reason? Because, when it comes to having what it takes for our children and us to live on Earth, we're dangerously close to making the choices that lead us beyond the "point of no return." This is the conclusion of an independent study on climate change co-chaired by Britain's former Secretary of State for Transport Stephen Byers and U.S. Senator Olympia Snowe (R-Maine), which was released in 2005. It stated that when it comes to the environment alone, we could reach that tipping point in as little as ten years and lose the fragile web of life that sustains us.[1] But the environment is only one of a host of crises facing us today, each leading us toward the same potentially deadly outcome for the human race.

The best minds of our time acknowledge that we're on multiple collision courses with disastrous outcomes—from the renewed threat of global war, the overuse of our resources, and the growing shortages of food and drinkable water; to the unprecedented stress we're placing on the world's oceans, forests, rivers, and lakes. The problem is that the experts can't seem to agree on what to do about these problems.

Act . . . but How?

Sometimes it's a good idea to study a problem thoroughly before we act. The more we know about a difficult situation, the more certain we can be that we've found the best solutions to the dilemma. But sometimes prolonged study is not so good. There are times when the best thing to do is act quickly to survive the immediate crisis, and only then to study the problem in detail from the safety of the time bought by taking decisive action.

Maybe the best way to illustrate what I mean here is with a make-believe scenario:

Let's say that on a beautiful, clear, and sunny day you're crossing a stretch of highway with a friend in order to get from your house on one side of the road to your friend's home on the other. Suddenly you both look up after being engrossed in deep conversation and see a huge 18-wheel tractor-trailer rig coming directly toward you.

Instantly your body's "fight or flight" response kicks in so that you can act. The question is: *How?* You have to decide quickly what to do. You and your friend both must choose, and choose fast.

So there you are, in the middle of the highway, with three lanes in front of you and three lanes behind you. Your dilemma is this: Do you have time to move forward to your destination—the other side—or is it best to move backward to the place you began? To answer the question with absolute certainty, you would need information that you simply don't have at your fingertips in this moment. You do not know, for instance, whether the truck is empty or loaded. You may not be able to tell precisely how fast it is moving or whether the driver can even see you on the road. You might not be able to recognize if it's a diesel- or gasoline-fueled truck that's coming your way, or what make the vehicle is.

And this is precisely the point. You don't need to know all of those details before you act. In the moment that you're crossing the highway, you already have all of the information necessary to tell you you're in a bad place. You already know that your life is in danger. You don't need such details to recognize the obvious: there's a big truck heading your way . . . and if you don't move quickly, in a matter of seconds nothing else is going to matter!

While this scenario may sound like a silly example, it's also precisely where we find ourselves on the world stage today. Our paths as individuals, families, and nations are like that of you and your friend walking across the highway. The "big truck" that's bearing down upon us is the perfect storm of multiple crises: situations such as climate change, terrorism, war, disease, the disappearance of food and water, and a host of unsustainable ways of dealing with everyday living here on Earth. Each crisis has the potential to end civilization and human life as we know it.

We may not be in agreement as to precisely why each of these events is occurring, but that doesn't change the fact that they are actually happening now. And, like two friends deciding to move forward across the highway or go back to the safety of where they've come from, we could study each crisis for another 100 years . . . yet the fact is that there are people, communities, and ways of life that will not survive the time it takes for all of the data to be compiled, the reports to be published, and the results to be debated.

The reason is that while we're evaluating the problem, people's homes will be destroyed by earthquakes, "superstorms," floods, and war; the land that sustained them will stop producing food; their wells will dry up; oceans will rise; coastlines will disappear— and those individuals will lose everything, including their lives. While these scenarios may sound extreme, the events I'm describing are already occurring in places such as Haiti, Japan, the Gulf Coast of the United States, and drought-ridden Africa . . . and it's getting worse.

Just as it makes tremendous sense to move out of the path of the big truck coming your way on the highway before you study the problem further, it makes tremendous sense to move out of the way of the multiple disasters looming on the horizon before they take an even greater toll.

And just as the direction you choose to move on the highway determines whether or not you get to your friend's house on the other side, the way we decide to take action in the face of the greatest threats to our existence will determine whether we succeed or fail, live or die. Our choices for survival all point back to the way we think about ourselves in the world, and how our thinking leads us to act.

The message of this book is that we must act wisely and quickly to head off the collision that awaits us on the highway of life we've chosen to cross. Maybe Albert Einstein said it best: "A new type of thinking is essential if mankind is to survive and move toward higher levels."[2] Developing a new level of thinking is precisely what we need to do today. We know the problems exist. We've already applied the best minds of our time, and the best science based upon the best theories available, to study those problems. If we were on the right track with our thinking, doesn't it make sense that we would have more answers and better solutions by now? The fact that we don't tells us we need to think differently.

The Dilemma

In recent years, an explosion of new discoveries throughout the sciences has left little doubt that many long-standing views about life, our world, and our bodies have to change. The reason is simple: *The ideas are wrong.* New evidence has given us new ways to think about the perennial questions of life, including where we've come from, how long we've been here, how we can best survive the crises that face our world, and what we can do now to make things better. While the new discoveries give us hope, despite the breakthroughs we still have a problem: the time required for us to integrate these discoveries into the accepted way of thinking may be longer than the time that's available to us to solve the crises. The state of biology is a perfect example of how this works.

The recently developed science of *epigenetics* is based upon scientific fact. It proves that the genetic code that we call the "blueprint of life," our DNA, changes with our environment. The piece that traditional scientists are reluctant to talk about is that the environment changing our DNA includes more than the toxins in our air and water, and more than the electromagnetic "noise" inundating those who live among the power lines, transformer stations, and cell-phone towers of the biggest cities in the world. The environment includes our very personal, subjective experiences of beliefs, emotions, and thoughts as well.

So while the scientific evidence tells us that we *can* change the DNA at the root of the life-threatening diseases that ravage our friends and loved ones, the textbooks that Western medical doctors rely upon still teach us that we can't, saying that we're victims of heredity and other factors beyond our control. Fortunately, this is beginning to change.

Through the work of visionary scientists such as stem-cell biologist Bruce Lipton, author of *The Biology of Belief* (Hay House, 2008), the surprising results of the latest studies are slowly percolating into the textbooks we rely upon for medical understanding. However, the conduit that carries these new discoveries about our cells—as well as those updating what we know of the origin of our species, our civilization, and the details of our past—is a system that is notoriously slow. The general rule for the lag time between a scientific discovery and its review, publication, and acceptance—before it shows up in the textbooks—is eight to ten years, and sometimes longer. And this is where the problem becomes obvious.

The best minds of today tell us in no uncertain terms that we're facing multiple crises posing threats of unprecedented magnitude, and that each of these crises must be dealt with immediately. We simply don't have eight to ten years to figure out how to adapt to the situation and head off the emerging threats of terrorism, war, and a nuclear arms race in the Middle East. These are issues that must be addressed *now*.

Our old ways of thinking—which include believing in survival of the fittest, the need for competition, and our separation from nature—have brought us to the brink of disaster. We're living at a time in history when we must confront the potential loss of all that we cherish as a civilization. It's precisely because we need new ways of thinking that the ancient question of who we are takes on a significance that is greater than ever. At the same time, a new mode of seeing the world, based upon a growing body of scientific evidence, is filling in the missing pieces of our knowledge and changing the way we think about ourselves.

In light of the new evidence regarding near–ice age civilizations, the false assumptions of human evolution, the origin and role of war in our past, and the undue emphasis on competition in our lives today, we must rethink the most basic beliefs that lie at the core of the decisions we make and the way we live. This is where *Deep Truth* comes in.

Why This Book?

While there is certainly no shortage of books that identify the extraordinary conditions threatening us today, they fall short of addressing the single element lying at the heart of how we deal with them. How can we possibly know what to choose—what policies to enact, what laws to pass—or how to build sustainable economies, share lifesaving technologies, and bridge the issues that are tearing at the fabric of our relationships and society . . . until we've answered the single question that lies at the very core of our existence: *Who are we?* As individuals, as families, as nations, and as a combined human civilization, we must first know who we are before we can make the right choices. It's especially important to do so now, at a time when every choice counts.

> How can we know what choices to make until we answer the single question that lies at the heart of each and every choice: Precisely *who* are we?

Without answering this fundamental question, making life-altering decisions is like trying to enter a house without knowing where the door is. While it's possible to break in through a window or knock down a wall, we'd damage the home in the process. And maybe this is a perfect metaphor for the quandary we find ourselves in. For our human family, which has more than quadrupled in size in a little over a century—from 1.6 billion in 1900 to about 7 billion in 2011—we can either use the key of understanding who we are to move through the door of successful solutions . . . or we can damage our home (Earth and ourselves) by responding to crises through the knee-jerk reactions of false assumptions based in incomplete science.

When we embrace the truths of our history on Earth, our planet's cycles of change, and the role these play in our lives, then we'll understand what we're really up against, what our options are, and what choices are available.

This book identifies six areas of discovery (and the facts they reveal) that will radically change the way we've been led to think about our world and ourselves in the past. As we address the great crises of our time, these are the most important truths we must consider:

— **Deep Truth 1:** Our ability to defuse the crises threatening our lives and our world hinges upon our willingness to accept what science is revealing about our origins and history.

As we face the never-before-seen threats that must be resolved within the next eight to ten years, how can we possibly know what choices to make, what laws to pass, and what policies to enact until we know who we are? The false assumptions of long-standing beliefs regarding evolution and human origins make little sense in the face of recent discoveries throughout the sciences.

— **Deep Truth 2:** The reluctance of mainstream educational systems to reflect new discoveries and explore new theories keeps us stuck in obsolete beliefs that fail to address the greatest crises of human history.

We base our choices of life, government, and civilization on the way we think about ourselves, our relationship to each other, and our relationship to planet Earth. For the last 300 years, these beliefs have come from the false assumptions of an outdated science. The sound principles of the scientific method have a built-in feature for self-correction of false assumptions that is effective when we allow the method to work as it was intended.

— **Deep Truth 3:** The key to addressing the crises threatening our survival lies in building partnerships based upon mutual aid and cooperation to adapt to the changes, rather than in pointing fingers and assigning blame, which makes such vital alliances difficult.

Our multiple crises (some induced by humans and some that have arisen naturally) have arrived at the tipping point of threatening the ultimate survival of our species. The industrial age has definitely contributed to the greenhouse gases in the atmosphere; and we certainly need to find clean, green, and alternative ways to provide electricity and fuel for the seven billion people who are presently living on our planet . . . however:

- *Fact:* Climate change is not human induced. The scientific evidence of 420,000 years of Earth's climate history shows a pattern of warming and cooling cycles at approximately 100,000-year intervals when no human industry was present.

- *Fact:* During the warming and cooling cycles of the past, the rise in greenhouse gases generally *lags behind* the temperature increase by an average of 400 to 800 years.

- *Fact:* It will take *never-before-seen* levels of synergy and teamwork to create sustainable lifestyles that help us adapt to natural cycles of change, as well as to address human-induced crises.

— **Deep Truth 4:** New discoveries of advanced civilizations dating to near the end of the last ice age provide insights into solving the crises in *our* time that our ancestors also faced in theirs.

While the scientific revelations involving near–ice age civilizations are upsetting the way historians traditionally think of humankind's journey through Earth's different ages, they support the oldest records of our past and the indigenous view of a cyclic world . . . with the rise and fall of civilizations, catastrophic events, and the consequences of poor choices repeating themselves.

— **Deep Truth 5:** A growing body of scientific data from multiple disciplines, gathered using new technology, provides evidence beyond any reasonable doubt that humankind reflects a design put into place at once, rather than a life-form emerging randomly through an evolutionary process over a long period of time.

While science may never identify precisely what, or who, is responsible for the design underlying our existence, the discoveries strongly challenge the conventional wisdom of evolutionary theory, and demonstrate that the chance that we resulted from random processes of biology is virtually nonexistent.

— **Deep Truth 6:** More than 400 peer-reviewed studies have concluded that violent competition and war directly contradict our deepest instincts of cooperation and nurturing. In other words, at the core of our truest nature we simply are not "wired" for war!

Why, then, has war played such a dominant role in shaping our history, our lives, and our world? Clues to the answer are found in the records of our early experiences on Earth, and the ancient accounts that hold instructions for ending the "war of the ages" and living at the heights of our destiny, rather than succumbing to the depths of our fate.

The sheer magnitude and number of crises converging in the first years of the 21st century pose a critical threat—a clear and present danger to our survival—and follow the cyclical trends that led to the loss and collapse of civilizations past. Knowing who we are, where we are in the cycles of civilization and nature, and the mistakes of past civilizations that we can learn from is the key to surviving the crises facing us today.

The best science of our time, when it is married to the wisdom of our past, confirms that we still have the ways and means to shift our time of crisis into a time of emergence. We can create a new world based upon actionable and sustainable principles rooted in the core understanding of our deepest truths.

In This Book

Through the seven chapters in this book, I invite you into an empowering, and possibly novel, way of thinking about your relationship to the world. For some people, this way of thinking may be nothing new. Maybe you were fortunate enough to be raised in a family that allowed current discoveries about civilization and life to fill in the missing pieces of your spiritual, religious, and historical views on the world.

For those who did not have such an upbringing, however, the chapters that follow open the door to a powerful, and practical, new path of self-discovery. Regardless of your beliefs, the evidence forcing humanity to rethink the traditional story of who we are, how long we've been here, and why the world seems to be "falling apart at the seams" is fascinating reading.

In the pages that follow, you will discover:

- Archaeological evidence leaving little doubt that advanced civilizations, with advanced technology, grew and flourished on Earth long before the traditionally accepted date of 5,000 to 5,500 years ago

- Why the wars we fight today stem from a way of thinking that began long ago, and why they're the modern continuation of an ancient battle that's not even ours

- Science-based evidence that human life is the result of an intelligent design

- A timeline illustrating when the human code of life is activated in the womb, when the first heartbeat of human life begins, and when consciousness awakens in human development

- A revised timeline of past civilizations (and how they fit into the world-age cycles) giving new meaning to the crises of today, as well as helping us define the choices that lie before us

It's important that you know up front what you can expect from your journey through these discoveries. For that reason, the following statements clearly explain what this book is, and what it is not:

- *Deep Truth* is <u>not</u> *a science book.* Although I will share the leading-edge science that invites us to rethink our relationship to the past, the cycles of time, our origins, and our habit of war, this work has not been written to conform to the format or standards of a classroom science textbook or a technical journal.

- *This is <u>not</u> a peer-reviewed research paper.* Each chapter and every report of research *has not* gone through the lengthy review process of a certified board or a selected panel of experts with a history of seeing our world through the eyes of a single field of study, such as physics, math, or psychology.

- *This book <u>is</u> well researched and well documented.* It has been written in a reader-friendly style that describes the experiments, case studies, historical records, and personal experiences supporting an empowering way of seeing ourselves in the world.

- *This book <u>is</u> an example of what can be accomplished when we cross the traditional boundaries between science and spirituality.* By marrying the 20th-century discoveries of genetics, archaeology, microbiology, and fractal time, we gain a powerful framework within which to place the dramatic changes of our age, and a context that helps us deal with those changes.

By its nature, the exploration of what and how we think of ourselves is different for everyone—it's a journey that is unique, intimate, and personal. So much of that difference stems from the experiences we share with our families, peer groups, and cultures. We've all been taught stories that explain our past and the origins of the earth and humanity, and that help us make sense of our world—stories based on what our community accepts as "truth" at a given point in time.

I invite you to consider the discoveries recounted in these pages and explore what they mean to you. Talk them over with the important people in your life; and discover if, and how, they may change the story that is shared in your family.

Deep Truth is written with one purpose in mind: to empower us (as we solve the crises of our lives and our world) to understand our relationship with the past. The key to empowerment is simply this: the better we know ourselves, the clearer the choices in our lives become.

No one knows for certain what the future holds. Quantum understanding tells us that we are always selecting our future through the choices we make in this very moment. But no matter which challenges await us or which choices we'll be faced with, one thing is absolutely certain: knowing who we are and understanding our relationship to one another, as well as to the world beyond, gives us the evolutionary edge that our ancient ancestors may not have had when they faced similar challenges in the past. With that edge, we tip the scales of life and balance in our favor. And it all begins with our awareness of the deepest truths of our existence, and how we rely on those truths each day for every choice in our lives.

— **Gregg Braden**
Santa Fe, New Mexico

CHAPTER ONE

WHO ARE WE?
IN SEARCH OF OURSELVES

*"Without an understanding of who we are, and from
where we came, I do not think we can truly advance."*

— LOUIS LEAKEY (1903–1972),
ARCHAEOLOGIST AND NATURALIST

"You imagine wonderful things and you imagine terrible things, and you take no responsibility for the choice. You say you have inside you both the power of good and the power of evil, the angel and the devil, but in truth you have just one thing inside you—the ability to imagine."[1] With these words from his novel *Sphere,* the late author Michael Crichton described the irony of our human experience as seen through the eyes of someone, or something, from beyond our world—in this case an alien sphere that has been on the bottom of the ocean for 300 years. And although the book itself is fictional, the insights revealed may hit closer to home than many of us would like to believe.

We are, in fact, mysterious beings of extremes and contradictions, which show up every day in the way we live and the choices we make. We say, for example, that we long for freedom in our lives, yet we allow ourselves to be bound by the fear of what we would do if we *had* all the freedom in the world. The fact that each cell in our bodies regenerates itself reminds us that we have the power to heal ourselves (we wouldn't be alive if we didn't), yet we refuse to acknowledge this power when it comes to healing our own diseases. We also claim to be beings of compassion, yet we are the only species that inflicts pain upon others to coerce information, or purely for entertainment. We say we desire peace in our world, while we continue to build the most destructive weapons of war ever known.

In our encounters with other worlds that may occur in the future, we will, no doubt, appear to any advanced forms of intelligent life as a conflicted species engaged in a constant struggle, wavering between the possibilities of a beautiful destiny and the death blows of our feared fate.

Now, having recently entered the second decade of the 21st century, we're faced with a humbling reality that brings the crises, extremes, and contradictions of our time into sobering focus. In the presence of the most advanced science in the history of our world, we still haven't answered the most basic question of our lives: *Who are we?*

The Jury Is Still Out

The U.S. Census Bureau tells us that we share our world with about seven billion fellow members of the human family. Although we may divide ourselves into separate groups, as defined by skin color, bloodlines, geography, and beliefs, we all share the same heritage when it comes to the origin of our species. And if each of us could be asked where we come from in a global door-to-door survey, there's a good chance that the responses would fall into one of three lines of thinking:

1. We are the product of a long line of miraculous synchronicities of biology (evolution) that have occurred over the last two million years.

2. We've been created, imbued with life, and placed on Earth directly by the hand of a greater power.

3. There is a grand cosmic pattern—an intelligent design—that makes us what we are; and this design was set into motion a long time ago by someone, or something, that we don't understand today.

While this quick summary may not entirely do these viewpoints justice, these three explanations, or some combination of them, form the core of all possibilities generally being considered today.

For thousands of years, the first and third explanations didn't even exist. Until 1859, essentially only one explanation was available to make sense of how we got here: the one invoked by the religious community. Based upon a literal interpretation of the biblical book of Genesis, the oldest document common to the world's three great monotheistic religions (Judaism, Christianity, and Islam), the belief essentially holds that we are here on purpose and were placed here personally by God.

This view remains popular in some communities today and is best recognized as *creationism,* a theory rooted in the religious doctrine proposed by Anglican bishop James Ussher more than 350 years ago. Combining the different biblical interpretations with the historical births and deaths recorded in the Bible of his time, Bishop Ussher created what he believed to be an accurate timeline for biblical events, commencing on the first day of creation.

Based upon his calculations, Ussher predicted that Sunday, October 23, 4004 b.c.e., was the first day of the world—the biblical "beginning" described in Genesis.[2] Using this date as the starting point, he followed the events and genealogies over time to arrive at the age that modern creationists, and specifically young Earth creationists, generally accept for the earth: 6,000 years.[3]

With this age as his benchmark, Ussher then calculated dates for key biblical events that relate to the origin and history of humankind. He determined, for example, that Adam was created in 4004 B.C.E., that Eve was created shortly thereafter, and that both were expelled from the Garden of Eden later the same year. Ussher's correlations were printed in authorized versions of the Bible in his day, and in 1701 the Church of England officially accepted Ussher's biblical chronology.

One of the creationist assumptions that stems directly from Ussher's work is that all life was created at once during Genesis. Additionally, the theory states that there are essentially no new species to be found in the world today. All life existing at present or in the past—including the human race—is supposedly the result of the original creation, and has remained fixed and unchanging.

These views are in direct conflict with two key points of modern science:

1. Geologists now place Earth's age at a staggering *4.5 billion* years old.

2. Mainstream biology largely accepts Darwin's theory of evolution as the mechanism responsible for the diversity of life on Earth today.

While the four-and-a-half-billion-year-old earth can sometimes be accepted by old Earth creationists, due to varying interpretations of how long a biblical day and year actually were, there is no such leeway when it comes to evolution. Charles Darwin's theory is in direct conflict with the theory of human origin through divine intervention, and there appears to be no middle ground for the two beliefs.

Darwin returned from his historic journey on the H.M.S. *Beagle* in 1836 and published his findings 23 years later, in 1859. His paradigm-shattering book, entitled *On the Origin of Species,* rocked the foundation of long-standing beliefs regarding our beginnings. While we will explore the ideas and implications of Darwin's work in greater depth later on, I mention them here because, for the first time, the theory of evolution challenged religious views in general, and specifically those of the Christian church.

I will state clearly at this point, however, that although Darwin's work was well thought out, meticulously documented, and performed within the guidelines of the scientific method, *a growing body of evidence now proves that it does not account for the facts of human origin as they're known today. Nor does it prove that we are the result of an evolutionary process.* This is not to say that evolution doesn't exist or hasn't occurred. It has. And the fossil record proves that it has for a number of specific species. The problem is that when we attempt to apply the processes observed in plants and some animals to humans—to us—the facts plainly don't support the theory.

So where does that leave us? What are we to believe? Which of the three viewpoints is the right one when it comes to our origin and our history? The jury is still out on this one, and the very topic is a trigger for heated debate. If we're relying upon the language of science, however, evolution is becoming less and less of a viable option to explain the complexities of human life.

In other words, the evolution that we see in nature may not apply to us. As you'll read about in the next section, there are things about our human family that simply cannot be explained by evolution, at least as we understand the theory today.

A Theory in Trouble

The scientific community since 1859, as well as much of the "modern" world since that time, has embraced evolution as the only plausible theory to explain human origins and how we've come to be what we are today. This widespread acceptance has led to the search for physical evidence to prove the theory: the fossilized "missing links" that should exist to document the stages of our journey. For reasons that are as controversial as the fossils themselves, for more than 150 years these missing links in our human ancestry have proven to be elusive at best.

More recently, the search for evidence of our ancestors has captured our collective imagination, as prestigious and credible journals such as *Science* and *Nature* have reported studies and featured full-page color plates documenting these discoveries. Seemingly overnight, recovered skulls with hollow eye sockets staring out at us from glossy images on magazine covers became members of our human family tree. They even took on names such as "Lucy" and "George" that made them seem more like family.

Growing up in the 1960s watching documentaries on my family's black-and-white television and reading about the search for our human origins in beautiful magazines like *National Geographic* and *Smithsonian,* it seemed as though there were updates almost on a daily basis regarding the search for our origins. While the search continues today, the latest discoveries appear to be less public, but are nonetheless ongoing. Some of the most productive areas for fossil evidence of our past have been located in remote portions of eastern Africa's Great Rift Valley. In northern Tanzania, for example, the Leakey family's multigenerational search for hominid remains—by Louis S. B. Leakey; his wife, Mary; their son Richard; and some of their other children—has pushed the accepted date of human origins back to about two million years ago.

During explorations since the 1950s, Leakey teams have painstakingly sifted through loose soil, pulverized rock, and grains of dust to recover bone fragments, teeth, stone tools, and sometimes entire skeletal sections of ancient beings that appear to have human characteristics. With complex-sounding names such as *Australopithecus afarensis* and *Homo neanderthalensis,* these are believed to be examples of human development along the ladder of evolution.

As impressive as these and similar findings are, and as much as they have added to our knowledge of the past, the search for human origins has been dogged by the lack of a single discovery that directly links such ancient forms of life to us.[4] And it may be that such a link will never be found. My sense is that, as interesting as the work in Africa is, and as much as it tells us about long-ago life-forms, it's probably not *our life history* that's being recovered.

Missing-Link Update: Still Missing

From 1859, when evolutionary theory was introduced, to the date of this writing, no clear evidence of a transitional species leading to us—the fossil evidence documenting our ancestors evolving into increasingly more humanlike beings—has surfaced. This fact remains despite the sophisticated technology and great manpower dedicated to resolving the question of our origins. A close look at the human family tree reveals that many of what are assumed to be undisputed links between fossil findings are, in fact, noted as suspected or *inferred* links.

In other words, the physical evidence that links *us* with the discovered remains of these creatures from the past has not been firmly established (see Figure 1.1).

**SPECULATIVE TREE
OF HUMAN EVOLUTION**

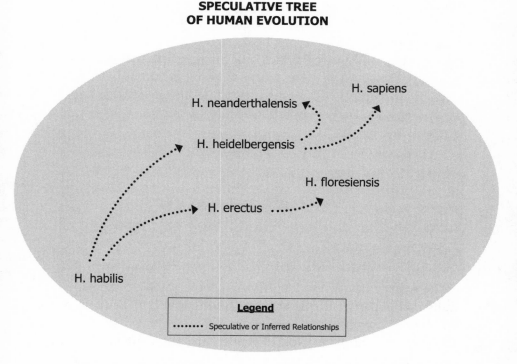

Figure 1.1. An example of the widely accepted chronology of ancient ancestors thought to lead to modern humans. Sequences such as this are largely interpreted from fossil evidence.

In *On the Origin of Species,* Darwin acknowledged this lack of evidence. He also acknowledged that it could be due to a flaw in one of two places: the way geologists think of the earth, or his theory of evolution. In his own words:

> As on the theory of natural selection an interminable number of intermediate forms must have existed . . . [w]hy do we not see these linking forms all around us? Why is not every geological formation charged with such links? We meet with no such evidence, and this is the most obvious and forcible of the many objections which may be urged against my theory.[5]

Reflecting upon this apparent quandary, Thomas H. Morgan, recipient of the 1933 Nobel Prize in physiology or medicine, stated that applying the "most rigid . . . tests used to distinguish wild species," we do not "know of a single instance of the transformation of one species into another."[6]

Two late-20th-century discoveries may begin to shed light on why the problem of a bridge between ancient and modern humans exists, and what the fact of a missing link may be saying to us about our history. For sound scientific reasons that will be explored in depth in a later chapter, while *Australopithecus afarensis* and Neanderthals may tell the story of *someone's* history, it's probably not *ours.*

What follows are two of the reasons why.

Interesting Fossils, but They're Not Us!

The first "map" describing the building blocks of life was established by James Watson and Francis Crick in 1953. Through their model of the DNA molecule, the door was opened for an entire science devoted to identifying people based on the genetic traits that make them who they are, and that also make them different from anyone else.

From eye and hair color, to gender, and the tendency toward developing certain diseases, the code for how our bodies look and work is stored in the blueprint of our genes, our DNA. Once

Watson and Crick unlocked the code holding the evidence of our past, the science of matching segments of DNA to determine paternity, identify missing persons, and link perpetrators to crime scenes has become a keystone in the fields of law enforcement and forensic medicine. It has also become the foundation for one of the most successful crime-solving series in the history of television: *CSI: Crime Scene Investigation.*

In 1987, the same techniques used in *CSI*-type investigations—the results of which are accepted as evidence in the highest courts of law today—were applied to the study of human origins for only the second time in history. In 2000, researchers at the University of Glasgow Human Identification Centre published the results of their investigation comparing DNA from a species believed to be our ancestor to that of modern humans.[7] Along with co-workers in Russia and Sweden, the Scottish scientists tested ancient DNA from an unusually well-preserved Neanderthal infant discovered in a limestone cave in northern Caucasus, at the border of Europe and Asia.

The exceptional condition of the child's remains is a story, and a mystery, unto itself. Normally this is the case only in frozen specimens, like those found in the icy polar regions. It was this state of preservation that allowed 30,000-year-old DNA from the infant to be compared to the DNA of humans today. It was also the first time that such tests could be performed on a body that had already been carbon-dated. The study concluded that the possibility of a genetic link between Neanderthals and modern humans is remote. The report suggests that modern humans are not, in fact, descended from Neanderthals.[8]

While in theory the science of genetic comparison should solve the mystery of our ancestry, the results are actually raising more questions regarding our evolutionary lineage and origins, and opening the door to "forbidden" territory.

The term *early modern human* (EMH), or *anatomically modern human* (AMH), has replaced *Cro-Magnon* as the descriptor for our closest ancestor. Scientists now believe that the physical differences between the bodies of contemporary humans and those of

EMHs are so slight that they don't justify a separate grouping. In other words, although ancient humans didn't necessarily behave like us, they *looked* like us. Or, conversely, we still look like them: our appearance hasn't changed much since our first ancestors appeared on Earth about 200,000 years ago. This fact has proven to be a problem for those who look to slow evolutionary changes over long periods of time to explain how we've come to be as we are.

In 2003, advances in DNA technology allowed for even more ambitious comparisons of ancient DNA. This time the tests compared Neanderthals and our earliest confirmed ancestors, the EMHs. The team of European scientists studied the DNA from two EMHs, one that was 23,000 years old and another that was 25,000 years old, with DNA from four Neanderthals between 29,000 and 42,000 years old. The findings, published in *Proceedings of the National Academy of Sciences,* stated: "Our results add to the evidence collected previously in different fields, making the hypothesis of a 'Neanderthal heritage' very unlikely."[9] In other words, the Neanderthals portrayed as the cavemen in motion pictures and cartoons are not the ancestors of EMHs. This means that we didn't evolve from them, and they cannot be *our* ancestors.

The Mystery of "Fused" DNA

Since the discovery of the genetic code, an additional mystery has emerged regarding the chromosomes that distinguish one species from another. Biological instructions are contained within the chromosomes for members of a species, determining things like the structure of their bones, the size of their brains, how they metabolize, and so on. Apes have 24 pairs of chromosomes, or a total of 48. Humans have 23 pairs, or a total of only 46. Although it looks like we're "missing" an entire set of chromosomes compared to our nearest relatives, our genetic maps reveal an interesting curiosity.

A closer look at where chromosomes appear to be absent from our genome shows that *human chromosome 2* is remarkably similar—and actually "corresponds"—to chromosomes 12 and 13 of the chimpanzee, *as if they somehow were combined* (fused) into a single larger piece of DNA.[10] Interestingly, this fusion occurred only in the case of humans.

I'm including the technical terminology from the *Proceedings of the National Academy of Sciences* (October 1991) that describes this fusion: "We conclude that the locus cloned in cosmids c8.1 and c29B is the relic of an *ancient telomere-telomere fusion* and marks the point at which two ancestral ape chromosomes fused to give rise to human chromosome 2."[11] (My italics.)

In other words, the two chromosomes that seem to be missing from our DNA appear to have been found, merged into a single new chromosome that is unique to us. Additionally, there are other characteristics of human and chimp genes that look almost identical.[12]

How did this merging of DNA happen? Scientists simply don't know. But the conclusion drawn from the studies opens a mysterious door that may allow us to ultimately find the answer to this question. It's the fact that these chromosomes are fused together, and the way they're fused, that has led scientists to conclude that only a rare process could have given rise to such a genetic phenomenon.[13] These studies are telling us that the arrangement of the DNA that makes human chromosome 2 (and us) unique is not something that we would normally expect from Darwin's evolution through natural selection.

What could have happened in the distant past to produce such changes in the fundamental code of life? The short answer is that we simply don't know. Based upon a comparison of human and primate physiology, however, there is a growing body of evidence suggesting that as *Homo sapiens,* we may not fit neatly into a traditional tree of evolutionary steps.

✻ ✻ ✻

New data from DNA, and the lack of fossil evidence support-ing the notion of human evolution from lower primates, suggests that we may, in fact, be a species unique unto ourselves. This theo-ry takes the approach that rather than being *descendants* of earlier forms of primates, we're separate and distinct from them. A com-parison of primate and human characteristics such as bone den-sity—and our ability to shed tears, perspire, and grow hair rather than fur—supports this theory, while fueling controversy for *both* proponents of creationism and evolutionary theory.

Although such findings may ultimately raise more questions than they answer, each stage of investigation adds to what we know about ourselves and further defines our place in the universe and our role in creation. Additional evidence in the fossil record lends credibility to these studies, indicating that, while we may share genetic characteristics with less evolved forms of life, *we've developed independently from them* along our own genetic timeline. Ours may be a much older species than previously thought, and we may have changed very little with respect to evolution during our time here.

Clearly, for both creationism and evolution, the sources of in-formation are incomplete, leaving interpretations open to revision as new evidence comes to light.

What We're Not

Sometimes we find the truth of what "is" in our lives by first discovering what "is not." Through the process of elimination, we eventually zero in on the understanding we're searching for. From our personal relationships with lovers, family, friends, and co-workers, to the war and peace between our nations, we seem to learn the great lessons of life in precisely this way. We *experience* what we don't want before we *learn* that we don't want it.

It was only after experiencing war on a global scale, for ex-ample, not once but twice, that we said no to more world wars. It was only after we experienced the unimaginable genocide of the mid-20th century that we said we would never allow events to unfold in that way again.

Many mainstream scientists, teachers, and researchers of our time are actively engaged in sifting through the discoveries of the last 100 years or so to discover what's true, and what's not, when it comes to human origins. Their discoveries are so numerous that they're being published on what sometimes feels like a daily basis. In fact, there is so much new information being reported so frequently now that scientific journals—such as *Science*, for example—have resorted to adding a weekly newsletter to their monthly publications to keep their subscribers up-to-date on the latest discoveries.

While all of this research is designed to help us understand what the 20th century revealed, many of the key discoveries that tip the scales one way or another on the issues scientists are investigating have yet to be presented in our textbooks and classrooms. This means that we're placing the hopes, trust, and promise of our future in the hands of young people who are learning science based upon obsolete beliefs.

Just as learning to operate a car without first understanding the rules of the road can't make for a healthy driving experience, reducing nature to atoms and molecules without learning about our relationship to them can't possibly lead to meaningful solutions for the crises facing us today. If we could bring the essence of the 20th-century discoveries regarding ourselves and our past together, what would they tell us? What does the best science of our time indicate about who we are and who we aren't?

The partial list that follows gives an idea where the new science may be headed. It is a fact that . . .

1. . . . the theory of living cells mutating randomly (evolving) over long periods of time does not explain the origin or complexities of human life.

2. . . . the biological link between humans and earlier humanlike life-forms in our ancestral tree is inferred and not proven.

3. . . . DNA studies prove that we did not descend from Neanderthal families, as previously believed.

4. . . . we have changed little since the early modern humans (EMHs) appeared about 200,000 years ago.

5. . . . it's unlikely that the DNA that makes us human and gives us our uniqueness could have formed in the way it has from natural processes of evolution.

So now that we know some of the things we're "not," what does the best science of our time tell us about who we *are?* The answer to this question is the key to the next six chapters of this book.

Three hundred years ago, the scientific thinking around Isaac Newton's laws of physics led us to view the universe, our world, and our bodies as if they were parts of a grand cosmic machine—that is, as huge and small systems that were separate from one another, independent from one another, and replaceable.

One hundred and fifty years ago, Charles Darwin proposed that we're the end product of a 200,000-year journey: survivors of an evolutionary competition who have had to fight for our place on Earth in the past, and must continue to do so today.

Also, the science of the last 100 years or so has led us to believe that technology is the answer to our problems, and that through science we will conquer nature and the threats to our survival.

Each of these ideas is based upon a false belief derived from scientific information that, at the very least, is incomplete. In some cases, it's just wrong.

Before we can answer the question of who are we, we must honestly consider the truths that we've asked science to reveal. In doing so, we quickly discover how the false assumptions of the past have led us into a proverbial rut on the road of discovery, where we are spinning our wheels in our search for the answers to life's mysteries.

The discoveries in the following chapters are real. They represent the kinds of news stories that should make for bold headlines in magazines and mainstream papers around the world. Instead, they are often relegated to obscure technical journals and news-letters with a limited number of technically minded subscribers. This may help us understand why our textbooks lag so far behind the discovery curve. It may also help us see where the thrust of exploration can lead with respect to the next great forays into the mysteries of our existence.

Deep Truth 1: Our ability to defuse the crises threatening our lives and our world hinges upon our willingness to accept what science is revealing about our origins and history.

CHAPTER TWO

THE DEEP TRUTH OF FALSE ASSUMPTIONS: DISCOVERIES THAT CHANGE EVERYTHING

"Sometimes a concept is baffling not because it is profound but because it is wrong."

— E. O. WILSON, BIOLOGIST AND NATURALIST

In 2008, two brothers released a film documenting their quest to answer some of the oldest and possibly most elusive questions out there, including "Who am I?" and "What is the meaning of life?" With critical recognition in the form of more than 30 major awards so far, Clifford and Jeffrey Azize created a stunning and powerfully moving film. It is simply titled *The Human Experience*.[1]

The poignant story line is highlighted through the brothers' sharing of images of rare personal encounters that range from meeting the lost children of Peru to visiting the abandoned lepers of Ghana. These life-altering encounters led them, and similarly lead viewers, on a journey to a deeper understanding of the universal experiences that bind us as a human family.

The questions posed in this film are among the same ancient and as-yet-unanswered ones that we humans have asked since our earliest ancestors tried to make sense of the cosmos, and our role in it, 200,000 years ago. Through the ages we have done our best to answer what have become known as the "perennial questions" of our existence: *Who are we? Where do we come from? How did we get here? Where are we going?* In every age, the best tools of the day have been used in this endeavor.

Our current era of science is no different. Science gives us a way of exploring the mysteries of the world and our bodies that makes sense out of the sometimes seemingly senseless things of life.

While I was trained as a scientist and taught to use the scientific method, no one ever really explained to me precisely what science *is* and *why* it has been such a successful way of exploring the world.

In the poetic language of a brilliant physicist, Einstein described science as the "attempt to make the chaotic diversity of our sense-experience correspond to a logically uniform system of thought."[2] In other words, it gives us a common language with which to explore the mysteries of life.

In its purest form, science is independent of the emotion or expectations that can sometimes change the way a scientist looks at the world. When scientists use the step-by-step procedures developed by other scientists in the past—what is known as the *scientific method*—it allows them to be certain that they're on solid ground when those accepted methods lead to new discoveries and these are shared with the world.

The dating of one of the world's most ancient archaeological sites is a perfect example of what I mean here. When researchers used ^{14}C (carbon-14) dating to find out how old the Göbekli Tepe (pronounced "Go-beckly Tep-ah") site in Turkey is, they followed an established method that has been widely accepted in the past. So when it showed that the site is between 11,517 and 11,623 years old—at least twice the age of ancient Sumer, long thought to be among the world's oldest civilizations—the data was based upon a proven approach, and the findings were taken seriously.

In general, the scientific method describes a sequence of steps that must be followed if an idea is to be accepted in the scientific community. Figure 2.1 illustrates this sequence.

The Scientific Method

1. We see something unexplained.
2. We develop an explanation (hypothesis).
3. We test the explanation with an experiment that gives us facts.
4. We evaluate the facts.
   a. If the facts support the explanation, we have a theory.
   b. If they don't, we need to go back to step 2, change our explanation, and repeat the process.

Figure 2.1. The four steps of the scientific method. This sequence gives us a consistent way to establish facts and discover where our thinking about something may not be supported by them. The scientific method is only as good, however, as the discipline and honesty of the individual who applies it.

There is a reason why I'm sharing the scientific method at this point in the book. From the sequence in Figure 2.1, we can see that if a new fact is uncovered that changes what we know about an existing idea, then the old belief must be updated to make room for the new information. The method allows for, *and expects,* new information to be discovered over time and assimilated into our existing canon of ideas and beliefs. When scientists discovered that the atom is not the smallest particle of matter, for example, and is actually made of even smaller particles, the old models of the atom became obsolete. They gave way to the new ones incorporating quarks, leptons, gluons, and so on. This updating of scientific knowledge with the confirmed facts of new discoveries is the key to keeping science honest, current, and meaningful.

To discount new and proven facts when they clearly do not support an existing scientific belief is, in fact, not scientific. But this is precisely what we see happening in the preparation of our textbooks and in our classrooms today. In the chapters that follow, we will explore new discoveries that have yet to be reflected in the educational curricula for a number of reasons, including reluctance to give up old models and ways of thinking. However, these are the very discoveries that help us make sense of the past, while holding the key to wise choices for our future.

In addition to giving us a good way to be consistent when we explore the natural world, science offers us a language with which to share what's been found in a meaningful way. So when a biologist says that something mysterious happens to a human embryo after the first three mitotic cell divisions, we can be certain of precisely the stage of development he or she is talking about.

I'd like to emphasize that there are other languages that describe our natural world. Some of them, such as alchemy and spirituality, have been around much longer than the brief lifetime of science. And while they're definitely not "scientific" (meaning they don't necessarily build upon the confirmed discoveries of the past to explain nature), they have been successful in helping us understand our relationship to the world, and to one another, for a very long time.

Apples, Magnets, and the Age of Science

It's generally accepted that modern science, and the scientific era, began in July 1687. It was then that Isaac Newton published his influential work *Philosophiae Naturalis Principia Mathematica* (in English, "The Mathematical Principles of Natural Philosophy") showing the mathematics that describes our everyday world.[3] For more than 200 years, Newton's observations of nature were the foundation of the scientific field now called *classical physics*.

Along with the theories of electricity and magnetism from the late 1800s and Albert Einstein's theories of relativity from the early 1900s, classical physics has been tremendously successful in explaining what we see as the "big things" in the world: the movement of planets and galaxies, apples falling from trees (according to a popular story, Newton discovered the law of gravitation after an apple fell on his head), and so forth. It has served us so well that using classical physics, we have been able to calculate the orbits for our satellites and even put men on the moon.

During the early 1900s, however, new discoveries showed us that there are places in nature where Newton's laws just don't seem to work. From the tiny world of particles within an atom, to the way atoms behave during the birth of stars in distant galaxies, some phenomena encountered by scientists simply could not be explained by this traditional brand of physics. The scientific way of answering questions says that if the existing thinking cannot explain what we see, then the way we think of the world must be updated to take into account the new observations and discoveries. The result of doing so in the world of physics produced what today is known as *quantum physics:* the study of the things that happen on a very small scale, dictated by forces underlying our physical world.

From the time that quantum physics appeared on the scientific stage, the great challenge has been to marry the two very different kinds of thinking represented by classical and quantum physics into a single view of the universe and life: a unified theory. So far, it hasn't happened. While some theorists have managed to solve individual pieces of the puzzle, none has yet solved the whole mystery. Just in the way new cracks seem to show up in a weak dam once existing ones are filled, the emerging theories have answered some questions while opening the doors to new ones—at times in places where no "doors" were even known to exist.

The evolution of *string theory* is a perfect example of such doors and cracks. In the 1980s, the idea that the universe is made of invisible vibrating strings of energy was believed to herald the next great revolution in physics. The deeper that physicists explored the theory, however, the more problems there appeared to be with the idea. "String theory was a bubble waiting to be pricked," says mathematician Peter Woit of Columbia University. "The fundamentals just weren't there anymore."[4]

Similarly, the initial promise of the Wheeler-DeWitt (WD) equation to unify classical and quantum physics faded quickly when the "fine print" became clear. To accomplish its seemingly impossible task, the WD equation left out the big factor that caused the problems: time itself. Although doing so helped with the mathematics, the fact remains that time is part of our world and our lives. Without it, any equations don't realistically represent the mystery they are trying to solve.

For now, however, the stark reality is this: It's been over a century since Max Planck formulated the core principles of quantum theory. After 100 years of the world's best scientific minds working with the best theories of mathematics and physics, testing these theories at the most advanced research facilities in the history of the world, it makes perfect sense to expect that by now we would have solved the big problems that plague our scientific worldview. That is, if we are on the right track.

It's because we haven't that we must now face the possibility that we may be on the *wrong* track.

Is Science on the Wrong Track?

If the basic ideas of how reality works are incomplete, then applying all of the brainpower and technology in the universe to those wrong ideas is not going to yield true answers. Regardless of a century's worth of teaching, millions of textbooks printed, and entire lifetimes and careers devoted to the theories—and the serious economic investment made to build and operate some of the most sophisticated machines ever devised to test them—if the ideas are wrong to begin with, they're never going to "get" right if we follow the same mistaken path that has led to them.

This is the big elephant of a concern that stands in the center of the room at each scientific symposium and conference being held anywhere in the world at present: Are we on the right track? When it comes to our relationship to our world, are we thinking the right way and asking the right questions?

In a 2010 article in *Prospect* entitled "Science's Dead End," physician James Le Fanu gives two examples of why many critics are questioning the value of new science and asking a question that looms even larger than "Is science on the right track?"[5] Le Fanu states his question boldly, asking out loud and publicly what others have only alluded to, or whispered behind closed doors. The question is this: *Is science stuck?*

Le Fanu explains why it's easy for us to think so:

> At a time when cosmologists can reliably infer what happened in the first few minutes of the birth of the universe and geologists can measure the movements of the continents to the nearest centimeter, it seems extraordinary that geneticists can't tell us why humans are so different from fruit flies, and neuroscientists are unable to clarify why we recall a telephone number.[6]

Le Fanu is right. And his example of humans and fruit flies is a perfect illustration of the problem.

Following the completion of the Human Genome Project (HGP) in 2001, scientists were astonished to learn that the genetic blueprint for a human is about 75 percent smaller than what had been expected. This is a huge discrepancy—about 75,000 genes were "missing"—and scientists had to acknowledge a difficult fact regarding what they had believed in the past. Before the results of this project, the thinking had been that there is a one-to-one correspondence between our genes and proteins. In other words, each of the proteins in our bodies comes from a single gene that holds instructions to make that protein.

After the HGP was completed, it was evident that this idea wasn't off just a little bit; it was *wrong!* The error was due to the belief that the one-to-one relationship between proteins and genes exists—a false assumption that scientists had made in the mid-20th century, and then built an entire belief system upon. In the end, the scientists also had to acknowledge that if so very few genes actually differentiate us from simpler forms of life, like Le Fanu's fruit flies or the common field mouse, then they were also wrong about what makes us unique.

Craig Venter, the president of a firm leading one of the gene-mapping teams, recognized this problem immediately when he stated, "We have only 300 unique genes in the human that are not in the mouse."[7] Taking the findings of his team one step further, Venter said, "This tells me genes can't possibly explain all of what makes us what we are."[8]

So this is one beautiful example of the quandary that a false assumption can create, and where it can lead. With only 300 genes separating us from a common mouse, where do we look to find out what makes us so different? If, as the evidence suggests, the difference is not in the DNA itself, then where is it? These questions have opened up what some have called a "Pandora's box" of possibilities leading us down a road from which there is no turning back. Scientists must now look *beyond* the DNA of the body to answer them. This puts us into the realm of unmeasured fields and unseen forces, a place where science has been reluctant to go in the past.

Ultimately, we may find that the key to discovering what makes us so different from other forms of life lies at the heart of our most ancient traditions and deeply held beliefs. Almost universally, these sources tell us that we are infused with what has been described as a special "spark" of a mysterious essence eternally joining us with one another and with something beyond our physical world that we can't see. It is this spark that sets us apart from all other forms of life on Earth.

The point of Le Fanu's comments and the discussion of mice and fruit flies is simply this: If we're really on the right track and we're really asking the right questions, then why haven't we bridged some of the great gaps in our understanding? Why can't we explain human consciousness or unite classical physics with quantum physics? Why is the question of when life begins in the womb still a mystery? And why don't we know who built the ancient civilizations that have now been dated back to the last ice age? Could it be that when it comes to the way we think of ourselves in the world, we have not only been *on* the wrong track, but we're *stuck* on that wrong track, which is leading us in the wrong direction?

New Discoveries, or Old Ones Improved?

These gaps of knowledge, coupled with what many see as diminishing returns on the investments we're pouring into scientific research, have led some critics to view the current lull in major scientific breakthroughs as a sort of holding pattern. In other words, while we continue to take leaps and bounds forward in the application of sciences such as genetics and computer technology, the advances are largely refinements of things we already know. They're based upon scientific breakthroughs that have already happened.

Advances in technologies related to information storage, telecommunications, and microprocessor speed—and the shrinking size of our computers as the computing power within them grows—are less about breakthroughs that shed new light on our world, and more about advances within the principles that are already understood. Microchips are a perfect example.

The microchip that makes computers possible was developed in 1958. It was based upon the scientific thinking of the time, which viewed information as energy that needs to be stored in a physical place and moved through physical wires that connect physical devices. With these ideas in mind, the first commercial chip needed only one transistor to accomplish its task. And while today's advanced microchip technology is hugely more sophisticated than the technology of the first chips made in 1958 (some now have more than 125 million transistors), the new ones are a refinement—a powerfully awesome and beautiful refinement using new materials—to streamline the original idea that information is "stuff" that needs to be stored in a place.

At the same time that microchip technology was being refined based on old ideas of energy, however, quantum discoveries showed scientists that the world we live in is *all* energy. And the energy of the world *is information itself.* In other words, information is everywhere, contained in the energy that is everything. This profound understanding tells us that the digital data of our books and communication devices doesn't have to be captured and stored as "stuff" in physical locations.

Instead, it can be stored beyond the bounds of a chip, in the place quantum theory describes as the foundation of reality: the quantum field. Here, the properties that make the field what it is (holography and entanglement) suggest that the distance and space limitations that plague today's manufacturers would disappear with fully realized quantum computing.

The knowledge already exists. The technology is already here. And while forward-thinking and visionary scientists such as Seth Lloyd, a professor of mechanical engineering at MIT, have proven that quantum computing is possible in the laboratory, we may discover that the biggest shift needed to embrace such possibilities on a large scale is less about the technology itself, and more about the way we think of it. The barrier to more scientists answering the big questions of life and the universe is the constraint of accepting theories based in false assumptions.

There Are Elephants in the Room

While some critics are asking if science is stuck, others are asking if it has failed us. As we find with any belief system that we look to for help in making sense of our world, there is a maturity curve that comes with it. When the early Christian church emerged in the 3rd century, for example, there was a belief that the new religion held the answers to the deepest questions about humankind's existence. As the religion matured and those who followed it evolved in their understanding, the beliefs changed. While the church still provides a powerful social core for families and communities, its ability to answer the questions of everyday life in a way that is useful has come into question.

Our world is arguably a better one, and we live better lives, because of the benefits of science. Science has certainly gotten it right in some places, and we all continue to reap rewards from scientific breakthroughs such as the advances in medicine adding years and even decades to our lives. But there are other places where the gaps and inconsistencies in the scientific view have become stubborn roadblocks in our quest to unlock the mysteries of life and nature. These are the proverbial elephants in the room: incomplete theories that form the foundation of scientific beliefs ... unresolved issues that, despite not having been fully explained, inform the way we think of ourselves.

In addition to the assumed one-to-one correspondence between genes and proteins previously mentioned, and the fact that we now know it doesn't exist, other elephants in the room of science include the failure to account for the field of energy that makes quantum entanglement possible, the failure of evolutionary theory to explain the origins of life and the origins of humankind, and the failure to acknowledge evidence of advanced civilizations in the past as part of a cyclical model of civilization.

The fact that traditional thinking has been unable to solve the deepest mysteries of our existence is casting a long shadow of doubt on what we use as the foundation of our reality. The scientific method states that when new evidence no longer supports an existing way of thinking, it's time to "rethink" the thinking.[9] And with the growing number of discoveries shifting us away from our past beliefs, the scientific evidence that has been considered anomalous in the past can no longer be discounted; it must be incorporated into mainstream science. As we'll see in the following sections, certain assumptions fall into the categories of beliefs that prevent us from advancing into a truly sustainable view of the world and our role in it.

To reconcile the crises in the way science defines us and our world means that we must do in the early 21st century what physicists had to do a hundred years ago. Just as they had to shift their thinking to accommodate the evidence of quantum theory, we must make room for more recent discoveries that have upset some of the most cherished beliefs of science. Our failure to do so will keep us locked into the beliefs, and the ways of living, that are leading us down the destructive path where we find ourselves today.

The False Assumptions of Science

A revolution in the way we think of ourselves is sweeping the world. It's forcing us to rewrite the story of our origins, our past, how long we've been here, and where we're going. Even though the revolution began in the early 20th century, it has gone unnoticed by average people going about their daily routines—that is, unless they're among the group of scientists who have dedicated their lives to understanding how life and the universe work.

For the archaeologists struggling to fit the discovery of advanced ice age civilizations into the traditional timeline of history, for example, and the biologists publishing more than 400 peer-reviewed studies showing that nature is based upon cooperation rather than "survival of the fittest," the revolution in thinking feels like a major-magnitude earthquake. It registers "off the scale" of new ideas as it levels some of the most cherished beliefs of conventional science. In its wake is left a wide swath of outdated teachings, demanding the reevaluation of long-held traditions and destroying the legacy of entire careers. The reason? Discoveries have shown that many of the scientific "facts" we've trusted for centuries to explain the universe and our role in it are flawed.

An obsolete paradigm of the universe and our relationship to it was based upon a series of scientific assumptions—*false assumptions*—that can no longer be taught as fact in light of new evidence. Examples of these include the following:

- *False Assumption 1:* Civilization is approximately 5,000 to 5,500 years old.

- *False Assumption 2:* Nature is based upon "survival of the fittest."

- *False Assumption 3:* Random events of evolution explain human origins.

- *False Assumption 4:* Consciousness is separate from our physical world.

- *False Assumption 5:* The space between things is empty.

When we think about everyday life—the way we care for ourselves and our families, how we solve our problems, the choices we make—we find that much of what we accept as common knowledge is rooted in the core beliefs of these false assumptions, which are holdovers of an outdated science that began 300 years ago. *It may be no coincidence that during this same period of time, the world has found itself facing the greatest crises of war, suffering, and disease in recorded history.* These ideas of our sterile-sounding chemical origins, of our relatively recent arrival on Earth, and of our separateness from nature have led us to believe that we're little more than specks of dust in the universe and a biological sidebar in the overall scheme of life.

Is it any wonder that we often feel powerless to help our loved ones and ourselves when we face life's great crises? Is it any wonder that we often feel just as helpless when we see our world changing so fast that it has been described as "falling apart at the seams"? At first blush there seems to be no reason for us to think any differently, to believe we have any control over ourselves or events. After all, there's nothing in our traditional textbooks or traditional way of seeing the world that allows for anything else. . . .

That is, however, until we take another look at the new discoveries of the last years of the 20th century. Although the results of paradigm-shattering research have been published in leading technical journals, they're often shared in the complex language of science, masking the power of their meaning from a nonscientific person. Average nonscientific, nontechnical people don't feel the impact of the new discoveries because they're being left out of the conversation. And that's where our revolution comes in.

Rather than following the first three centuries of scientific imagery portraying us as insignificant beings that originated through a miraculous series of biological "flukes" and then survived 5,000 years of civilization as powerless victims separate from the harsh world we've found ourselves in, the new science suggests something radically different. In the late 1990s and early 2000s, peer-reviewed scientific studies revealed the following facts:

- *Fact 1:* Civilization is at least twice as old as the approximately 5,000 to 5,500 years estimated by conventional timelines.[10]

- *Fact 2:* Nature relies upon cooperation and mutual aid, not competition, for survival.[11]

- *Fact 3:* Human life shows unmistakable signs of an intelligent design.[12]

- *Fact 4:* Our emotions directly influence what happens in the sea of energy we are bathed in.[13]

- *Fact 5:* The universe, our world, and our bodies are made of a shared field of energy—a matrix—that makes the unity known as "entanglement" possible.[14]

It's been said that "insanity" is doing the same thing over and over again in the same way and expecting different results. To attempt to resolve the unprecedented crises of our time, looking at them through the eyes of the same beliefs that paved the way *to* the crises makes little sense. Doing so *now,* knowing that those beliefs are no longer true, makes even less sense.

To meet the challenges of our time, we must be willing to think differently about ourselves than we have for at least the last three centuries. And to do so means that we must cross some of the traditional boundaries that have isolated the discoveries in one area of scientific study from those in another. When we do, something wonderful begins to happen.

Science Was Wrong . . . Then It Was Right!

There is a chain of knowledge that links our modern world with the past, and each time that chain is broken, we lose valuable knowledge about ourselves. We know that the chain has been broken at least twice in recorded history: once with the burning of the Great Library of Alexandria in Egypt during the Roman conquest, and again with the biblical edits of the 4th century C.E. My thinking has been that the closer we can get to the original teachings that existed before the knowledge was lost, the more clearly we can understand what our ancestors knew that we've forgotten.

For the bulk of my adult life, I've searched the places least disturbed by the modern world to find sources of ancient and indigenous wisdom. My journey has taken me to some of the most amazing sites remaining on Earth. From the magnificent monasteries of the Tibetan plateau and the humble monasteries in the mountains of Egypt and southern Peru, to the recovered texts of the Dead Sea and the oral histories of native peoples throughout the world, I've listened to stories and studied records. As different as each of the traditions I've encountered appears to be from the others, there are common themes weaving them into the collective fabric of our past.

One of the overriding themes is our relationship with nature and our world, a relationship whose depths have been confirmed only recently in the language of modern science. The question that comes to me again and again is this: if our ancestors had such a deep understanding of the earth and our relationship to it, and science is just now able to validate that relationship, then what else did advanced civilizations of the past know that we've forgotten?

The Deep Truths

During a conversation with Albert Einstein, Nobel Prize–winning physicist Niels Bohr once shared what seems to be a contradiction regarding what we think of as "truth." He described how there are two very different kinds of truth: "To the one kind belong statements so simple and clear that the opposite assertion obviously could not be defended. The other kind—the so-called *deep truths*—are statements in which the opposite also contains deep truth."[15]

The scientific belief that everything is separate from everything else is an example of a deep truth, one established by the Michelson-Morley experiment in 1887.[16] This was the much-anticipated culmination of efforts in the scientific community to settle once and for all the question of whether or not a universal field of energy connects all things. The thinking at the time was that, if present, it should be a moving field, and it should be possible to detect its movement.

The results of the experiment were interpreted by scientists of the time to show that no field exists. The implication of the results—the scientific assumption—was that everything is separate from everything else. This meant that what happens in one place has little, if any, effect on what happens somewhere else.

The results of the Michelson-Morley experiment were the foundation of scientific theory and classroom teachings. Multiple generations grew up believing that we live in a world where everything is separate from everything else. This belief is reflected in many facets of our lives and civilization, ranging from the way we think of ourselves and our relationship to the earth, to the economic systems that benefit some people at the expense of others. For nearly a century, the assumptions of Michelson and Morley (the two scientists for whom the experiment was named) were accepted as fact . . . that is, until the experiment was repeated 99 years later.

In 1986, a scientist named E. W. Silvertooth duplicated the Michelson-Morley experiment in a study sponsored by the U.S.

Air Force. Under the unassuming title "Special Relativity," *Nature* published the results. Using equipment that was much more sensitive than what Michelson and Morley had in their day, Silvertooth *did detect movement* in the field. And the movement was precisely linked to the motion of Earth through space, just as Michelson and Morley had predicted a century before.[17] I'm sharing this experiment here to illustrate how a deep truth accepted at one time can later change.

> *Deep truths* are statements of which the opposite also contains a deep truth.

It's the profound and mysterious relationship between the deep truths of our past (false assumptions that we've long accepted as truths) and those emerging from new discoveries (which now reveal those earlier "truths" to be false) that is dividing us at all levels of society today. These divisions show up in everything from terrorism and wars between nations to the conflicting beliefs that tear us apart as families. Left unchecked, they pose a clear and present danger to our world.

At a later time, Bohr restated the paradox of deep truths in simpler terms, saying, "It is the hallmark of any deep truth that its negation is also a deep truth."[18] In the example above, it's what Bohr called the "negation" of the old scientific assumption (meaning the discovery that it no longer makes sense in the presence of new evidence) that makes the *opposite* a deep truth. And this is where the news of a recent discovery becomes a proverbial double-edged sword.

The good news is that the new information gives us an updated and presumably more correct way of thinking about things. The downside is that entire paradigms have already been built upon the false assumptions. Everything from the curricula approved by school boards and taught in our classrooms; to the careers of teachers, authors, and academics whose lives have been devoted to teaching the paradigm—along with political decisions and the policies that have been made into law in the highest courts of the land—is based upon what is accepted as "true" in our culture. We may well discover that our beliefs about global warming, for example, fall precisely into this category of deep truth.

The prospect of realigning so many legal, political, and academic systems already in place to reflect a deep truth is, for some, overwhelming. On the other hand, how can we hope to confront the great crises facing us *without* doing so? Clearly, the greatest threats to our lives and our world lie in the beliefs that we fight and die for, as these beliefs are based on assumptions about the past. For this very reason, the key to our survival lies in uncovering the deep truths of our very nature.

The Pyramid of Knowledge

We live in a world where everything has meaning, and is meaningful to everything else. What happens in the oceans has meaning for the climate of the mountains. What happens in a river has meaning for the life that depends upon the river. The choices that you and I make as we express our beliefs in our living rooms and around family dinner tables have meaning for the people in our immediate lives, as well as for those living halfway around the world. In the world of nature, there are no boundaries separating one part of life from another. It's for precisely this reason that it's always been a mystery to me why we *create* boundaries when we study the universe and nature.

We tend to think of geology, for example, as somehow distinct from physics, and imagine that biology is somehow detached from everyday life. While this separation may make it easier to study rocks and living things for a few years in a university, at some point we must begin to think of them as part of our everyday reality in order for them to become useful in our lives. And this is where scientific study of our world is emerging into an entirely new paradigm based upon the way in which one kind of knowledge is related to other kinds of knowledge.

There's a hierarchy in terms of the scientific disciplines. Sometimes it helps to illustrate this relationship visually as an upside-down pyramid. The smallest part of the pyramid, the capstone on the bottom, represents the key to everything that is stacked above it. In the world of science, that capstone is mathematics. It's for this reason that the words of one of the first scientists, Galileo Galilei, continue to ring as true today as they did when he wrote them 500 years ago. He said that the universe is like a "grand book, which stands continually open to our gaze, but cannot be understood unless one first learns to comprehend the language and interpret the characters in which it is written. It is written in the language of mathematics."[19]

Clearly, our mathematical knowledge is the tool that allows us to describe what happens in each successive field of knowledge as we move up the pyramid, shown in Figure 2.2 below.

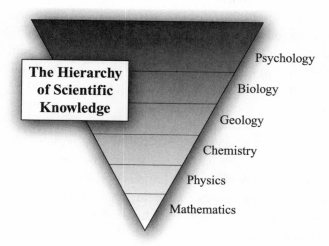

Figure 2.2. The relationship between the sciences expressed as a pyramid of knowledge to show their hierarchy. Mathematics is the foundation that each of the subsequent sciences is based upon. With this relationship in mind, it's easy to see how a change in scientific understanding at any level of the pyramid must be taken into consideration by each science above it in order to remain truly scientific.

After mathematics, physics forms the next layer of knowledge on the pyramid, as the ideas of mathematics are applied to the forces of nature, what we call the "laws" of the universe. These things—such as gravity, the speed of light, and so on—are then applied to the study of chemistry, the next layer in our model. Through chemistry, the forces of the universe act upon the elements of nature to create the foundation of our world, which we study as geology. Directly or indirectly, the expression of each underlying field of knowledge comes to bear upon the way in which life is expressed in our world. Biology is the study of that life; and directly above it is psychology, the science that helps us understand why life behaves as it does.

From this simple chart, two things become obvious: (1) each field plays a vital role in nature and is directly related to all of the fields below it; and (2) when new discoveries change the way we think of ourselves at any point in the hierarchy, everything above it must reflect the new thinking. For example, when the quantum principles of interconnection (nonlocality) emerged in physics, every scientific discipline above physics on the chart should have changed to reflect that understanding. And while chemistry has begun to adapt the ideas and offer them in the classroom, biology still teaches that biofields, such as the magnetic field of the heart, are localized and have little, if any, effect on the world beyond the body itself.

In the compartmentalized way we've chosen to study our world, science is enmeshed in a continual struggle to catch up with itself. And, if the past is any gauge, the higher the scientific discipline is on the chart, the longer it will take for the new discoveries to be reflected in that field. The key to reaping the benefits of science is all about *us* and the wisdom with which we apply what we discover.

Maybe evolutionary biologist E. O. Wilson said it best when he noted: "We are drowning in information, while starving for wisdom. The world henceforth will be run by synthesizers, people able to put together the right information at the right time, think critically about it, and make important choices wisely."[20] From the invention of the wheel (which could be used for transportation or torture) to the invention of weapons (which could provide food for entire communities or kill other people in war), the tension between knowledge and wisdom appears to be a species-wide struggle that has been with us for a very long time.

Later on, we'll take a look at the reasons why we've struggled and why our struggle may be near its end. For now, I'd like to say that science's value may be calculated less by its failure and more by how we use it, what we expect from it, and our relationship to knowledge and wisdom.

Beyond Knowledge and Wisdom: Common Sense

By any measure, the 20th century was a wild ride for the people of Earth. Between 1900 and 2000, we went from a world of about 1.6 billion to over 6 billion people, survived two world wars, squeaked through 44 years of the Cold War and 70,000 ready-to-go-at-the-touch-of-a-button nuclear missiles, unlocked the DNA code of life, walked on the moon, and ultimately made the computers that took the first humans into space look like children's toys. It was 100 years of the most accelerated population growth, and the greatest threat of our extinction, in 5,000 years of recorded history. Many historians look upon the 20th century as the age of knowledge, and it's easy to see why.

Along with the scientific discoveries about nature and life, we also made great discoveries about our past. Written records addressing concepts at the foundation of three major world religions were discovered midway through the century. New interpretations were made of even older artifacts from places like Egypt, Sumer, and Mexico's Yucatán Peninsula. Clearly the last century was one of recovering the knowledge of our past. And while we will undoubtedly continue to make new discoveries that shed additional light on our history, it's also clear that in this new century, we find ourselves once again living in a very different world than our parents and grandparents did.

The 21st century will be seen as the century of wisdom, as a time when we are forced to apply what we've learned in order to survive the world we've created. To do so, we will have to approach our problems very differently than we have in the past. We will be challenged to draw upon all that we know and use it in new, creative, and innovative ways. But to do so will require another kind of information that is seldom talked about in the science books of theories, proofs, and facts.

We will have to temper the facts of scientific knowledge—the data of the data sheets and the results of computer-generated models, graphs, and predictions—with the very ability that sets us apart from other forms of life. We will have to use what generations past simply called "common sense." The term *common sense,* however, may not be as ordinary as we make it sound.

Rather, it's the kind of thinking that comes from a systematic and organized process, one where we consider knowledge from many sources of information, mix it all together, and weigh it carefully before making our choices. And when we seem to be on the fence about the final decision, it's then that we add the intangible factor of common sense, often based on what we call "gut feeling" or "instinct."

It's a good thing that we do, because there are times in the recent past when it's precisely that undefined quality of human decision making that may have saved the world from disaster! An event during the height of the Cold War is a beautiful example of the power of common sense.

On September 26, 1983, Stanislav Petrov, a high-ranking Soviet military man, was in command of an early-warning system designed to detect any signs of an American attack. Tensions were already at an all-time high following the Soviet interception and shooting down of a civilian jumbo jet and the loss of all 269 people on board, including U.S. Congressman Lawrence McDonald, earlier that month.

At 30 minutes after midnight, the moment Petrov and his command team hoped would never happen did, in fact, occur. Warning lights flashed, sirens sounded, and the computer screens in their room at the top of the Soviet Ballistic Missile Early Warning System (BMEWS) showed five nuclear missiles coming from the U.S. headed directly for the Soviet Union. In a matter of moments, Petrov had to make the choice he dreaded—to return the fire, or not—knowing that, in that moment, the potential beginning of World War III and the fate of humanity was in his hands.

He and the men under his command were military professionals. They had trained for precisely such a moment. His instructions were clear. In the event of attack, he was to push the START button at his console to launch a counterattack against the U.S. Once he did so, he knew that he would set into motion a fail-proof system designed for all-out war. Once the button was pushed, the sequence could not be stopped. It was designed so that it operated from that point forward without the help of humans. "The main computer wouldn't ask me [what to do]," Petrov later explained. "It was specially constructed in such a way that [once the button was pushed] no one could affect the system's operations."[21]

To Petrov, his operators, and the equipment, the emergency looked real. All of the data checked out. The system seemed to be working, and as far as the radar detectors were concerned, Russia was under the nuclear attack that would begin a third world war.

But Petrov had second thoughts. Something didn't seem right to him. With only five missiles detected, it wasn't an "all-out" attack from the U.S., and that was the part that didn't make sense. It just didn't seem like any scenario considered by military intelligence.

Petrov had to act immediately, but before he did, he had to be clear about what was happening. Did he actually *feel* that the Soviet Union was under a nuclear attack from the U.S., or was it something else? In less than one minute he made his decision.

Petrov reported the alarm to his superiors and the other command posts, but he declared it as a "false" reading. And then he waited. If he was wrong, the incoming missiles would strike their Russian targets within 15 minutes. After what must have been a very long quarter of an hour, he—and no doubt countless others in command posts throughout the former Soviet Union—breathed a sigh of relief. Nothing had happened: the complex network of satellites and computers *had* issued a false warning.

A later investigation confirmed that the readings were due to a "glitch" in the radar.

The reason why I'm sharing the story is because of what it illustrates. Even when all of the sophisticated technology told Petrov that Russia was under attack; even though it was the height of the Cold War tensions of 1983; and even with all of his conditioning as a military man trained to follow orders, protocols, and procedures, Stanislav Petrov tempered all he knew with the intangible experience of common sense and a gut feeling—an experience that can't be taught in a classroom or taken in pill form. In this case, one man's common sense is the reason World War III did not begin in September 1983. Twenty-one years later, in 2004, Petrov was recognized as the "man who saved the world" and honored for his courage to trust his instincts by the Association of World Citizens.[22]

While hopefully none of us will ever be asked to make the kind of choice that Petrov did in 1983, I have no doubt that common sense will play a key role in assessing the knowledge that science puts at our fingertips. It will be our skillful use of that knowledge, tempered with a generous portion of common sense, that will help us bridge the gap between science and its application . . . the age of knowledge and the age of wisdom. And it doesn't have to happen in a big global way.

I have a dear friend who has been involved in more traffic accidents in the last 10 years of his life than I have in my 40-plus years of driving. Fortunately, he's survived each one with relatively mild injuries.

When I ask him about his experiences, a common theme runs through each detailed account. In every instance, he is in "the right." He always has the green light. It's always his turn to *go* at the four-way stop. And he is always allowed to park where he is parked because there is no sign telling him not to.

So while he might not have legally been at fault in each instance, the conditions may not have been the best for him to make the choices he made. In other words, just because the light is *green* doesn't mean that it's okay to drive through an intersection. Just because there's no sign saying that the curb next to a loading dock is a vulnerable place to park doesn't mean that the trucks unloading there don't miss the mark sometimes and run over the curb. In each instance, his common sense could have told my friend to use caution. He insists that he's right, and he is. But right doesn't mean safe.

While this may sound like a silly example, it illustrates how rules are meant as guidelines only, and not as absolute guarantees of safety.

In a similar vein, when the rules of science make no sense within the context of new discoveries, it's probably because we don't have all of the information. But just because we don't have it yet doesn't mean that we are meant to keep following the old way merely because "that's the way it's always been done."

It makes no sense to follow scientific dogma to our detriment. Yet this is precisely what we do each time we teach a room of students ideas that we now know are not true. As we'll discover in subsequent chapters, it is becoming more and more critical to wed wisdom, knowledge, and the scientific method with common sense as we struggle to answer questions about life, war, and survival.

If a line of thinking has led to a dead end, then we must decide whether we return to the drawing board and start again or continue down a dead-end path. Genetics experienced a huge dead end with the completion of the Human Genome Project at the turn of the millennium. We may very well witness an example of this in the search for the "God particle" in physics.

If we're honest with ourselves, I believe we're looking for answers to help us understand the world and meet the challenges of everyday life. And for us to do so, it's clear that knowledge is not enough. As we enter the age of wisdom, we will need to draw upon everything at our disposal to navigate the uncharted territory of the deep truths that emerge. I cannot help but believe that the undefined quality of common sense will play a crucial role in our journey.

How Do We Know What's True?

Many of the ideas addressed in this book are "hot" topics in our world today: issues that have triggered some of the most passionate and, occasionally, violent debates of modern times. In order to move beyond the emotional arguments of the past—from the court and media battles over the theory of evolution, creationism, and what's printed in our children's textbooks; to the way we help other nations in times of crisis—we need a consistent way of evaluating our new discoveries. What does each one really tell us? How do we know where speculation ends and evidence begins? What's the difference between a fact and a theory? How much evidence does it take to replace an existing theory with a new one?

To answer these questions and make sure we're talking apples and apples with each topic, not apples and oranges, I'll begin by clarifying the words that are often used in connection with such hot topics to justify various assumptions—words such as *science, fact, theory,* and *proof.*

Because so many of the ideas we'll explore are based in scientific discoveries, I'll define the words from a scientific perspective. So a *scientific theory,* for example, may have a different definition than a "theory" in everyday life. With a clear understanding of what each term means, and how we're using it, we can build a reliable way to help make sense of hot topics—a kind of mental "truth template" that gives us a consistent way to evaluate what we find. So let's begin. . . .

What Is a Scientific Fact?

Definition: A *fact* is "something having real, demonstrable existence."[23]

Example: If we're in the Los Angeles International Airport (LAX) at 4 P.M. Pacific Standard Time on a Thursday, and a business partner speaking on the phone asks us where we are in that moment, then it's a fact that we're in a precise city, at a precise airport, at a precise time, on a precise day. If our friend calls the ticket counter at LAX and the agent confirms that we are, in fact, standing in line at the counter, then the fact has been verified; and it was done by an objective witness who does not benefit one way or the other if we're actually there or not. The fact tells us what "is," but it may not explain how things came to be as they are. In other words, the fact does not describe when or how we actually got to the airport, although we make an assumption, as scientists often do, based on the fact.

What Is a Theory?

Definition: In the everyday world, we often think of a *theory* as little more than an idea that is unproven, or a guess. In the world of science, however, a theory means something that may surprise a non-science-based person. It is something that's been verified and accepted to be true. The definition of a *theory* is an "assumption based on limited information or knowledge."[24]

Example: A theory is formed on the basis of facts that are known at the time. For the previous example, because we are at the airport—something that is an observed fact—it's reasonable for our business partner to assume that we used local transportation to get there. And that assumption is our partner's *theory* of how we got to the airport. It can remain a theory, and even be a good one, as long as there's no evidence to prove it wrong. When it comes to a theory, there's no limit as to when, and how much, new evidence can show up. This is the key to understanding a theory. It can be modified and changed again and again to take new evidence into account as it comes to light. To make things even more interesting, a theory does not have to be a fact.

What Is Proof?

Definition: Proof is the "evidence or argument that compels the mind to accept an assertion as true."[25]

Example: The fact that the agent at the ticket counter confirmed that we're at LAX is the evidence—the proof—that leads our colleague on the phone to believe that we're actually at LAX.

What Forms Scientific Proof?

Definition: Based upon the previous definitions, *scientific proof* is the proof that comes from facts as a result of scientific methods of discovery.

Example: When we talk about evolution or the history of civilization in terms of fact, theory, and proof, keeping in mind what these terms mean will help us determine credibility. The new discoveries regarding the false assumptions of modern science present us with beautiful examples of Bohr's *deep truths*.

From the belief that everything is separate from everything else, to the notion that emotion has no effect upon the world beyond the person experiencing it, for the last 100 years or so science appears to have been in a holding pattern when it comes to understanding the nature of reality and our role in it. Now that we face what the experts view as the greatest number and magnitude of crises ever to threaten human existence, it is more important than ever that we move beyond the false assumptions of science that have derailed our ability to deal effectively with everything from war and terrorism to climate change.

If science is, in fact, "stuck," then the way to get *un*stuck is to honor the process of inquiry and openly acknowledge when discoveries change the way we see the world.

Now Is the Time

Clearly we don't know all that there is to know about how the universe works and our role in it. As in the analogy of crossing the highway with a big truck fast approaching (discussed in the Introduction), while future studies will undoubtedly reveal greater insights, it's sometimes best to make choices based upon what we know in the moment—so that we can live to refine our choices.

A powerful voice in the scientific community, Sir Martin Rees, professor of astrophysics at the University of Cambridge, suggests that we have only a "50/50 chance of surviving the 21st century without a major setback."[26] While we've always had natural disasters to contend with, a new class of threats that Rees calls "human induced" now has to be taken into account as well. Emerging studies, such as those reported in a special edition of *Scientific American,* "Crossroads for Planet Earth" (September 2005), echo Rees's warning, telling us, "The next 50 years will be decisive in determining whether the human race—now entering a unique period in its history—can ensure the best possible future for itself."[27] The good news echoed by the experts almost universally, however, is that "if decision makers can get the framework right, the future of humanity will be secured by thousands of mundane decisions."[28] It's in the details of everyday life that "the most profound advances are made."[29]

Without a doubt, there are countless decisions that each of us will be asked to make in the near future. I can't help thinking, however, that one of the most profound, and perhaps the simplest, will be to embrace what the new science has shown us about who we are and our role in the world.

If we can accept, rather than deny, the powerful evidence that the individual sciences are showing us, then everything changes. With that change we can begin anew. This makes us part of, rather than separate from, all that we see and experience. And that's why the new discoveries, such as those in physics and biology, are so powerful. They write us—all of humankind—right back into the equation of life and the universe. They also write us into the role of solving the great crises of our day, rather than leaving them to a future generation or simply to fate. What problem can we—as architects of our reality, with the power to rearrange the atoms of matter itself—fail to solve? What solution could possibly be beyond our reach?

While for some people the possibilities hinted at by new discoveries are a refreshing way to view the world, for others they shake the foundation of long-standing tradition. It's not unusual to see leading-edge scientists themselves reluctant to acknowledge the implications of their own research when it reveals that we are, in fact, powerful creators in the universe. It's sometimes easier to rest on the false assumptions of outdated science than to embrace information that changes everything we understand. When we take the easier course, however, we live in the illusion of a lie. We lie to ourselves about who we are and the possibilities that await us. We lie to those who trust and rely upon us to teach them the latest and greatest truths about our world.

When I share this irony with live audiences, often the response echoes the wisdom of science-fiction author Tad Williams, who wrote: "We tell lies when we are afraid . . . afraid of what we don't know, afraid of what others will think, afraid of what will be found out about us. But every time we tell a lie, the thing that we fear grows stronger."[30]

When the discoveries of today tell us that the teachings of the past are no longer true, we must make a choice. Do we continue teaching the false principles and suffering the consequences of wrong assumptions? If we do, then we must answer an even deeper question: *What are we afraid of?* What is it about knowing the truth of who we are, how we arrived here, and how long we've been on Earth that is so threatening to our way of life?

Figuring this out may become the greatest challenge of our time in history. *Can we face the truth that we have asked ourselves to discover?* Do we have the courage to accept who we are in the universe, and the role that our existence implies? If the answer to these questions is yes, then we must also accept the responsibility that comes with knowing we can change the world by changing ourselves.

We've already seen that widely held beliefs leading to hate, separation, and fear can destroy our bodies and our world faster than we could have ever imagined. Maybe all we need is a little shift in the way we think of ourselves to recognize the great truth that we are, in fact, the architects of our experience. If the experts are right, nothing short of the survival of civilization and humankind hinges upon the choices that we make in the next few years. And to make them, we must think of ourselves and our relationship to one another, as well as to the world at large, differently than we ever have before.

Our willingness to accept the deep truths of life is the key to whether or not our children will survive our choices and have the opportunity to explore the *next* deep truths in their adulthood.

> **Deep Truth 2:** The reluctance of mainstream educational systems to reflect new discoveries and explore new theories keeps us stuck in obsolete beliefs that fail to address the greatest crises of human history.

CHAPTER THREE

LIVING ON THE EDGE: SURVIVING THE TIPPING POINTS OF CHANGE

*"Every great and deep difficulty bears in itself its own solution.
It forces us to change our thinking in order to find it."*

— NIELS BOHR (1885–1962), NOBEL PRIZE–WINNING PHYSICIST

We're dangerously close to losing all that we cherish as individuals and as a civilization. Across the board, scientists are telling us in clear and direct terms that we are perilously near the point of no return when it comes to the destruction of the natural systems that sustain our lives. At the same time, the world is reeling from the growing impact of climate change that has happened faster than anyone dreamed it would. There's been a tendency to lump all of these crises together and deal with them in the same way and from the same perspective.

The mainstream belief is that all of the tipping points are human induced. The thinking has been that we caused the problems—from climate change and an unsustainable global population, to extreme poverty and shortages of food and fresh water—and we need to fix them. The truth is that we have caused *some* of them, and others we have not. While we can, and are, addressing how we grow our food, use natural resources, and sustain our growing population, we simply can't view climate change in the same way.

As we'll explore in this chapter, the very science that tells us the climate is changing also shows us that *we* are not the cause. Four hundred and twenty thousand years of history clearly demonstrate that the planet's position in space creates patterns of warming and cooling that repeat on a cyclical basis, and that the rise in greenhouse gases actually *lags behind* the warming by hundreds of years. The irony is that the cyclical rhythms in Earth's temperature—one factor of life that we cannot control—represent where the focus, resources, and energy of the best minds of our time are being directed in an attempt to stop this phenomenon.

Living on the edge of so many tipping points all at once gives us the reason, and the rare opportunity, to change the way we think and live. The people of the world, including its leaders, must cooperate and pool resources on an unprecedented level to adapt to the natural changes we all face together—changes beyond our control. And the only way to begin to do so is to think differently about who we are and how we live.

If we can choose this path rather than create the atmosphere of mistrust and separation that comes from the finger-pointing, blame, and economic penalties linked to a century of industrial development, I have no doubt that we will not only survive our multiple crises, but transcend our difficulty in coping with the factors that cause them. The benefits that stem from cooperation will lead to a lasting civilization that thrives upon healthy lifestyles of sustainability and mutual aid. The following pages give us the reasons why.

Solving Big Problems

It's not just our imagination.

It's not some unspoken experience of collective fear telling us that something's changing in our world—something very big and very real. Respected think tanks such as the Worldwatch Institute, founded in 1974 to independently research critical global issues; and the World Resources Institute, founded in 1982 to analyze environmental policy—as well as the United Nations Educational, Scientific and Cultural Organization (UNESCO)[1]—have gone beyond the warnings that began with environmental movements in the 1960s and '70s. They're all telling us that the time they warned us about is now here.

The "Crossroads for Planet Earth" edition of *Scientific American* confirms our sense that this is no ordinary time in the world, stating that the human race is, in fact, "now entering a unique period in its history."[2] The purpose of the special magazine issue was to identify a number of global crises that, if left unchecked, hold the potential to end human life and civilization as we know it today. Citing new diseases with no known cures and energy-intensive nations exhausting our finite resources; never-before-seen levels of global poverty; and the habitual disregard for Earth's oceans, rivers, and rain forests, the conclusions drawn were unanimous. We simply cannot continue living as we have in the past if we expect to survive even another 100 years. The planet cannot sustain our habits.

The point that organizations such as the ones mentioned previously are bringing into the public awareness is that each of the scenarios identified in their reports is catastrophic, and *all* of them are playing out right now. The contributors to the special publications and reports are certainly not alone in their assessment of our situation. From university professors and other scientists; to the research communities of the Central Intelligence Agency, and even the U.S. Pentagon, who see our world crises as a national security issue, all are ringing the alarms of concern loudly and clearly. They're all telling us that we're *already* in trouble. We're *already* at the tipping point of losing the oceans, forests, climate conditions, and animals that give us life in the world as we've known it. We've *already* arrived at the delicate place in our relationship with nature where doing nothing to head off the impending disaster is no longer an option. If we're to avoid the immense suffering that looms on the horizon, we must act now to change the way we think, and the way we live.

Complicating all of these problems is the renewed threat of world war. What sets this threat apart from the world wars of the last century, however, is that it's driven in part by crises like those described in the *Scientific American* special edition, rather than the historical reasons of borders and power. E. O. Wilson captures the uniqueness of our moment in history, stating that we are in what he calls the "bottleneck" in time, when the stress upon both our resources and our ability to solve the problems of our day will be pushed to their limits.[3]

In 2003, Jeffrey Sachs, the director of The Earth Institute at Columbia University, summed up our situation in unmistakable and sobering terms:

> We have nearly seven billion people. And they're on the search for enough food, water, energy to meet their needs, to make economic progress. But when you add it all up, we are already a globally unsustainable world society. Climate change, water stress, environmental degradation, species extinction; all of this is now impinging on us in ways that are becoming more and more painful and dangerous over time.[4]

Sachs also affirmed his confidence that the science and technology of resource-rich nations can abolish the extreme levels of poverty contributing to many of the crises in the developing world: "For the first time in history, global economic prosperity, brought on by continuing scientific and technological progress and the self-reinforcing accumulation of wealth, has placed the world within reach of eliminating extreme poverty altogether."[5]

I like Sachs's ideas. And I like the way he thinks. I was trained as a scientist . . . and I share his belief that science-based technologies—such as water purification; the generation and distribution of electricity; and the sharing of powerful drugs to eradicate malaria, HIV/AIDS, and hepatitis—*could* end the suffering of millions of people in the developing world. I hope that Sachs's optimism, power, and influence can truly make the kind of difference in the world that he envisions. But I am also practical.

I know that before technology can be applied in the world at the level that Sachs, I, and others envision, the thinking that gives a priority to those goals must first be in place. That kind of thinking calls for a radical shift away from the beliefs and false assumptions that have led to many of the crises. Clearly our choices to wage war and deplete finite resources, such as our reserves of fossil fuels, as well as doing little to alleviate huge and growing levels of poverty around the globe, are no longer sustainable if we want our civilization to last beyond the next century. If we hope to remain here on Earth, we've got to change the way we live. And to do so, we've got to change the way we think, which can only come from a powerful shift in the way we see the world and ourselves in it. The controversy and debate over global warming is a beautiful illustration of what I mean.

Climate Change in Our Living Rooms

In 2006, former vice president Al Gore brought the topic of climate change into the living rooms and classrooms of people throughout the world. He and film director Davis Guggenheim premiered their documentary film, *An Inconvenient Truth,* at the Sundance Film Festival. The film eventually garnered two Academy Awards, and Al Gore went on to share the Nobel Peace Prize with the United Nation's Intergovernmental Panel on Climate Change (IPCC) in 2007.

Along with the conversation and accolades surrounding the film came controversy. In the documentary, Gore offered convincing statistics and compelling images—from huge cliffs of ice breaking and falling into the Antarctic Ocean, to exhausted polar bears swimming in the waters of a near-iceless North Pole search-ing for solid ground (ice) to rest on—telling us two things about our world: (1) climate change is already here, and (2) we're the cause of it. Climate change was suddenly front and center among the issues determining the direction of global policy. And because it coincided with an election cycle, it also became a determining factor in the 2008 presidential race.

Seemingly overnight, the subject of global warming was no longer just an interesting dilemma that the experts were ponder-ing. What has been causing dramatic shifts in Earth's climate and what to do about it became, and remain, major topics of everyday conversation and talking points of the political process. Candi-dates' perspectives on climate change can now make or break their election prospects throughout the world.

While many of us know that the weather we see in our own backyards is changing, the debate over why it's happening, what it means, and where it's headed shows that people's views couldn't be more divided. The crux of the debate hinges upon the way two key questions are answered:

1. Is climate change really occurring?

2. Do the changes caused by greenhouse gases such as carbon dioxide stem from human sources?

The barrage of data available to justify an answer to either question is enough to make a scientist dizzy. To the average person on the street, it's nothing short of overwhelming. We feel as if we need an advanced degree just to read through the reams of reports before we can even begin to think about what we're being told. But it's the same information that points us in the right direction and helps us know the facts so we can understand what's really happening and make informed decisions.

✹ ✹ ✹

To begin with, the only way to determine if we're living through an anomalous period of climate extremes is to compare Earth's climate today to conditions in the past. By doing so, we can assess whether variants such as the average temperature above and below the equator, for example, are really so very different from what they were hundreds or thousands of years ago. Maybe even more important, we can tell if the temperature changes we're seeing today are part of a natural cycle. In 1999, a press release announced the successful completion of a scientific project that gives us just such a window into the past.

Each year, for hundreds of thousands of years, a natural process "freezes" a record of Earth's climate. As the seasons change annually and the temperature drops, a new sheet of ice forms that's added to the top of the ice caps of the world. When the new layer freezes, it preserves oxygen, carbon dioxide, and other elements and compounds, along with the rain, snow, microscopic life, and dust that are accumulated before the freezing occurs. Each year's accumulation covers and seals in place whatever was captured the previous year, creating a permanent record as it adds to the thickness of the ice.

As long as the ice in polar regions stays frozen, a virtual library of our planet's history, captured in the thousands of layers that have built up over thousands of years, is available to us. This history tells scientists about the global temperatures, as well as available sunlight, sea levels, and the thickness of the ice caps, in Earth's distant past. This record also gives us a way to determine if today's conditions are really "out in left field" when it comes to normal cycles of climate.

In June 1999, an international team of scientists completed a drilling project to the bottom of the thickest portions of the ice—the Vostok, Antarctica, "drill down." The layers of ice they sampled give us a continuous window for 420,000 years into the past, further into Earth's history than had ever been possible before.[6] The information revealed by these ice cores, along with additional data from the Greenland ice sheets, now offers a powerful key for understanding the climate of the past and determining whether or not what is happening in our world today is beyond the range of normal cycles.

During the research for my book *Fractal Time* (Hay House, 2009), I used the ice-core database retrieved in 1999 to compare today's conditions of temperature, magnetic strength, radiant energy from the sun, and ice thickness to times past. Based on that information, we can answer the two big questions about Earth's climate:

Question 1: Is climate change happening?
Answer 1: Absolutely, yes.

Question 2: Have we caused the change?
Answer 2: Absolutely not.

Now that we have the answers, let's take a closer look at where they come from.

Since we know that yes, climate change is happening, the next question becomes: *Is Earth warming up?* The answer is yes, and then it's no. *Is Earth cooling down?* The answer is, once again, absolutely yes . . . and then, the answer is absolutely no.

We have to say yes and no to both questions because both warming *and* cooling have occurred during the time that is the subject of the controversy and debate. In the last years of the 20th century and now in the early years of the 21st century, the world has seen not only record cooling and warming, but other extremes of weather such as hurricanes, torrential rainfall, blizzards, ice storms, tornadoes, and nearly every other meteorological phenomenon imaginable.

For example, in January 2011 an arctic chill felt throughout the U.S. kept people home from their offices and classrooms due to record low temperatures—for example, 25 degrees in Tallahassee, Florida; and 0 degrees in Bridgeport, Connecticut—while portions of Western Australia were drenched in nearly 53 inches of relentless rainfall in that same month alone. It's obvious that we're living in a time of weather extremes. The question now isn't whether or not a change is occurring, but what is *causing* the change . . .

and whether it is due to the warming or cooling of our planet. This is where an understanding of climate history and the cycles that trigger shifts comes in handy.

Much of the controversy regarding global warming is based upon the interpretation of temperature records of the past, which stem from two different sources. It was only about 130 years ago— in 1880, to be specific—that a reliable record of the climate of the "modern" era began being kept. To study any year prior to that date, scientists rely on indirect ways to measure trends of warming and cooling. These include the ice cores I mentioned previously, as well as tree-ring and ocean-floor-sediment data. Scientists are continually updating and refining our understanding of the planet's climate history using a combination of these sources.

Today, there are three main sources of data that researchers use when they want to know about Earth's climate in the past. Briefly, these databases are maintained by:

- The National Climatic Data Center, the National Oceanic and Atmospheric Administration

- Remote Sensing Systems, the University of Alabama at Birmingham

- The Climatic Research Unit, the University of East Anglia in England

Additionally, data is collected and maintained by the NASA Goddard Institute for Space Studies.

Scientists rely largely upon these databases, individually or together, to supply a picture of climate trends from the past and data to model future ones. All of these sources leave little doubt that Earth has warmed over the last 120 years or so. In fact, it's done so two times—once between the mid-1930s and the late 1950s; and then again, beginning in the late 1970s (see Figure 3.1). The experts appear to be undecided as to whether the most recent round of warming is still occurring or it has ended and the cyclical cooling that follows has already begun.

Recent periods of global cooling include those seen in the late 1800s and in the mid-20th century. During the 1960s and '70s, alarms about global warming were dampened by the sudden shift to cooler temperatures.

So any honest answer to the question of warming and cooling must be a *yes* to both. However, this may not be the question that people really mean to ask. The next part of the equation for understanding climate change is to identify how such brief cycles of warming and cooling fit into the bigger picture of Earth's history. And this is where the cycles of the past begin to tell a very interesting story.

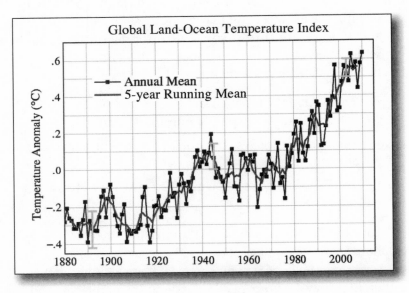

Figure 3.1. This illustration shows the global mean land-ocean temperature change between 1880, when consistent records began, and 2010. The vertical bars show areas of uncertainty, the lines linking the dots are the global mean, and the solid line is the five-year mean. (Credit: NASA Goddard Institute for Space Studies.)

What Figure 3.1 cannot show is the bigger picture of what happened immediately prior to 1880. The temperatures before that time appear on the left portion of the chart as the final stages of a cooling trend that lasted from 1400 c.e. until the mid-1860s.

Although this pre-dates the modern readings, it is well within the span of written records and the technical reports of navigators, as well as the journals and diaries of pioneers.

Along with additional stores of information, such as tree-ring data, these sources tell of a particularly harsh period called the "Little Ice Age." This global cooling, especially in the northern latitudes, is believed to have been responsible for monumental changes in the way people of the time lived. For example, it may have caused the devastating Irish Potato Famine that began in 1845 and killed more than one million people before it ended six years later, as well as a host of other crop failures, livestock deaths, and the loss of some colonies in Greenland.

For some people, the 130-plus years of modern temperature records may sound like a long time. But in terms of Earth's history and climate cycles, it's actually very short. In fact, on the timescale described in the charts of Earth's past, it's little more than a brief blip.

If we're going to set new policies, enact new laws, and ask a planetful of people to change the way they live, it makes perfect sense to look at a much bigger picture. Since we have no direct measurements of world temperatures before 1880, scientists use other tools to determine the climatic conditions of ages past. And this is where the previously discussed ice cores come in.

Evidence on Ice

With the successful drilling to the bottom of the Antarctic ice at Vostok, we now have 420,000 years of data on Earth's history to compare with the phenomena we're experiencing today to tell us the real story of climate change—and the comparison is sobering.

A glance at the temperature data from the Antarctic cores in Figure 3.2 on the facing page tells us one thing immediately: There's definitely a rhythm involved in the warming and cooling of the Earth, and that rhythm is based upon cycles that each last about 100,000 years. Furthermore, within those huge cycles there are smaller ones. Scientists now know that these are actually nested cycles—that is, cycles within cycles within cycles . . . and so on. And the cycles are based upon something that is predictable and can be calculated. It's all about Earth's location in space: the tilt, wobble, and angle of our planet relative to the sun and the core of the Milky Way.

Scientists believe that the roughly 100,000-year temperature cycles are largely caused by the changing shape of Earth's orbit around the sun over time—a natural phenomenon called *eccentricity*. Sometimes the path that our planet traces through its solar orbit looks like an elongated oval, or ellipsis, and at other times it looks more like a circle. As the path changes over the course of 100,000 years, the distance from Earth to the sun changes.

Within this 100,000-year cycle are a series of smaller 41,000-year-long cycles linked to Earth's wobble. This tilting motion tips us 1.5 degrees toward or away from the sun; and contains smaller cycles of approximately 21,000 years that contain even smaller, 11-year-long sunspot cycles.

The top line of Figure 3.2, which is labeled "Temperature variation," shows the periodic rise and fall of temperatures as indicated in the Antarctic ice cores. On this particular graph we can also see a similar rhythm for CO_2 for the same period of time, indicated by the line on the middle chart labeled "Carbon dioxide." We'll explore the details of the temperature–carbon dioxide relationship in the next section. From the data in Figure 3.2 alone, however, we gain two key insights into climate change: (1) the rise and fall of temperatures is cyclical; and (2) each big cycle is made of smaller, nested cycles of warming and cooling.

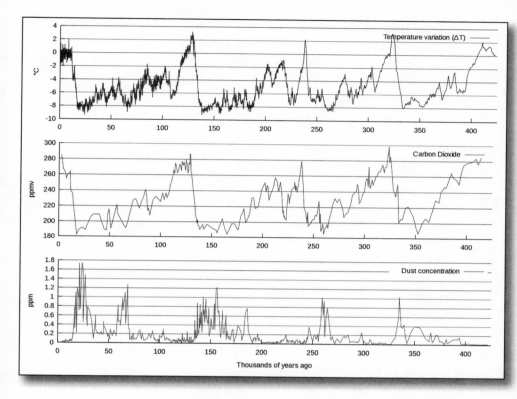

Figure 3.2. The rhythmic rise and fall of temperatures registered in the ice cores of Antarctica show beyond any reasonable doubt that Earth's cycles of warming and cooling have occurred in a regular pattern of approximately 100,000-year intervals for at least the last 420,000 years. (Credit: Petit/NOAA/GNU Free Documentation License.)

When we step back and look at the nested cycles within the bigger picture of tens of thousands of years, the larger perspective shows us that the recent changes in temperature are part of a well-established pattern. Within that pattern, the so-called anomalies of today fall well within the range of what would be expected for our time in the cycles. And this is precisely the point: if we know about the cycles of the past, then we can reasonably anticipate when those cycles will repeat again.

Understanding the rhythms of nature begins to put the recent extremes of climate into perspective. And the pattern of warming and cooling is only one of a number of factors that follow such cycles. Others include the strength of the Earth's magnetic fields, the intensity of the sun's energy, and the thickness of the polar ice caps. So let's look at what the cycles show us first, and then we can explore what they mean.

We can see from Figure 3.2 that the cyclical periods of warming are temporary and last between 15,000 and 20,000 years, before the Earth's temperature returns to being colder. Barring any unforeseen catastrophic events, such as a meteor impact, a super solar flare, a global earthquake, or a galactic "superwave" of electromagnetic pulses from the center of the Milky Way, there is no reason to believe that the cycles of the future will vary from the cycles of the past.

Maybe this is precisely what our indigenous ancestors were trying to tell us in the language of their time. While they may not have had the GPS, satellites, or computers that we have today, they did have a history of living through the cycles and the changes they bring to the world. Today we happen to be living during a time when one cycle (a cycle of warming) is ending and the next (a cycle of cooling) is beginning.

Did We Cause Global Warming?

The politics of recent years has been on a direct collision course with scientific interpretation and public opinion on the issue of whether or not global warming and the rise in certain greenhouse gases are actually connected. In other words, did we humans and our industrial habits of the past century cause or contribute to the temperatures that we see today?

While I was trained as a geologist and worked in the industry from the mid-'70s through the mid-'80s, I am definitely not a climate scientist. So although the evidence confirming the cycles of warming is based upon clear geological data, I rely upon the same sources of information that you do to determine if, in fact, the human race is a significant factor in the warming that has occurred. For that data I go back to the record of carbon dioxide (CO_2) and methane (CH_4) in the atmosphere of the past.

The first long ice cores from the Vostok drilling project provided an unprecedented 150,000-year history of the composition of gases from Earth's atmosphere, including greenhouse gases. The 1999 drilling has now extended that history to 420,000 years. With these samples, scientists now have the opportunity to look at the big picture (150,000 years into the past), and then the *really* big picture (420,000 years back) to see precisely how the cycles of global temperatures and greenhouse gases play out. And the picture this data gives us is stunning.

Figure 3.3 is a graph of information from the analysis of the Vostok ice cores. Three types of data are compared with one another to find out what relationship, if any, exists between carbon dioxide (CO_2), seen in the middle of the graph; methane (CH_4), at the top; and temperatures, as shown at the bottom of the graph. While there is definitely a relationship between temperature and CO_2, it may not be the one that global-warming alarmists had hoped to establish.

According to the journal *CO_2 Science,* scientists analyzing the cores made a remarkable discovery, one with a pivotal bearing upon the global-warming controversy: "Changes in atmospheric CO_2 content *never precede* changes in air temperature, when going from glacial to interglacial conditions; and when going from interglacial to glacial conditions, the change in CO_2 concentration actually lags the change in air temperature."[7] (My emphasis.)

Another study, published in *Science,* leaves no doubt as to precisely what the findings demonstrate: "High-resolution records from Antarctic ice cores show that carbon dioxide concentrations increased by 80 to 100 parts per million by volume 600 ± 400 years after the warming of the last three deglaciations."[8] One additional technical note indicates just how far off the correlations between greenhouse gases and temperature have been: "The lag time of the rise in CO_2 concentrations with respect to temperature change is on the order of 400 to 1,000 years during all three glacial-interglacial transitions."[9]

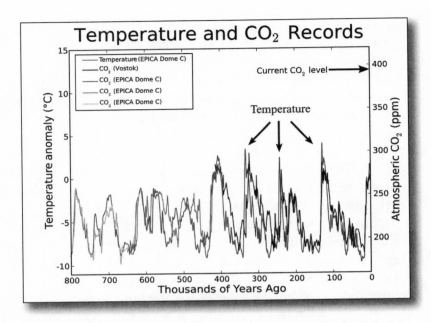

Figure 3.3. Comparison of cycles of methane levels (CH_4) and carbon dioxide levels (CO_2) to temperatures for the last 800,000 years. This data from the Antarctic ice cores shows that the CO_2 levels actually lag behind the rise in temperature and cannot be the reason for the warming. (Credit: LeLand McInnes/GNU Free Documentation License.)

So what's the bottom line with respect to all of this data on climate change? How are we to answer the questions that introduced this section? Is climate change a fact? Have *we* caused global warming? In the absence of another source of information that suggests otherwise, the deep truth of global warming is as follows, according to the present data:

1. Global warming is a fact in modern times.

2. The cooling cycle that follows warming is also a fact in modern times.

3. Ice-core data shows that greenhouse gases, specifically CO_2, *are not* the cause of global warming, as the higher temperatures precede the increase in gas levels by between 400 and 1,000 years.

4. Ice-core data shows that CO_2 levels have been as high as or even higher than today over the last 400,000 years. There are no known industrial sources for these gases in our distant past.

5. We're in a general cycle of warming that began about 18,000 years ago, as we emerged from the Pleistocene ice age. Historically, such warming cycles last between 15,000 and 20,000 years and are punctuated by brief periods of cooling, such as the Little Ice Age of the mid-1800s. The cycles and data suggest that we are within the window of time when a cooling cycle can be expected, and we may now be entering one.

The average household relies upon mainstream media and "official" statements from governmental agencies of the world, including the Intergovernmental Panel on Climate Change, for information. I'm in awe of the number of people in audiences throughout the U.S. who believe global warming is an open-and-shut case. They believe that it's a recent problem, we caused it, and now we've got to pay to fix it. But while I'm in awe, I'm also not all that surprised.

The reason is because the same media that gave global warming its "popularity" also authoritatively told us that we're the ones responsible for it. In *An Inconvenient Truth,* Al Gore states plainly that each one of us is a cause of global warming, but we can make choices to reduce our individual carbon footprint.[10]

While I like Gore's ideas about lifestyle changes (we definitely need to go "green" ASAP), there remains considerable resistance to the reasons he uses to justify them. *Contrary to what many assume to be a consensus, the scientists of the world are not in universal agreement that greenhouse gases and human industry are the cause of the warming.* Because there are so many sources telling us why we have triggered global warming, I'd like to take this opportunity to give a voice to some of the esteemed scientists who have caused ripples in their communities, and even risked their careers, because they could not, in good conscience, go with the flow on this topic.

While most scientists acknowledge the fact that Earth has warmed, these scientists are not among those who believe that we caused this. What follows is a small but representative sample of their comments, preceded by each scientist's name, field of specialization, and the institution where he or she works:

— **Sallie Baliunas,** astronomer, Harvard-Smithsonian Center for Astrophysics: "The recent warming trend in the surface temperature record cannot be caused by the increase of human-made greenhouse gases in the air."[11]

— **Khabibullo Abdusamatov,** mathematician and astronomer, the Pulkovo Observatory of the Russian Academy of Sciences: "Global warming results not from the emission of greenhouse gases into the atmosphere, but from an unusually high level of solar radiation and a lengthy—almost throughout the last century—growth in its intensity. . . . Ascribing 'greenhouse' effect properties to the Earth's atmosphere is not scientifically substantiated. . . . Heated greenhouse gases, which become lighter as a result of expansion, ascend to the atmosphere only to give the absorbed heat away."[12]

— **William M. Gray,** professor emeritus, head of the Tropical Meteorology Project, Department of Atmospheric Science, Colorado State University: "This small warming is likely a result of the natural alterations in global ocean currents which are driven by ocean salinity variations. Ocean circulation variations are as yet little understood. Human kind has little or nothing to do with the recent temperature changes. We are not that influential."[13] Also: "I am of the opinion that [global warming] is one of the greatest hoaxes ever perpetrated on the American people.[14]

— **George V. Chilingar,** professor of civil and petroleum engineering, University of Southern California: "[T]he following global forces of nature [are] driving the Earth's climate: (1) solar radiation . . . , (2) outgassing as a major supplier of gases to the World Ocean and the atmosphere, and, possibly, (3) microbial activities. . . . [Q]uantitative estimates of the scope and extent of their corresponding effects on the Earth's climate . . . show that the human-induced climatic changes are negligible."[15]

— **Ian Clark,** geologist, professor of earth sciences, University of Ottawa: "That portion of the scientific community that attributes climate warming to CO_2 relies on the hypothesis that increasing CO_2, which is in fact a minor greenhouse gas, triggers a much larger water vapor response to warm the atmosphere. This mechanism has never been tested scientifically beyond the mathematical models that predict extensive warming, and are confounded by the complexity of cloud formation—which has a cooling effect. . . . We know that [the sun] was responsible for climate change in the past, and so is clearly going to play the lead role in present and future climate change. And interestingly . . . solar activity has recently begun a downward cycle."[16]

— **Chris de Freitas,** associate professor of geology and environmental science, University of Auckland: "There is evidence of global warming. . . . But warming does not confirm that carbon dioxide is causing it. Climate is always warming or cooling. There are natural variability theories of warming. To support the argument that carbon dioxide is causing it, the evidence would have to distinguish between human-caused and natural warming. This has not been done."[17]

— **David Douglass,** professor of physics and astronomy, University of Rochester: "The observed pattern of warming, comparing surface and atmospheric temperature trends, does not show the characteristic fingerprint associated with greenhouse warming. The inescapable conclusion is that the human contribution is not significant and that observed increases in carbon dioxide and other greenhouse gases make only a negligible contribution to climate warming."[18]

— **Don Easterbrook,** emeritus professor of geology, Western Washington University: "Global warming since 1900 could well have happened without any effect of CO_2. If the cycles continue as in the past, the current warm cycle should end soon and global temperatures should cool slightly until about 2035."[19]

It's because of the number and depth of opinions such as these that the remedy for, and direction of, climate change is so uncertain. Because of the uncertainty, it's also probably no surprise that the next step in deciding what to do about the change has become a moving target eluding even the most powerful and influential people in the world.

The Hope

In 2010, the hopes of the world were high as we witnessed an unprecedented gathering of world leaders in Denmark to determine how to respond to Earth's changing climate: the Copenhagen Climate Summit. The purpose of the series of meetings was to discuss, and hopefully agree upon, some kind of action, akin to a treaty, that would address the change threatening the world's way of life.

As the conference began, there were powerful signs of promise and cooperation among the leaders themselves (rather than their representatives); presidents, prime ministers, kings, queens, and dictators alike had gathered to address a problem that transcends our differences of politics and policy. By the end of the conference, however, hope faded into disappointment, then turned to despair over the outcome. Despite the best minds of the day preparing the research that brought the leaders together, and the best diplomatic channels supposedly being cleared to pave the way for agreements, the leaders of the world were ultimately unable to find a way to work together toward solutions.

What happened instead is the very crux of why this book is so important. In my opinion, the summit was a tragic missed opportunity, and I say so for the following reason.

The Opportunity

In Copenhagen, the world's leaders had a rare moment to show their respective countries, and also demonstrate to one another, that there is a bond among people of all nations greater than the differences of borders, governments, cultures, and beliefs that have separated us in the past. They could have agreed, for example, that although we don't know precisely why the climate is changing, the simple fact is that it *is*—and this change is threatening civilization as we know it. Coastlines are disappearing; great cities of the world are being destroyed by extreme weather; entire peoples and ways of life are vanishing; and the ability to grow food in the Northern Hemisphere, where the bulk of the world's population lives, is diminishing quickly.

They could have simply agreed that although we don't know precisely why these things are happening, as a community of nations we can pledge to use our resources, our money, our militaries, our technology, and our labor to ease the transition. Our leaders could have agreed to something along these lines . . . but they didn't.

One of the comments heard again and again by those in attendance was that the wealthier countries simply hadn't done their homework. They didn't understand the mind-set of the poorer countries that had experienced thousands of deaths and billions of dollars in economic losses due to climate change in one year alone: 2008. That year, Cyclone Nargis in Myanmar, for example, took at least 100,000 lives. Many people became homeless in a matter of hours, as the storm washed away entire villages. Then approximately 200,000 people were affected by heavy rains and severe flooding, as four storms (Fay, Gustav, Hanna, and Ike) devastated much of Haiti's infrastructure and made the country even more vulnerable to the disastrous earthquake that occurred less than two years later. Typhoon Hagupit killed about 70,000 people in China and left at least 18,000 missing soon after a 7.9-magnitude earthquake struck that same year.

In the words of British economist Nicolas Stern, chair of the Grantham Research Institute on Climate Change and the Environment, the outcome of the Copenhagen Climate Summit was disappointing due, at least in part, to the attitude of the wealthier nations. And while there was "less arrogance than in previous years . . ." he said, "it could have been much better handled by the rich countries."[20]

The Opportunity: Missed

Instead of acknowledging the problem and admitting that the jury is out as to what has caused climate change (although the data for warming and cooling cycles looks extremely convincing to *me*), participants at the summit attempted first to find fault with specific countries and industries; second, to assign blame and degrees of guilt to specific nations; and last, to attach a financial penalty for the assumed guilt. Clearly, there was more than one agenda playing out in Copenhagen.

My personal feeling is that this is the essence of the missed opportunity of so many leaders—with so much support from the people they represent, with so much in common, and with so much at stake . . . going home empty-handed. It also explains why there was so little to show for the conference in terms of a meaningful framework to address the multiple crises that everyone agrees exist.

And while it is sad, it should probably come as no surprise.

The Copenhagen Climate Summit offers a perfect real-life example of why this book was written, and illustrates a way of thinking that's based upon the false assumptions of science. The failure to reach a meaningful framework of action is a direct result of a way of life built upon scientific assumptions valuing competition and separation above cooperation and unity.

Specifically, our civilization is built upon the series of false assumptions identified earlier in the book—namely, that nature is based upon "survival of the fittest," everything is separate from everything else, and consciousness is separate from our physical world.

If the leaders of our world, and their representatives, had really understood and lived from the deep scientific truths—that the universe, the planet, and our bodies are made of a shared field of energy, a matrix that makes the unity of entanglement possible; that human emotion directly influences what happens in the matrix; and also that nature relies on cooperation, not competition, for survival—they would certainly have made different choices. Then it is very likely that the Copenhagen Climate Summit of 2010 would have had a better outcome.

If participants had acknowledged the evidence of Fact 1 (civilization is at least twice as old as the 5,000 years or so accepted in conventional timelines), they would have known that the changes in climate that prompted the conference are cyclical. They've occurred in the past and are precisely the kinds of changes that we should expect to show up for our period in a cyclical history.

Deep truths give us the sound scientific reasons to think differently than we did when we made the choices that led us to the crises we're now facing. For the Copenhagen Climate Summit, thinking differently would entail a shift away from seeing the world as a single pie with finite slices, where some must lose their portions in order for others to benefit . . . to realizing that we can make many pies, and even new ones of different flavors, to meet the needs of our entire global family.

While the events in Copenhagen illustrate one example of how a small shift in thinking could lead to a radically different outcome, the following sections will show the same principle in other crises. Unlike climate change and global warming, however, these crises are directly linked to the choices we have made. And because they are, they represent an unprecedented opportunity to change the thinking and actions that led to them.

Where Have All the Species Gone?

When I was growing up in northern Missouri, one of the things I looked forward to most were the daylong hikes I took during the long summer vacations from school. From early in the morning until late in the day, I would walk alone over the trails that weave through the dense, green forests covering the bluffs overlooking the Missouri River. I was always amazed that I could look straight up and not see the sky through the intertwined branches, leaves, and vines above me.

To me, those walks through the Missouri forests felt like an adventure backward in time, as if I were walking into a prehistoric jungle. At any moment I expected some ancient creature to suddenly jump onto the trail from out of nowhere just to let me know that it still existed, and then disappear back to its mystical hiding place.

The point of this story is that I assumed the forest, and everything in it, went on forever, had existed forever, and would remain there for me to enjoy . . . forever. I couldn't imagine it any other way.

Today, the Missouri River and the ecosystem that surrounds it has become one of the tragic stories of modern technology. Due to "progress" in the form of dams, water-diversion structures, and artificial channels that change the direction of water flow in what has become the largest reservoir system in the country, the Missouri is one of the most "endangered" rivers in the United States, as is much of the wildlife dependent on it.[21]

There are at least three species in the Missouri River ecosystem presently at risk of becoming extinct—two kinds of birds and one kind of fish. Each of these animals is a key to maintaining the balance of the delicate food chain that supports the ecosystem. The U.S. Fish and Wildlife Service has now issued a report recommending that the man-made controls on the river be changed. The purpose of doing so is to allow a return to the natural rise and fall in temperatures and water levels that the endangered wildlife in the area depend upon.[22]

It wasn't until I was in a seventh-grade science class near the very forests I loved to hike through that I learned the sad reality about such beautiful places. For any of a number of reasons, history shows that they don't last forever. There were times in the past when the unthinkable happened: Some kind of disaster came along and wiped every single member of a plant or animal species completely from the face of the Earth. It became *extinct.*

While some extinctions were due to natural causes—such as climate change or, 65 million years ago, an asteroid slamming into Earth—I was shocked to discover that at times they result from something much more familiar and closer to home: our presence. We humans have been the disaster that has ended, or threatened, the existence of entire species.

A classic illustration of this phenomenon is the fate of the dodo that once lived on the island of Mauritius in the Indian Ocean. This animal's extinction is the archetype of human-induced extinctions.

The dodo was a large, flightless bird that weighed 45 to 50 pounds and has been linked to the pigeon family by modern DNA studies. When the first Portuguese explorers reached the island in 1507, the birds were said to be so numerous that they were uncountable.

Then, a combination of human causes—including deforestation, which limited the dodos' nesting grounds; the presence of dogs, pigs, and other predators that the explorers brought with them; and hunting, because the birds nested on the ground and were easy prey—the dodo population quickly dwindled until it could no longer sustain itself. While textbooks say that the last confirmed sighting was in 1662, eyewitness accounts have surfaced for sightings as late as 1693.

The sad fact is that within about 150 years or so of our first encounter with these fearless, flightless birds, human activity led to the extinction of the dodo. It was the first documented case in modern times to prove that living populations are not inexhaustible, and we are capable of hunting a species to the point of extinction.

Unfortunately, the same lesson has resurfaced in more recent years with other species, including the American buffalo, whose population dwindled from 75 million in the 1870s to fewer than 1,000 by 1900; and the blue whale, the largest mammal ever to inhabit the earth, whose population was reduced from 350,000 before commercial whaling began to somewhere between 8,000 and 14,000 today. Many more species have been hunted dangerously close to extinction. As is the case for both the American buffalo and the blue whale, through a shift in the way we think of these animals, it is possible to save them from extinction. That is, unless the number of species that is dying off is so large that it's impossible to focus on one or two with specific acts of conservation.

This is precisely where we find ourselves today.

While many people believe that all of the life-forms on Earth have already been discovered, nothing could be further from the truth. An estimated 18,000 or so new species are identified every year. Some of these are found in surprising places where we'd least expect such discoveries. In July 2010, for example, scientists found 11 new species of insects living in a place visited by many people every year: Mercantour National Park in France.

But while new species are being discovered every year, at the same time the extinction rate of Earth's life is speeding up. The estimates are that as many as 26,000 species are now vanishing from Earth each year, some before they are even discovered. For this reason UN Secretary-General Ban Ki-moon advises, "To tackle the root causes of biodiversity loss, we must give it higher priority in all areas of decision making and in all economic sectors."[23] Clearly the accelerated extinction rates of so many species are sending a powerful message to us—the life-forms creating the greatest amount of change on the planet. The question is: *Are we listening to the message?*

Are We Next?

Evolutionary biologists make their living by looking into the past to help us understand the present and identify the trends that are shaping our future. There is nearly universal agreement among biologists that there have been periods in the past when huge portions of life on Earth disappeared. They chalk the disappearances up to a number of causes, and while theories on the reasons may vary, the outcome isn't up for debate.

Mass extinctions are a fact of the past. According to biologists, there have been at least five mass extinctions in the history of Earth. Each was separated from the ones that preceded and followed it by a period of time measured in hundreds of millions of years. The first mass extinction, for example, was 440 million years ago (MYA); the second, 370 MYA; the third, 245 MYA; the fourth, 210 MYA. The fifth and last mass extinction on Earth, about 65 MYA, was a time when 60 to 80 percent of all life on Earth disappeared. While these extinctions may seem like they happened long ago (and they did), they are still important to us today because *we* are part of the next one.[24]

Biologists tell us in no uncertain terms that we are in the midst of a sixth great mass extinction—and the loss of huge amounts of life on Earth is not something that suddenly snuck up on scientists. E. O. Wilson estimates that our planet was already losing as many as 30,000 species each year in the early part of the 20th century. More recent estimates suggest that the problem may be even worse than he believes. This fact certainly sounds ominous and is definitely bad news. The good news is that there is a key factor that makes "our" mass extinction different from the previous ones. This is our ray of hope.

In the summer of 2008, I shared a lecture tour in Europe with my dear friend and esteemed colleague Bruce Lipton. He and I had both published our most recent books with Hay House (*The Biology of Belief* and *The Divine Matrix,* respectively) and decided to combine our book tours through the German-speaking countries to share our new material together. It was during a long travel day on the train from Zurich, Switzerland, to Frankfurt, Germany, that Bruce and I had the opportunity to sit back; take in the beauty of the European countryside; and share a few meals and thoughts on life, love, and the fate of the Earth—and do so in precisely that order.

Toward the end of lunch, I asked Bruce the question I'd wanted to pose to him for years, but I had never really found the time to do justice to the conversation or his answer.

"Just how bad are things in the overall scheme of biology and life on Earth?" I asked. "Just between us, how bad are they, really?"

His answer sent me reeling. Bruce, a man whom I love as a friend and respect tremendously for his professional integrity, gave me the simple, elegant, and laser-sharp kind of response that has made his teachings so accessible and popular. Using the imagery of our indigenous ancestors, he described how our home here on Earth is essentially a "garden": a huge, planet-sized one.

"Everything on Earth is part of the garden," he said, "including us. Mother Earth has a way of dealing with the things that don't fit into her garden—they are kicked out!" Then he turned and looked directly across the table at me. With a glimmer in his eyes that comes from a lifetime of study leading him to something huge and profound, he summed up our situation in just a few words. "Either we figure out how to live in peace in nature's garden and take care of it," he said, "or we'll be turned into *mulch* to feed the rest of the garden!"

In the way that only Bruce can do so well, with his garden analogy he had just described what we can expect our fate to be unless something changes, and fast. But he had skillfully explained even more. He had offered the key to what it is that makes our time of extinction different from those of the past: While the first five extinctions appear to have been caused by nature (asteroids, climate change, and so on), ours is not from nature. It's from *us*. The sixth great mass extinction of life on Earth, including of human life, is human induced.

According to Niles Eldredge, former curator-in-chief of the Hall of Biodiversity at the American Museum of Natural History,

"There is little doubt that humans are the direct cause of ecosystem stress and species destruction in the modern world through such activities as: transformation of the landscape, overexploitation of species, pollution and the introduction of alien species."[25]

Eldredge is not alone in his assessment. The Millennium Ecosystem Assessment has been tasked with studying the state of the world's ecosystems and their impact on "human well-being." The first of seven planned reports was published in 2005. While the studies are ongoing and more data is being gathered, the implications so far are clear: "The ongoing degradation of 15 of the 24 ecosystem services examined—including fresh water; capture fisheries; air and water regulation; and the regulation of regional climate, natural hazards and pests—increases the likelihood of potentially abrupt changes that will seriously affect human well-being."[26]

Specifically the report describes the kinds of crises that can be expected if there is no change in our policies of land and resource use. "Abrupt changes" may include the emergence of new diseases, sudden drops in water quality, creation of "dead zones" along the coasts, the collapse of fisheries, and shifts in regional climate. The bottom line to the Millennium Ecosystem Assessment can be summed up in a single, sobering sentence. The stark reality is that, in effect, *one species (us) is now a hazard to the other ten million or so species on the planet, as well as to itself.*

Ignoring the Crises . . . Until We Can't

Recently, a well-known financial advisor was asked when the next economic crisis in the world would begin. He framed his answer in precisely the same way I often reply to the question "When will all of the dreaded crises of the indigenous 'new world age' predictions begin?" The advisor responded by asking several brief and poignant questions of his own:

What will have to happen before you say we're in a crisis right now? How high will gas prices have to get before your neighbors notice something is wrong? How high will gold have to get, or silver? How many banks will have to go under? How high will unemployment have to rise? How many cities will have to go bankrupt? Where's your threshold? How bad will things have to be before you begin to see what's really happening?[27]

The way the advisor answered is the whole point of this section of *Deep Truth*.

The best minds of our time are telling us that we're already in crisis, and actually facing multiple critical situations all happening at the same time—*now*. How scarce does fresh water need to become before we acknowledge there's a problem? How many financial institutions need to fail? How many times does the world's population need to double while its resources shrink? How close do we have to come to another global war?

I guess my new-and-improved answer to the "When?" question would be: "How bad do things have to get before we acknowledge that we're already in multiple crises, and heading for even bigger trouble unless we change the way we think?"

While there's probably nothing in the list of crises in the previous sections that comes as a surprise to anyone reading this book, there's a strange trait that we humans exhibit when it comes to bad news. And it seems that the worse the news is, the more pronounced the trait becomes. We seem to deal with really devastating information in one of two possible ways: either we minimize it to the point of insignificance or we ignore it altogether. The phenomenon is called "normalcy bias," and it tends to be strongest among people who have never before encountered the extremes facing them.

People living today who experienced the Great Depression of the 1930s, for example, know what it was like to have unemployment at nearly 25 percent, stand in soup lines blocks long, and wait hours for a loaf of rationed bread. And they understand just how quickly the worst can come to pass. Those people are always prepared for it in case it does happen again. To the young people in America today, the Great Depression seems like a dark fairy tale. The old black-and-white photos make it look antiquated, remote, and impossible. They just can't imagine how it could ever happen again.

How people responded to rumors of the human holocaust that was occurring during World War II offers a powerful example of how this bias in our psyche seems to work.

In 1944, as boxcars packed with people left the ghettos of Hungary and Poland during daylight hours, in plain sight of townspeople, those left behind were convinced that the trains were taking the "lucky ones" to relocation sites. It was there, they believed, that those aboard would have better homes and find a better way of life. Even though the horrors of the death camps were whispered of in their communities, no one could believe the rumors. No one wanted to believe them. And so they didn't. They ignored them.

In 2009, Kitty Williams, a survivor of the Nazi death camps, shared her story with the public and the press for the first time since she was freed at the end of the war.[28] Ironically, before she actually found herself in one of those boxcars headed for Auschwitz-Birkenau, like so many others she and her family heard the stories of what was happening, but could not accept that they were true.

Kitty recalled:

> I remember young Polish and probably Czechoslovakian men knocking on our door, saying they were trying to escape, trying to get to Israel, going through Hungary, and of course we always fed them and gave them some supplies. When they were telling us about the atrocities I don't think we really believed them. The human mind cannot imagine this can happen. It's an exaggeration, it can't be true, it just can't be.[29]

Eventually Kitty, her family, and others who had denied the rumors for so long became victims of the horrors they'd heard about. And while she survived to tell her story, many of her friends and family members were among the approximately 5.8 million people who didn't. The point is that they were warned but either did not accept or could not believe the facts that faced them each day.

* * *

In a similar vein, it's no secret that our world is in trouble. To many people, the problems just seem too big, and the solutions too unlikely, for them to take any kind of action. When we're feeling overwhelmed, it's often easier to deal with it all by ignoring the crises. A perfect example of this, but one in no way comparable to the magnitude of suffering of the Holocaust, is what was happening to the world's economic system in 2007.

Even with the warning signs of the analysts blazing and the alarms of the experts blaring, no one wanted to believe what was happening to the financial systems of the world, and where the economy was headed. *It's too big to fail,* was the thinking. *They* [the governments] *could never let it break.* And precisely this kind of thinking was the basis for the way in which loans were handled, and how money was disbursed and spent in the U.S. at the time.

In July 2008, I was speaking with the financial advisor who was responsible for the life savings of a retired family friend. The family had asked if I could help get her assets into a more secure place. On the phone I asked the advisor how we could best safeguard some of the savings out of the stocks and mutual funds in which they were invested. The conversation didn't go the way I thought it would.

At the very mention of financial safety, the voice on the other end of the phone became indignant and even dismissive. "I'm a professional financial advisor," he said. "I do this for a living." That's when I knew the conversation was in trouble. "What could be safer than these mutual funds and blue-chip stocks?" he asked. "They've been around forever. In the long term, they can't lose."

"I hear what you're saying," I answered, "and in the past I would've agreed with you. But those stocks are only as safe as the market is. And something's wrong with the market. The traditional indicators don't mean what they used to mean—everything's 'up.' Tangible assets like gold, silver, and oil shouldn't be up if the stocks are up. There's no sound reason for the market to be so high, to be up in so many sectors, and to stay so high for so long. Something's got to give, and when it does, Mary [not her real name] is going to lose everything her husband worked for throughout their marriage before he died."

I couldn't believe the words that I heard next. "The market can't fail," the advisor told me. "It's too big and too strong. There's just too much momentum." Less than eight weeks later, it did. And when it fell, it *crashed*.

I watched in awe as the numbers on the TV continued to drop throughout the day. The LED screen showing the Dow Jones Industrial Average became a continuous blur of red morphing, in fractions of a second, into lower and lower numbers, as values plummeted in a free fall.

It was September 29, 2008, and the unthinkable had just occurred. Contrary to what the advisor on the phone had said to me only two months before, big institutions—such as Freddie Mac, Fannie Mae, Lehman Brothers, Goldman Sachs, and Bear Stearns—which have traditionally been thought to be too big to fail, had just done so.

By the end of the day, the stock market had dropped 777.68 points, to set the record for the largest single-day loss in history. When it did, the $1.2 trillion loss in the stock market translated into huge personal losses for nearly everyone invested in it, and it was the beginning of the shift that has impacted nearly everyone in the world financially since then.

I called Mary from the airport the next day, and the news wasn't good. Sadly, in less than 48 hours, she had lost almost half of the savings she and her husband had built, nurtured, and protected during their 40-plus years of marriage. What was even more disheartening about the situation was that she now could no longer employ the caregivers she needed each day to help with her daily routines.

While I was in awe as I watched massive amounts of wealth drain from the American economy throughout that day, I was not surprised. And neither were the people who follow the economic policies for such things as national interest, national debt, and housing loans. The trends had been in place for years, and the unmistakable signs of the collapse were recognized at least 15 months *before* it actually happened. On June 14, 2007, Richard C. Cook published a paper with the Centre for Research on Globalization. The first sentence of the report tells the whole story: "It's official: the crash of the U.S. economy has begun."[30]

Cook's paper cited the work of two leading economists who looked deeper than the outward signs of a booming stock market. Steven Pearlstein, a Pulitzer Prize–winning columnist for *The Washington Post;* and Robert Samuelson, a contributing editor for *Newsweek* and *The Washington Post,* both saw the same bubble forming in the economy. And they both saw it at the same time. The red flag for them came when they recognized the growing number of companies carrying massive amounts of debt compared to the money they were bringing in.

"Across the board stock prices and company valuations will fall," Pearlstein said. "Banks will announce painful write-offs, some hedge funds will close their doors. Some companies will be forced into bankruptcy or restructuring."[31]

The message of Pearlstein, Samuelson, and others was clear: 2007 was the year that the conditions for a perfect global economic storm converged, and when the storm struck, the U.S. economy was directly in its path. Of course, while they predicted the scenario, even Pearlstein and Samuelson may not have known just how bad things would become, or how long the crisis would last.

The reason I've shared this story is to demonstrate how crises tend to be discounted or ignored until they hit close to home and it's too late to do anything about them. In this case, it was so close to home that it was in everyone's pocketbooks. Suddenly people were asking the obvious questions: *What happened? Why did it happen? How could it have happened so quickly?* And this is the key point to understand in this part of this book.

The global economic collapse didn't happen "quickly" as an independent event. It cannot be isolated from the larger scenario of multiple tipping points facing our global community. And just as climate change was largely ignored by policymakers and the public alike until the ice caps of the earth began to melt and islands began to disappear under rising sea levels, the collapse of the economy sent a signal to those who could step back and look at the big picture. The signal was part of what may be thought of as the "Earth Code," showing us how systems that are not sustainable can no longer continue.

As demonstrated in my book *Fractal Time,* economic systems follow the same natural rhythms that create patterns in nature and cycles in climate. Because the patterns can be calculated and their returning conditions can be predicted, it should come as no surprise that the global conditions of economic collapse are converging once again in the same window of time as so many other unsustainable systems, including population growth, resource depletion, and cycles of war.

A World of Broken Systems

Everyone learns in different ways. Some people do so through hours of repetition, while others can read and remember information with a quick glance at the page of a book. The way we "hear" information, and what we do after we hear it, has a lot to do with how we learn. And precisely because we do learn differently, it's a good thing so many different people are sounding the same call for global change in so many different ways.

What makes no sense to one person may be the wake-up call for another, and vice versa. And while those sounding the call may be using different words to describe what's happening—from the technical perspective of *Scientific American* and the Worldwatch Institute, to the everyday language of Al Gore's *An Inconvenient Truth*—the message that our fragile way of life is in trouble is being heard throughout the world.

One of the most influential voices leading the effort to educate and mobilize the masses toward a conscious shift in the way we live is environmentalist and author Lester Brown, the former head of the Worldwatch Institute. "We are in a race between tipping points in nature and our political systems," Brown says.[32]

In a masterful attempt to curb the suffering of what is now acknowledged to be a collapsing civilization, he released his straight-talking book *Plan B 3.0: Mobilizing to Save Civilization.*[33] In it, Brown described just how bad things were at the time the book was written, and how much worse they might get. Since then, many of his warnings have become reality.

He identifies how critical times in nature—when a species' population is shrinking, for example—mark the point of no return for the system in question. Brown then describes the state of a number of different yet related systems on Earth, and where we are with respect to the point of no return for each one.

It's a sobering yet necessary assessment that offers the hope of an action plan, as well as highlighting the problems. Without a doubt, *Plan B 3.0* is making a difference in the way we think of our world. And for many organizations, agencies, and individuals, Brown's book has become a bible for identifying potential solutions.

From the publication of *Plan B 3.0* to the efforts of the Worldwatch Institute, an obvious movement is afoot to alert the general public to the conditions threatening life and civilization as we know it. And the effort is gaining momentum. While the studies, reports, books, and institutes may not agree on each and every detail of the crises or how to deal with them, there are concerns that all have identified in their unique ways. In general, they fall into broad categories that can be defined as follows:

- *Crisis Point 1:* An unsustainable world population

- *Crisis Point 2:* Climate change

- *Crisis Point 3:* Growing shortages of food and fresh water

- *Crisis Point 4:* The widening gap between poverty and wealth, health and disease, and illiteracy and education

- *Crisis Point 5:* The growing threat of war and the renewed threat of atomic war

The overriding factors that make our moment in history so different from times past are the sheer number, magnitude, and timing of the problems we face today. Each tipping point listed above holds the potential to wreak tremendous suffering upon humanity and bring the world as we know it to a grinding halt if we ignore the problem and do nothing. And, as you can plainly see, all are already happening. Each item identified here has already reached the crisis proportions predicted by environmentalists, scientists, and economists nearly 40 years ago.

So this takes us back to the important question asked in the previous section: *What will have to happen before we say that things are already bad—that we're already in a crisis right now?* Knowing that each crisis is already upon us right now is the answer that needs no further explanation. Throughout the remainder of this book, we'll take a closer look at some of the key crisis points that appear to be the triggers for yet others.

We'll begin with **Crisis Point 1:** the sheer number of people sharing our world. This factor alone only worsens the magnitude of **Crisis Point 3:** the growing shortages of food and water; and of **Crisis Point 4:** the widening gap between poverty and wealth, health and disease, and illiteracy and education.

While each of these crisis points stems from a system that has already broken down, the stress that climate change, **Crisis Point 2**, has brought to the world has forced our unsustainable ways of life to reach a breaking point in recent years. This same stress has contributed to **Crisis Point 5:** the growing threat of war and the renewed threat of atomic war. (I'll defer our exploration of this crisis point until Chapter 6: War Doesn't Work Anymore.)

As we examine the crises, new discoveries will help us separate false assumptions from facts.

People, People, and More People!

Many "firsts" happened in the 20th century: some good, some not so good, and some simply mind-boggling. Since 1900 the world has witnessed the first airplane and television, the first computers, and the first humans on the moon . . . along with the invention of microchips, the discovery of DNA, and the splitting of the atom. The world has also witnessed explosive, never-before-seen growth in population.

From the end of the last ice age until about the year 1650, the total population of the planet is estimated to have been stable at less than 500 million people. To put this into perspective, it means that for the last 9,000 years or so, the number of people living on the earth and being sustained by its resources has only been about half the number now living in India today.

After 1650, that number changed. The graph in Figure 3.4 gives us an appreciation of just how quickly the population of Earth has grown in only 350 years' time, and the rate at which it has doubled.

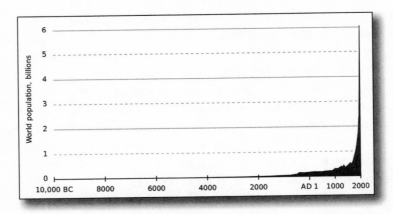

Figure 3.4. Estimate of Earth's total population from 10,000 B.C.E. to 2000 C.E. The steep increase approaching the year 2000 began in 1804 when the global population reached the one-billion mark. The dramatic population growth since that time is unprecedented in the history of the world and is key to the multiple crises of disappearing food, shrinking supplies of fresh water, and the decreasing availability of cropland necessary to sustain our global family. (Credit: El T, public domain.)

Between the years 1650 and 1804, the population of the earth, which had remained under 500 million for so long, suddenly jumped to 1 billion people. Then, it took only 123 years to reach 2 billion. After that it seems there was no looking back. As the number of people in the world increased to 3, 4, 5, and 6 billion, the number of years it took to add each additional billion shrank from hundreds to 33, 14, 13, and 12, respectively. While our global family had reached the new record of about 6.89 billion by the year 2010 and is still growing, the rate of growth seems to have slowed from a peak, estimated by the United Nations, of 88 million people per year, in 1989, to the current 75 million people per year.[34]

The rate of population growth in the recent past, and where that growth is believed to be headed, has signaled an alarm for the governments, universities, and agencies whose job it is to track this kind of information. The above data is powerful evidence of an unsustainable trend: the doubling of the world's population on a timescale that follows a predictable rhythm of cycles. And while the current trend suggests that the next doubling of our global family, from 4 billion (in 1974) to 8 billion, will occur by 2025, the experts believe that, *if it happens at all,* this will be the last time a doubling occurs until sometime in the 22nd century.

Another doubling in this century is doubtful, largely due to the sheer number of people likely to be involved in any crisis we'll face during that time. Whether a pandemic disease, a shortage of food and water, or the death toll of war will prevent the next doubling is uncertain. What *is* certain is that each of these potential crises poses a very real threat—one that, if realized, would impact a huge number of people quickly. Although such a dramatic drop in global population is rare, it has occurred in the past.

The spread of disease in the 14th century is a powerful reminder that such things are possible. Between 1348 and 1351 the "Black Death" spread throughout most of Europe. Although the sporadic record keeping of that time makes determining the exact death toll difficult, the estimated number of people killed by the plague ranges between 75 million and 200 million.

While today's antibiotics make such a mortality rate unlikely, they only work to treat bacterial infections. The increase in the number of new viral infections that have no known cure, combined with modern air travel, which makes it possible for people to transport themselves in a matter of hours from areas of high infection rates to the biggest cities with the densest populations, makes this threat a very real source of concern.

For reasons such as these, our ability to forecast population trends is a powerful tool in our toolkit to deal with a changing world and predict the demands that growing numbers of people are placing on the land that supports them. The CIA described the need for such information, saying: "The [population] growth rate is a factor in determining how great a burden would be imposed on a country by the changing needs of its people for infrastructure (e.g., schools, hospitals, housing, roads), resources (e.g., food, water, electricity), and jobs. Rapid population growth can be seen as threatening by neighboring countries."[35]

As Joel E. Cohen, mathematical biologist and head of the Laboratory of Populations at The Rockefeller University, states in *Scientific American*, "The peak population growth rate ever reached, about 2.1 percent a year, occurred between 1965 and 1970. Human population never grew with such speed before the 20th century and is never again likely to grow with such speed."[36]

The good news in Cohen's assessment is that the population explosion appears to have peaked about 40 years ago. The flip side is that most of those born during that peak are still alive and need to find the resources of food, water, shelter, and jobs to sustain them through their life expectancy, now estimated to be an average of 67 years worldwide. This is where politics, technology, lifestyle, and age-old customs are converging to create the hotbed of crises that we see today.

UNESCO's *Millennium Ecosystem Assessment Synthesis Report*

To address any of the tipping-point crises, they must first be identified clearly and concisely. In this way, issues that seem like problems too big to overcome can be broken into smaller, manageable portions that can be approached one at a time.

Due to its clarity, I've chosen to use the *Millennium Ecosystem Assessment Synthesis Report,* drafted by 1,300 contributing scientists in 95 countries, as a summary here to tie some of the major crisis points together. Its findings describe the impact that human activity has had upon key ecosystems that we depend upon, and detail how disappearing resources are affecting the quality of human life. It's the violent competition over the loss of these resources that fuels already-strained international tensions and adds to the threat of war.

Here is the essence of the four key findings from the UNESCO report in the original words:

1. Humans have changed ecosystems more rapidly and extensively in the last 50 years than in any other period. This was done largely to meet rapidly growing demands for food, fresh water, timber, fiber, and fuel. More land was converted to agriculture since 1945 than in the 18th and 19th centuries combined. More than half of all the synthetic nitrogen fertilizers, first made in 1913, ever used on the planet have been used since 1985. Experts say that this resulted in a substantial and largely irreversible loss in diversity of life on Earth, with some 10 to 30 percent of the mammal, bird, and amphibian species currently threatened with extinction.

2. Ecosystem changes that have contributed substantial net gains in human well-being and economic development have been achieved at growing costs in the form of degradation of other services. Only four ecosystem services have been enhanced in the last 50 years: increases in crop, livestock, and aquaculture production, and increased carbon sequestration for global climate regulation. Two services—capture fisheries and fresh water—are now well beyond levels that can sustain

current, much less future, demands. Experts say that these problems will substantially diminish the benefits for future generations.

3. The degradation of ecosystem services could become significantly worse during the first half of this century and is a barrier to achieving the UN Millennium Development Goals. In all the four plausible futures explored by the scientists, they project progress in eliminating hunger, but at far slower rates than needed to halve the number of people suffering from hunger by 2015. Experts warn that changes in ecosystems such as deforestation influence the abundance of human pathogens such as malaria and cholera, as well as the risk of emergence of new diseases. Malaria, for example, accounts for 11 percent of the disease burden in Africa and had it been eliminated 35 years ago, the continent's gross domestic product would have increased by $100 billion.

4. The challenge of reversing the degradation of ecosystems while meeting increasing demands can be met under some scenarios involving significant policy and institutional changes. However, these changes will be large and are not currently under way. The report mentions options that exist to conserve or enhance ecosystem services that reduce negative trade-offs or that will positively impact other services. Protection of natural forests, for example, not only conserves wildlife but also supplies fresh water and reduces carbon emissions.[37]

Summing up all of the research, all of the expertise, and all of the recommendations that the Millennium Assessment (MA) has created in this document, the MA board of directors conclude: "It lies within the power of human societies to ease the strains we are putting on the nature services of the planet, while continuing to use them to bring better living standards to all." They go on to say, "Achieving this, however, will require radical changes in the way nature is treated at every level of decision-making and new ways of cooperation between government, business and civil society. The warning signs are there for all of us to see. The future now lies in our hands."[38]

Clearly, as a species we're on a learning curve with regard to the way we live, and we're teetering on the brink of making choices with very dire consequences. As we saw with the 2010 Copenhagen Climate

Summit, the choices of the past have been based in a way of seeing the world that is, at the very least, incomplete; and is, in some instances, absolutely wrong.

This is one of those places where common sense enters into the picture in a big way.

Getting It Right

Common sense tells us that it is illogical to attempt solving the greatest crises in human history through the vision of an incomplete understanding of the problem. We are discovering that many of the tools we used in the past no longer work. They are ineffective in dealing with the scale of issues that face us, and the problems are only getting worse. Meanwhile, our future and our very lives are at stake.

With the sheer number and magnitude of crises we face today, the consequences of a wrong decision have never been greater. At the same time, the opportunities have never been clearer. The crises are forcing us to rethink old ideas and set our course in a new and life-affirming direction. For precisely this reason, we must take a long, hard look at the core assumptions underlying our relationships to ourselves and to the world, and ask ourselves why it is that we believe as we do.

So where do we start? How do we come to think of ourselves so differently in the world? Our ancient past is a great place to begin.

> **Deep Truth 3:** The key to addressing the crises threatening our survival lies in building partnerships based upon mutual aid and cooperation to adapt to the changes, rather than in pointing fingers and assigning blame, which makes such vital alliances difficult.

CHAPTER FOUR

THE HIDDEN HISTORY OF OUR FORGOTTEN PAST: PLACES THAT SHOULD NOT EXIST

"Those who cannot remember the past
are condemned to repeat their mistakes."

— GEORGE SANTAYANA (1863–1952), PHILOSOPHER

When I was in school during the '60s and '70s, I was taught that civilization began about 5,500 years ago. The traditional thinking was that around then the two earliest civilizations, those of Sumer and Egypt, developed in the area where Africa and Asia come together. The rest, as the saying goes, is history.

With the exception of a few leading-edge textbooks and forward-thinking teachers, schools today are still teaching the same history. This traditional view of our past makes it sound as if primitive peoples came together about 3100 B.C.E. near areas of food and water, and began to build simple homes for their families—structures that progressed over centuries into the steel-and-glass skyscrapers that we see today. It's a great story, and it makes perfect sense. There's one big problem, however: the story doesn't fit the evidence. And because it doesn't, it's not based in science.

A growing body of scientific evidence from multiple locations around the world shows beyond any reasonable doubt that the "first civilizations" of traditional history are really not the first at all. Instead, ancient Sumer and Egypt followed in the footsteps of even older and, in some respects, even more advanced civilizations that appeared, and then disappeared, much earlier than 5,000 years ago. And while there's a lot that we don't know about these ancient civilizations that are twice as old as traditional history says they should be, one thing is absolutely certain: the history that we're teaching in our classrooms is one piece of a much larger picture.

The existence of older civilizations opens the door to some big questions that have yet to be answered. Who built them? Where did they come from? And perhaps the question that is most important to us today: What happened to them? How is it possible that huge urban centers could have existed near the last ice age—massive cities and temple complexes built using advanced technologies that cannot be duplicated today—and then vanished from the face of the earth?

The answers to these questions may hold clues to surviving the crises that face our world today. It's for this reason that I've placed the topic of our ancient history among our deepest truths.

Saving the Past

For a brief moment, I closed my eyes and listened as the wind moved through the branches towering above me. The breeze that found its way to me through the dense forest, past the layer of sweat and dust that was clinging to my face and arms, was a welcome relief that morning. Even though the air was hot, at least it was moving and provided a break from the stifling heat and humidity of a late-summer afternoon in northern Missouri.

I remember thinking that there is a timeless quality to moments like the one I was experiencing. Surely the ancient peoples whose campsite I was excavating that day had had the same experience as they cooked their meals over the fire pit I was uncovering hundreds of years later. Streams of sweat rolled off my face and fell to the ground as I opened my eyes and leaned forward over the shallow depression where my trawl scraped away the next layer of earth.

Only a few weeks before, I had been at this same archaeological dig, which was exposing an ancient village, with my anthropology class in college. We had been asked to help with the emergency recovery of this surprising discovery. It was surprising because the ^{14}C dating on initial artifacts recovered showed that it was the home of an indigenous people thought to have lived in the area only at a later time. The hunting camp beneath my feet was the first evidence that this group of people, the ancient Hopewell (100–500 C.E.), had migrated to the bluffs overlooking the Missouri River much earlier than had been known.

The emergency aspect of the dig was due to the fact that it was located directly in the path of an oncoming highway project that would cover the area. For reasons ranging from the cold weather that would soon make the construction difficult, to planning, priorities, and schedules, the timing of the project, we were told, could not be changed. In just a few weeks, the blades of heavy equipment would cut directly through the mound where I knelt, and the evidence of this site would rapidly be buried under tons of asphalt and concrete . . . or destroyed forever.

Before the construction began, no one knew the ancient campsite was there. As happens so often with archaeological discoveries, it wasn't years of scholarly research that had brought the site to the attention of the authorities. Instead, it was the sharp eye of a heavy-equipment operator clearing the area. For just an instant, as the driver had raised the massive steel blade of his bull-dozer from the ground, the glimmer of something shiny caught his eye. Maybe it was because he looked in just the right place at just the right moment. Or maybe it was because he cared enough to investigate what he'd seen. For whatever the reason, on that day the construction worker stopped his work long enough to follow the ray of sunlight that reflected off the slick, shiny surface of a piece of pottery that had been buried for centuries.

That driver's discovery was the reason why my class had been asked to help. Rather than the orderly documentation and exca-vation that would normally characterize such a dig, we had been working on a countdown. Within a matter of days, the evidence and history of whoever had made their home at this site long ago was due to disappear.

On that day, I was at the site alone. While the construction project continued, classes had concluded and, for reasons of time and money, the official dig was considered finished. Nonetheless, I wanted to save as much of the site and the evidence of the people who lived there as possible. As I uncovered bits of bone, pottery, flint chips, and arrowheads, I wondered how this single find would change the way we see the history of America's ancient heartland.

Then I began to think in larger terms, and to ask a bigger ques-tion: If our knowledge of local history was still changing, could the same thing be occurring on a global level? What else had hap-pened to the people and cultures from our distant past that we've now forgotten? Have there been advanced civilizations that ex-isted long before the accepted timeline of history suggests? And, if so, what changed them and their world so drastically? It would not be until decades later that I would discover some of the answers to my questions.

In just a few days of scraping away the wet, black earth of the ancient forest, the charred bits of bone and pottery changed the entire story of what had happened beneath the weathered cliffs of northern Missouri long ago. It changed what would be taught in the classrooms of high schools and colleges throughout the country. It changed the timelines and maps of where people lived and how they migrated in the past. It changed the course of careers for archaeologists and historians who had based their work on theories and assumptions made from incomplete knowledge. All of these things changed. They had to, because of the new evidence.

The existence of physical artifacts and the science linking them to a specific date long ago told researchers a story that could not be ignored. And just as the local history of cultures along the bluffs and river valleys of northern Missouri had to be revised to reflect the new evidence found at our dig, the global history of humankind throughout the world must now change to accommodate new science-based discoveries.

The Moving Target of History

"History is the invention of historians." This quote, attributed to Napoléon Bonaparte (1769–1821), self-designated Emperor of France, is a beautiful reminder of why it's important to keep our view of the past current using the revisions called for by the scientific method, even when new discoveries don't fit the accepted timeline of history. In this way we keep our window to the past honest, and our historians current.

Until the mid-20th century, the history of civilization seemed pretty much to be an open-and-shut case. The traditional "story" of civilization suggests that it developed through a continual progression of improvements in agriculture, technology, and culture (see Figure 4.1). It's a linear story that looks good on a textbook timeline: simple beginnings that have resulted in the complex world of today. This story is neat and tidy. Perhaps, most important, it's believable.

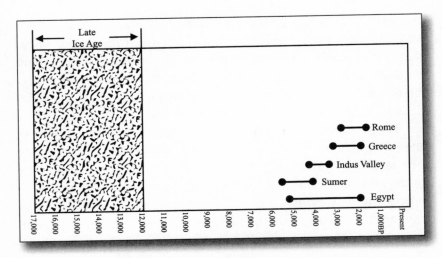

Figure 4.1. The traditional timeline of civilization. This graph is a composite from various sources and shows the beginning and end dates of the major civilizations relative to one another. Note that Sumer has traditionally been accepted as the oldest civilization, believed to have emerged approximately 5,500 years ago.

Each time a new archaeological site confirms another piece of the traditional story of our past, it becomes easier to give a "green light" of acceptance to the rest of the story. The problem with this, however, is that a growing body of evidence doesn't support the accepted story. Anytime we discover even one piece of evidence that doesn't fit the timeline of history, and that evidence is verified by the best science of our day, then we are forced to change the timeline to make room for it. Amateur archaeologist Heinrich Schliemann's discovery of ancient Troy in 1870 is a beautiful example of how just such an adjustment was made.

Schliemann had long been fascinated by *The Iliad*—Homer's literary classic about the legendary Trojan War—as well as the story of the Trojan horse and how it was used to accomplish what no army had accomplished before: the capture of the ancient city of Troy. He asked himself a simple question: *What if the age-old legend that the Greeks told to their children was more than a fairy tale? What if it was true?* What if *The Iliad* was the description of an actual event that took place so long ago that the story was all that was left to keep its memory alive?

Acting on his intuition, Schliemann used *The Iliad* as a literal map, and followed its clues to make one of the greatest archaeological discoveries of the 19th century. Schliemann excavated eight layers of earth, representing eight previous civilizations buried under a small mound in Hisarlik (at the time part of the Ottoman Empire, now an area of Turkey) that lay in the exact location where *The Iliad* said the ancient battle occurred.

In the ninth layer of the dig site, Schliemann found the gates of the ancient city of Troy. It was then that the world accepted the physical reality of what most people had believed to be a fairy tale, and the timeline of world history was changed to include Schliemann's discovery.

Similarly, Hiram Bingham's 1911 discovery of Machu Picchu, the so-called lost city of the Incas, resulted directly from the investigation of ancient legends and myths.

Following both these discoveries, history books and lessons had to be updated and changed, and entire careers that had been based upon one way of thinking and teaching had to be adjusted to reflect the new discoveries. A growing body of scientific evidence now suggests that we're in a very similar situation today, and on a much larger scale.

Figure 4.2. *Top:* The remains of Peru's "lost" city of the Incas, Machu Picchu, as they appeared in 1911 after archaeologists burned away thick jungle overgrowth from the site. (Credit: Hiram Bingham, 1911/public domain.) *Bottom:* Machu Picchu as it appears today, showing portions of the complex reconstructed. (Credit: © Jerry Miner/sacredspaces.org.) *Facing page:* A portion of the ancient city of Troy, believed to be mythical until amateur archaeologist Heinrich Schliemann discovered it in 1870. (Credit: iStockphoto: © MaxFX.)

Recent evidence is casting a long shadow of doubt on the traditional story of our past. The new story that's emerging has implications that shake the foundation of what we've believed and have been taught in schools for nearly 300 years. Those implications may hold clues informing us of how we can survive the same types of crises today that brought an end to great civilizations of the past.

Civilizations That Time Forgot?

While there have always been reports of ancient civilizations and artifacts that seemed too fantastic to be true (and many of them probably *were*), since the mid-1800s there has been an increase in the number of discoveries that fall into this category. From the sonar that enabled the seafloor discovery of an ancient city in India's Gulf of Khambhat, to the earth-penetrating radar showing the unexcavated remains of the oldest temples in the world, recent advances in technology have contributed to a growing body of information telling us that our picture of the past is anything but complete.

Of course, not all of our astounding recent discoveries take place on remote mountaintops or in isolated rain forests. Some are near the largest cities in the world, with hundreds of thousands of tourists each year walking around them, staring in awe, and photographing them each day.

Let's take a look at four of those discoveries now.

Discovery 1

Where: Giza Plateau, Egypt.

What: Physical evidence pushes the construction date of Egypt's Great Sphinx to a time near the last ice age.

Implication: The scientific evidence, which was produced using a valid and reliable methodology, proves beyond a reasonable doubt that the core-body of the Sphinx existed during the torrential rains that followed the end of the last ice age, placing the monument's age into the 7,000- to 9,000-year range. The peer-reviewed data is accepted by members of the geological sciences.

The problem rests with the historians who must now reconcile the new data about the Great Sphinx with the traditionally established timeline of civilization.

While there have always been conflicting opinions and heated debates about discoveries that don't seem to fit the traditional story of the past, there has been a tendency to set them aside and label them as "anomalous." The thinking has been that there could be a mistake in the techniques that dated objects, for example; or that while the data may be good, the interpretation of the data is not so good. Since the 1980s, the age of Egypt's Great Sphinx has been a perfect example of such a controversy, and the debate about the matter has been played out in the mainstream media as well as at scientific conferences.

The Great Sphinx is located on the Giza Plateau at the edge of Cairo. It is traditionally believed to have been built between 2558 and 2532 B.C.E., meaning that it is around 4,500 years old. Through the work of pioneering Egyptologist R. A. Schwaller de Lubicz and the later work of independent researcher John Anthony West, however, the traditional dates have been brought into question.

One of the mysteries of the Sphinx temple complex, as well as the Great Pyramid and other monuments on the Giza Plateau, is that unlike many other temples in Egypt's Nile River Valley, there are no written records on the monuments themselves to tell us about their history—or at least none that have been discovered so far.

With the exception of four letters from the Greek alphabet near the upper chamber of the Great Pyramid, believed to have been inscribed centuries after it was built, archaeologists have found no lettering or hieroglyphics carved into the Sphinx or the Pyramid, nor any ancient papyrus scrolls tucked away in a tomb that tell us precisely when, and how, these massive structures were built or who built them. In the absence of such direct evidence, we are left to consider another kind: *circumstantial* evidence. And that is where the controversy comes in.

In the 1980s and '90s, John Anthony West was reexamining the earlier work of scholar Schwaller de Lubicz for clues regarding the age of the Great Sphinx. During his 15 years of exploring and documenting the monuments of Egypt early in the 20th century, Schwaller de Lubicz found that the traditional explanations of how, and when, structures such as the various pyramids and the Sphinx were built didn't agree with what he was seeing for himself. As a result, he began to question the accepted stories from a purely geological perspective.

It's generally accepted by Egyptologists, geologists, and historians alike that the main body of the Sphinx was carved in place from the existing bedrock of the Giza Plateau. As the natural rock was removed to create the half-human, half-lion body, the structure became surrounded by the hollowed-out trough that we can still see today.

Standing in the trough, both West and Schwaller de Lubicz were struck by the erosion marks on the back and sides of the Sphinx, some of which are many feet deep. While the experts seem to agree that the marks are definitely due to erosion, the traditional explanation is that they resulted from the wind blowing loose sand onto the structure. The belief has been that after a long period of time, this process carved the deep furrows clearly visible on the surface of the Sphinx today (see Figure 4.3).

Close examination of the erosion marks themselves led Schwaller de Lubicz to question the traditional "windblown sand" idea. The reason was that the marks looked more like the work of water-based erosion than what would be expected from a wind-related process. As it turns out, scientists investigating late in the 20th century agreed.

Figure 4.3. Erosion marks on the shoulders *(top)* and back *(bottom)* of Egypt's Great Sphinx show the telltale signs of fluvial erosion–the wear from large amounts of fast-moving water over long periods of time. The last time this kind of erosion was possible for the deserts of northern Africa was when the climate changed at the end of the last ice age 8,000 to 12,000 years ago. (Credit: © Gregg Braden.)

In 1989, West enlisted the aid of Robert M. Schoch, a stratigrapher and paleontologist from Boston University, to bring a scientific eye to the mystery. Schoch made his first trip to the Giza Plateau in 1990. During the multiple trips in the years that have followed, he's made a number of discoveries—powerful scientific contributions that move us toward unlocking the mystery of the age of the Great Sphinx. What he's found, however, has also opened the door to even more questions, and deeper mysteries.

"I discovered that the geological evidence was not compatible with what the Egyptologists were saying," Schoch states. "I came to the conclusion that the oldest portions of the Great Sphinx, what I refer to as the core-body, must date back to an earlier period (at least 5000 B.C., and maybe as early as 7000 B.C. or 9000 B.C.), a time when the climate was very different and included more rain."[1]

In the years following Schoch's first site visit, his investigation into the natural structures and the geology of the surrounding area has led to new discoveries that add to the growing body of research regarding the origin and age of the Sphinx. The first is that the deep erosion marks in the body of the Sphinx are definitely not caused from windblown sand, but are the "telltale marks of water weathering."[2] Additionally, the vertical cracks in the bedrock walls surrounding the structure show "diagnostic signs of having been formed by precipitation and water runoff."[3]

To determine just how far underground the erosion patterns on the buried portions of the Sphinx continue, Schoch and his team used seismic studies, similar to those used to tell how deeply a well must be drilled to reach water. Basically, sound waves travel into the earth and are reflected by buried surfaces back to measuring devices located at ground level. The studies conducted on the area beneath the body of the Sphinx revealed that the erosion patterns we see aboveground continue to a portion of the structure not visible at ground level, and possess what Schoch calls an "extraordinary depth of subsurface weathering."[4]

It's generally agreed by scientists that Egypt experienced a period of heavy rains following the end of the last ice age approximately 12,000 years ago. The scientific data shows that the rains lasted about 4,000 years and stopped around 8,000 years ago. The dates that Schoch gives for the carving of the Sphinx range conservatively from 5000 to 7000 B.C.E., or even possibly as far back as 9000 B.C.E. (in other words, the Sphinx is at least 7,000 years old, and may be as much as 9,000 to 11,000 years old), placing it well within the span of time when the heavy rains inundated present-day Egypt's Sahara region.[5]

So even though the geological evidence supports these conclusions, and they've been accepted by the geological community, they present a huge problem for historians.

Discovery 2

Where: Göbekli Tepe, Turkey.

What: Physical evidence of the ceremonial complex at Göbekli Tepe, the earliest civilization documented on Earth, has been scientifically dated to 11,500 years ago, pushing the date of this site close to the end of the last ice age.

Implication: This scientific evidence proves beyond a reasonable doubt that civilization is at least twice as old as previously believed. German archaeologist Klaus Schmidt knew that he had found something extraordinary the first day he explored Göbekli Tepe (Turkish for "hill of the navel"). A single tree stands on the top of the highest hill at the site, and the locals tell a story that holds the tree to be a marker of sacred significance. Schmidt knew this story, and says that when he arrived, "I thought we might be onto something."[6] As he looked over the site and saw the hillside covered with broken pieces of flint and evidence of ancient occupation, he remembers, "Within the first minute, I knew that if I didn't walk away immediately, I would be here the rest of my life."[7]

He stayed, and has been excavating the site since that pivotal day in 1994.

Göbekli Tepe wasn't completely unknown to archaeologists. It's just that the American-led team who had originally found and documented the site 30 years earlier, in 1964, had falsely assumed that the mounds surrounding it were burial grounds that would date to a much more recent time. No one could have known, or even suspected, just how far from the truth that assumption would be.

The bottom line is that Göbekli Tepe turns out to be older—much, much older—than anyone could have ever dared to imagine. The find of a lifetime, it's an archaeologist's dream. In the words of Patrick Symmes, the journalist who wrote about the discovery for *Newsweek* magazine in February 2010, "The site isn't just old, it redefines old."[8]

How old? The scientifically accepted method for determining the age of the Göbekli Tepe site dates the temples excavated so far to 11,550 years ago.[9] For the sake of comparison, this means that they were built 6,000 years *before* the ancient stone circles of Stonehenge in England.

Göbekli Tepe contains a number of circular temples that vary in size, but appear to have similar layouts. Each temple has two large T-shaped pillars in the center and is surrounded by smaller pillars that form the ring of the circle (see Figure 4.4). Even though the site is not as large as Stonehenge, and does not contain the distinctive overhead slabs found there, as I pored over the first images of the excavations from Göbekli Tepe, the vertical stones arranged in circles certainly reminded me of the celestial markers and other observatory-like features familiar from Stonehenge.

As of spring 2010, four of the circular temples and 50 of the pillars had been excavated. Earth-imaging radar, however, shows that another 15 to 20 circles still remain covered beneath the surface. The largest of the circular temples is about 98 feet across, and the tallest pillars are about 17 feet high. One of the things that make the site especially valuable to archaeologists is that it appears to have been intentionally buried about 8,000 B.C.E. The reason is a mystery.

This means that the slabs are still intact—still vertical, just as they were at the time they were used. And they're well preserved. About half of the pillars uncovered so far have images carved on them in high relief. And while these images appear hieroglyph-like, they are not believed to be a form of language. (Traditional history suggests that writing did not appear until about 6,000 years later.)

✳ ✳ ✳

Figure 4.4. *Above:* The layout of the vertical stone pillars that make up the circles at the Göbekli Tepe site. (Credit: © Berthold Steinhilber/laif/Redux.) *Facing page:* A close-up of the detailed images on the pillars. (Credit: © Berthold Steinhilber/laif/ Redux.)

The carvings on the pillars depict animals such as foxes, cows, and lions, but no humans per se. The pillars, however, appear to be made in the likeness of human forms, with arms, hands, and fingers, although without faces or even heads. This has suggested to some historians that the pillars represent deities with human qualities. Johns Hopkins University archaeologist Glenn Schwartz observed how the Bible describes man as created in God's image, and Göbekli Tepe "is the first time you can see humans with that idea, that they resemble gods," he says.[10]

When I first heard of Göbekli Tepe, my reaction was to suspect that there had been a mistake in the dating: either in the method or in the interpretation. The technique used was carbon dating (called carbon-14, or ^{14}C, dating), a process commonly used to determine the age of everything from ancient mummies to the fur on prehistoric woolly mammoths found frozen in the ice sheets of Siberia.

I was skeptical of the reported age because I know, as a former geologist, that stone relics themselves cannot be dated. The technique of carbon dating works only for something that has lived at some point in the past and absorbed carbon from the environment while it was alive.

The preliminary dating of Göbekli Tepe is based upon samples from two different sources: (1) charcoal deposits (remnants of ancient wood) buried at the lowest levels of the site excavated so far, noted as "Hd" samples, which give us an idea of how long ago the site was actually occupied; and (2) carbonate deposits found on some of the stone pillars, noted as "Ua" samples, which can only be used to tell us about the time after the site was abandoned. (The *Hd* and *Ua* notations are unique identifiers that the researchers have given to their samples.)

I researched this kind of dating personally to assure myself that it is reliable. A 2007 report in the science journal *The Holocene* addressed my concerns precisely. The conclusion of this in-depth study was that the kind of deposits used to fix the age of Göbekli Tepe can actually be "dated more accurately with ^{14}C than has been generally appreciated."[11]

With the accuracy of this kind of dating established, the results of the preliminary tests are nothing short of stunning. The "Hd" samples shown in Figure 4.5, taken from the top levels of the earliest layers excavated so far, date to 9559 B.C.E., plus or minus 53 years, or 11,570 years ago! While this date already places Göbekli

Tepe among the oldest known temple sites in the world, we may discover that the earliest levels of occupation are much older. The reason why is that the samples used for the preliminary dating were taken from the *top portions* of the sites that the excavations had exposed. This means that they are only the most recent layers of the oldest levels of occupation. Because the base of the site is even deeper in the ground, it's likely that the lower layers will reveal dates that are even older. Experts working at the site suspect that ^{14}C tests from the deepest layers will push the date for Göbekli Tepe back to at least 11,000 B.C.E. (13,000 years ago), and possibly earlier!

Figure 4.5 is a brief summary of the samples used to establish the dates. The "Years Old" column shows the age of each sample after factoring in the years that account for B.C.E. notation, as well as the margin of error shown in the "Calibrated Date" column.

Sample Number Used by Lab	Calibrated Date (Years B.C.E.)	Years Old	Site Description
Ua-19561	7560–7370	9,370–9,560	Enclosure C
Ua-19562	8280–7970	9,970–10,280	Enclosure B
Hd-20025	9110–8620	11,110–11,370	Layer III
Hd-20036	9130–8800	11,370–11,560	Layer III

Figure 4.5. Four samples used for ^{14}C dating of Göbekli Tepe. The "Hd" samples, from carbon remains, are from the most recent layers of the oldest levels of occupation. They date to an astonishing 11,517 to 11,623 years ago.[12] It's believed that when the excavations reach the deepest levels of occupation, the date of the site may be pushed into the last years of the ice age, more than 12,000 years ago.

The mysteries of Göbekli Tepe are far from being solved. We may never know, for example, why the entire site was covered up around 8,000 B.C.E. or who built it in the first place. It may take years or even decades more to decipher the glyphs that cover the pillars, or to understand if the site could have served astronomical purposes, such as those confirmed in some Mayan and Egyptian temples. Schmidt says that decades of work remain, and it's obvious that anyone who undertakes the task of understanding Göbekli Tepe may find that he or she has just committed a lifetime to this endeavor.

Robert Schoch and John Anthony West explored Göbekli Tepe personally in 2010.[13] One of the questions that the critics of the geologist and the Egyptologist's near–ice age dating for the Great Sphinx (described in the previous section) have consistently asked is: "Where are the potsherds?" In other words, where is the hard, physical evidence of the people, technology, and civilization that would have had to exist to create a structure like the Sphinx? Following their exploration of Göbekli Tepe, West remarked, "We don't need a potsherd. We've got a whole gigantic, ceremonial site with carved reliefs."[14]

One thing is certain: The evidence is in, and the scientists agree. Something happened at Göbekli Tepe 11,500 years ago that our modern worldview can no longer ignore. And when we consider this site in the revised timeline of our past, along with other additional findings from around the world, an entirely new view of our history begins to emerge. It doesn't end with Göbekli Tepe alone.

Discovery 3

Where: Gulf of Khambhat, India.

What: Physical evidence of a "lost" civilization that dates back to about 9,500 years ago has been identified under the waters of the Indian Ocean.

Implication: While there is controversy surrounding this discovery, it comes as a result of the techniques used for the site's excavation and the collection of samples. The controversy does not change the fact that an ancient city has been discovered off the coast of India, hidden beneath 120 feet of water. This fact implies that the city was built before the land was submerged, and may have existed during the time of the sea-level rise that occurred at the end of the last ice age. I'm offering it here as additional evidence that other late–ice age civilizations, such as those in Egypt and Turkey, are more than isolated anomalies.

Maybe it's not surprising that so many new discoveries of ancient civilizations seem to be coming from the watery depths of our world. These are the places least obvious to the naked eye, and least disturbed by modern civilization. Once discovered, they are also some of the hardest to explore. Nevertheless, throughout the 20th century, there were reports of "lost" cities being found under the lakes and oceans throughout the globe. From the grainy images of roads and walls discovered just off the coast of Bimini Island in the 1960s, and of similar finds near the Bahamas; to the video footage of massive pyramid-like structures discovered off the coast of Japan in 1986, it's obvious that we're on the verge of discovering an entirely new era of human history that changes what we've believed about the past.

In January 2002, the British Broadcasting Company (BBC) reported on an archaeological discovery with the enthusiasm that generally comes with stories of lost cities and forgotten civilizations. The headline trumpeted: "Lost City 'Could Rewrite History.'" As I read the report, I was reminded of similar claims made about the Dead Sea Scrolls. Journalist Tom Housden was speculating that the discovery "may force historians and archaeologists to radically reconsider their view of ancient history."[15]

The more I read, the more I understood that this discovery was different from many others.

— **First**, its location was significant: Underneath 120 feet of water near the west coast of India, the site is in a place where such a find would not be expected. Having dived at such depths as an oceanography major in college, I knew how something could be there in plain sight and still go unnoticed for years.

I remember searching for an ancient shipwreck off the eastern coast of Florida with friends in the 1970s, for example. We found ourselves swimming in tropical waters directly above the mound of coral-encrusted remains, and passing by them multiple times, without even realizing that we were just a few feet away. It was only when our expert guide pointed out the wreck that we could see the shape and make our way to what was left of the ship. So it comes as no surprise to me that a stretch of ocean could have been heavily traversed by ships for centuries, yet still hold the secret of an undiscovered civilization.

The BBC report said that Indian scientists from the National Institute of Oceanographic Technology (NIOT) were not *looking* for the remains of an ancient site that could rewrite the history of the world. They were in the area to test the water quality and the impact of pollution when their equipment registered unexpected signals. When they investigated where the signals were coming from, their sonar maps revealed the regular forms and intentional angles that are the telltale signs of walls created by human civilization. It was then that they knew they'd found a forgotten city.

— The **second** piece of information that told me this was no ordinary find was the sheer size of the underwater complex. This wasn't a typical archaeological site identified by a single out-of-place mound measuring only a few hundred feet across, like I'd seen with the shipwreck in Florida. The Gulf of Khambhat site, as it is now known, was being measured in terms of *miles*. The report said that a strip of ruins was preserved that extended continuously for two miles in one direction and five miles in another. In archaeological terms, this is huge, and it tells us that whatever the scientists discovered in India's coastal waters is more than an ancient campsite or a single temple. It appears to be the remains of a huge and ancient city.

I've studied the archaeology and history of India, and there is no room in the traditional timeline of Indian archaeology that allows for what the NIOT discovery seems to be revealing.

Questions immediately began to race through my mind: *Who built this city? Why did it disappear?* And the biggest question was the most obvious: *How old is it?* This last question is where the controversy begins to heat up.

The initial age of the site, based on the dating of recovered artifacts such as human bones, teeth, pottery, and beads, reverberated above the chatter of archaeological reports of other new findings in the world. It was *9,500 years old,* a full 5,000 years older than even the earliest dates assigned to the mysterious sites of Mohenjo Daro and Harappa, which were discovered in the Indus Valley in the 1920s.

As we've seen from the sites of Göbekli Tepe and the Great Sphinx, dating in this range poses a huge problem for historians. Scientists are in general agreement that the last ice age ended about 12,000 years ago. As mentioned in the discussion of the erosion marks on the Sphinx, it was after this time that temperatures warmed; a period of tremendous rainfall began, lasting somewhere in the neighborhood of 4,000 years; the ice that covered much of the Northern Hemisphere began to melt; and sea levels started to rise. When they did, many areas on low-lying coastlines disappeared under the water. Because it's unlikely (although not impossible) that massive cities like the one discovered at the Gulf of Khambhat were originally constructed underwater, the implication is that they had to exist before the rains began. That is, they had to be built at some time *during* the last ice age.

In a BBC News Online interview, archaeologist Justin Morris, working with the British Museum, explained why this implication poses such a problem. "Culturally speaking," he said, "in that part of the world there were no civilizations prior to about 2500 B.C."[16] The time frame he described here reflects the traditional thinking of the current scientific paradigm—specifically, that civilization itself began only about 5,000 years ago, and first appeared in the area of India and what is now Pakistan about 4,500 years ago. But 2500 B.C.E. is a full 5,000 years later than the ^{14}C dates for the artifacts found at the Gulf of Khambhat site.

Further commenting about the find in the Gulf of Khambhat, Morris notes that the ^{14}C dating process is not without its error margins: "More work would need to be undertaken before the site could be categorically said to belong to a 9,000-year old civilization."[17]

Morris is right on both counts. The ^{14}C dating process has certainly had its share of controversy in the past, and there certainly are conditions that can skew the accuracy of the results. It's precisely for this reason that ^{14}C dates are generally given with a margin of error.

The studies I've seen from the initial reports do not include this margin of error, so at the time of this writing I cannot say specifically how much time it involves. However, it certainly is a factor of tens to hundreds of years, as in the ranges we saw previously for the Göbekli Tepe dates—not *thousands* of years, covering the entire time span of civilization as we know it. And this is where Morris's second comment is especially important.

While ^{14}C dating methods are scientifically accepted and commonly used, the techniques employed to bring the first artifacts from the Gulf of Khambhat site to the surface so they could be dated have been called into question by scientists and historians alike. The objects were unconventionally dredged up from the site by machine, rather than acquired through painstaking excavation using precise grids that are explored systematically. This certainly makes it hard to tell exactly where the artifacts came from within the site, and if the bones and teeth, for example, are from the same time and place as the bits of wood.

Without a doubt, the depth of the site, and the poor visibility at such a depth, has something to do with why the artifacts have initially been recovered in the way they have. Researchers have said in response to their critics that this round of collection was intended as a preliminary "look and see" to (1) determine that a site actually exists, and (2) to give scientists some idea of what they may be dealing with.

Based on the preliminary findings, I have no doubt that a full-on archaeological excavation—complete with all of the trusted features of traditional underwater archaeology—will take place in the near future in the Gulf of Khambhat. Until that happens, however, we cannot say with scientific certainty whether the objects that have already been dated actually originated at the time of the structures themselves or were carried by sea currents and deposited at the site. Until the next phase of the excavation answers some of these lingering questions, we have to view the site for what it is: additional evidence of a near–ice age civilization forgotten at some point in history, and now submerged under 120 feet of seawater. It is a city whose secrets may help us gain a better understanding of our ancient past.

If India's Gulf of Khambhat site indeed confirms what the preliminary evidence suggests, and supports the mounting body of evidence for advanced civilizations during the last ice age, then we must reconsider our current beliefs about the history of civilization. In an interview with the BBC regarding the implications of such a site, independent researcher and scholar Graham Hancock stated the problem beautifully, saying, "It means that the whole model of the origins of civilization with which archaeologists have been working will have to be remade from scratch."[18]

Discovery 4

Where: Caral, Peru.

What: Physical evidence of a "lost" civilization in northern Peru has been scientifically dated to between 5,000 and 6,900 years ago.

Implication: The discovery of an advanced civilization that collapsed during the time when it has traditionally been suggested that civilization was beginning is forcing historians to rewrite the history of the Americas. The physical evidence from Caral now makes it the oldest civilization known to have existed in any of the Americas.

✳ ✳ ✳

The first thing I noticed as we neared the top of the ridge was the lack of color. For as far as I could see in the ancient valley stretching in front of me, there were no trees; no fields of corn; nor any beautiful, exposed formations of rock that we were so used to seeing in other places in Peru. From the gray skies that hung just above the mountains surrounding us, to the muted earth tones of the ground, it all looked the same extending in every direction. Flat, dull, and barren.

I had waited six years to stand where I was standing, but it was not the dullness of the soil that I had come to see. In the valley just below me proceeded the ongoing excavations of something that the traditional archaeologists said should not exist, and which the traditional historians knew would cause them to rewrite every textbook, and change what is being taught, in every high school history class throughout the Americas.

Spreading out for 150 acres in front of where I was standing with my guide, his friend, and my fiancée was the site of the ancient city of Caral in north central Peru. And we were there at a very auspicious time: the day that the results of ^{14}C dating for multiple artifacts would be completed and the age of the site would be revealed.

The Place That Time Forgot

Together we walked another half mile or so down into the main excavations, where my guide had arranged for us to meet with one of the researchers working at the site. I could see immediately that we had very different ideas about what would be discussed.

The young archaeologist wanted to focus on what the last six years of intensive excavation had unearthed. Interestingly, there was no pottery found (the official explanation is that it was not invented yet), but 32 flutes made of bones from birds and other animals were uncovered. Looking closer, we could see that these ancient instruments were engraved with the images of animals such as monkeys and birds. What made this find especially interesting is that the animals portrayed are only found in the Amazon region of Peru, hours away by car from where we were standing.

While I was certainly interested to hear what our archaeologist friend had to say, it was the things that he didn't say that brought the familiar set of questions to my mind. Who built the site? Where did the people come from? Were they part of the Incan lineage, or did they represent a people and way of life that was completely separate from known Andean cultures? What happened to them, and where did they go?

The official answer for each of these questions was the same: "We don't know." While they are all questions that the archaeologist knew would arise, I could see that it was not easy for our new friend to acknowledge that so much is unknown about the site he was excavating. By any measure, the mysterious site of Caral is an anomaly for a number of reasons.

Figure 4.6. *Top:* The author at the Caral, Peru, excavation site in 2010. This is one of the two circular plazas discovered at the 150-acre complex. (Credit: © Martha Reich.) *Bottom:* A close-up showing one of the five pyramids still under excavation. (Credit: © Gregg Braden.)

Although it was known to locals as early as 1905, it was not until 1994 that fresh interest triggered a renewed attempt to excavate the site and, hopefully, explain the mystery that lay weathering in the Peruvian desert. In 1996, under the direction and guidance of Ruth Shady Solis, the director of the Museum of Archaeology and Anthropology of National University of San Marcos in Lima, Peru; and in cooperation with Jonathan Haas, MacArthur Curator in the Department of Anthropology of The Field Museum in Chicago, Illinois, the five pyramids and two circular plazas that form the bulk of the main site were excavated and restored, and scientific dating of the site began in earnest.

The results of their joint efforts were nothing short of astounding. Before the carbon dating pushed the age of the site into a realm archaeologists long had thought impossible for civilization in that part of Peru, historians believed they had the history of North America, Central America, and South America solidly "buttoned up," as one explained to me. There is a tidy story that includes cultures such the Olmecs, the Maya, the Aztecs, and the Anasazi, for example. They each have their time in history and made contributions to civilization. It's a story that's been told and retold in classrooms throughout the world.

The recent dating of material found inside of the buried walls has now changed all of that.

The very day we arrived, the results of several ^{14}C dating tests were to be released. Materials studied included plant fibers located within the hollow portions of the buried walls themselves, as well as a rare information-storage system of woven fiber knots known as *quipus*. As remote as the site is, the local cell towers were in full operation that day, and our guide's mobile phone rang as we were nearing the end of our exploration.

At first his face froze with apprehension when he heard the voice on the other end. He knew that he was about to hear something important, something that would either tell us that we were standing on top of another Incan city, previously unknown, which would fall into the accepted timeline of civilization . . . or that the history of the world had just changed.

His face lit up with a huge smile as he heard the results first-hand, and then immediately shared them with us. The scientific dating of the site was confirmed. The independent labs had each returned dates that were within the same range, a timeline that would immediately catapult the remote site of Caral onto the global stage: somewhere between 4900 B.C.E. and 3000 B.C.E.—5,000 to 6,900 years before the present day. This officially made it the oldest advanced civilization (advanced in terms of architecture, astronomy, agriculture, art, and mathematics) known to exist anywhere in the Americas.[19]

How an advanced civilization, located so close to known sites from the Incan Empire, could have gone unrecognized for so long is a mystery unto itself. The list of unknowns is significant, and because of the implications they may hold, it doesn't help put the minds of historians at ease.

It may be no coincidence that Caral shares so many of the mysteries with Chaco Canyon, the UNESCO World Heritage Site in America's Desert Southwest. For both sites, there are no written records, or at least none that have been discovered so far. Both sites appear to have been capable of supporting large numbers of people, yet only a few bodies, dating to a more recent age, have been found at either. At both sites, an advanced form of architecture appears to have been used to build the multistory buildings that have survived the elements (and in the case of Caral, have lasted for thousands of years). And, for both Caral and Chaco Canyon, while there are theories as to why the builders of the sites abandoned the fruits of their labor, the fact is that no one knows the reasons for certain.

✱ ✱ ✱

While Caral is more than 5,000 years older than the Mayan civilization, indigenous to the Yucatán region of Mexico, we may discover that the key to the mystery of both Caral and Chaco Canyon is in the legacy that the Maya left behind: the calendars describing huge cycles of time. The present world age, which has been accurately identified by Mayan calendars, began about the time that Caral was abandoned 5,000 years ago. And it ends in our time in December 2012, when the *next* world age begins. We may discover that the Andean knowledge of cosmic cycles preserved in Caral is actually part of a great wisdom that has been preserved, albeit hidden, *throughout* the Americas over the centuries—and that perhaps leads directly to understanding the crises of our world today.

Mayan Time

Any discussion of the accomplishments of the Maya must acknowledge what is arguably the single most sophisticated achievement of all: their unsurpassed calculation of time and cosmic cycles, made using their calendars. But Mayan calendars represent much more than simply counting the number of days between the full moon and the new moon. These ancients were tracking *cycles* of time, and the celestial events that occur during those cycles.

The Mayan calendar is believed to be the most sophisticated method of measuring galactic time in existence before the 20th century. Even today, modern descendants of the ancient Maya keep track of galactic, as well as local, time using this system that experts such as Michael D. Coe, author of *The Maya*, tell us has "not slipped one day in over 25 centuries."[20]

The key to the Maya's galactic "timer" was a 260-day count called the *Tzolkin*, or Sacred Calendar, intermeshed with another 365-day calendar known as the *Vague Year*. These two cycles of time progressed like the cogs of two wheels, continuing until the rare moment when one day on the Sacred Calendar matched the same day on the Vague Year. That powerful event marked the end of a 52-year cycle, and was part of an even greater expanse of time called the *Great Cycle*.

At present, there is no single artifact known to represent the calendar in its entirety. While modern scholars are able to interpret the Mayan system of timekeeping from inscriptions and codices, another ancient artifact has preserved the Mayan view of time as a single calendar that is still in use today. It's the Aztec Stone of the Sun *(Piedra del Sol)*, the ancient calendar disk pictured in Figure 4.7.

Figure 4.7. There is no single artifact that represents the entire system of Mayan calendars. The ancient Aztec calendar in this illustration is believed to be derived from the Mayan calculations of time. The themes of the four previous world ages are clearly seen as the four boxes surrounding the glyph in the center of the disk that represents the present world age. (Credit: Fotosearch Lushpix Value/Unlisted Images, Inc.)

The original disk that the image in Figure 4.7 was modeled after was discovered during excavations in Mexico City's main plaza in 1790. In *Fractal Time,* I share a detailed description of how the inscriptions on it are interpreted and what they're believed to reveal. Rather than being redundant with that description here, the key is that the images on the Aztec disk are intact, readable, and still used today by the indigenous peoples of Central America. To those who know the language of the disk, it's a beautiful map depicting our relationship to time, covering everything from thousands of years to the present moment.

Reading the Map of Time

The Maya used the calculations on the Stone of the Sun to predict how the movements in the heavens would affect our world and human life over long periods of time, which they described as a series of shorter cycles. The last in the present series of those cycles concludes with the winter solstice on December 21, 2012. On this date, the Great Cycle of the present Mayan world age ends, and the calendar is reset to begin the new cycle of the next world age.

Similar to the way the odometer on some cars returns to all zeros after reaching the 100,000-mile mark, the Mayan calendar "resets" to a fresh start date as the cycle begins anew. The Mayan timekeepers encoded the end date, and the system that keeps track of it, into the massive tablets and temples that they built throughout what is now Mexico and Guatemala.

While the Mayan priests marked the key dates for these cycles on their monuments more than 2,000 years ago, it was not until early in the 20th century that their meaning made sense within the framework of our familiar Gregorian calendar, and the message of world-age cycles became clear. The original work of Mayan scholar Joseph T. Goodman (1905), confirmed by archaeologists J. Eric S. Thompson (1927) and Juan Martínez Hernández (1928), arrived at the generally accepted date for the beginning of the Mayan Great Cycle, known as the *GMT correlation* in recognition of each man's contribution (although there is still some controversy surrounding the correlation). Based in these understandings and the traditions of the Mayan priests themselves, the ancient calendars indicate that the last Great Cycle began on the Mayan date 0.0.0.0.0, which translates to August 11, 3114 B.C.E.[21]

Whenever I read about such a long-ago date, it helps me grasp its meaning if I can think of it in terms of something else that was happening at the same time. So as a reference point for the start of the Mayan Great Cycle, the beginning identified by the ancient calendar is about the same time that the first hieroglyphs appeared in ancient Egypt. From that point to today, the balance of the Great Cycle encompasses the entire span of time we typically think of as recorded human history.

The Mayan mystery makes little sense without placing it in the context of the advanced civilizations that preceded it. When we think of the ancient Maya as part of a chain of knowledge that continues into the mists of our past, a continuity of human experience begins to emerge that seems to center around a repeating event reshaping the landscape and the lives of those who experience it. The event is so rare that no one living in an age when it occurs is ever around in the next age when it happens again. Knowing this, our ancestors did in their time precisely what we are doing in ours: They recorded their experiences. They preserved them in multiple media as the inscriptions in the stone of temple walls, the codices of ancient paper, and the stories passed from one generation to the next. We're preserving ours in the multiple media of audio recordings, film, and the stories of our day.

We'll do our very best to preserve for the future everything we learn in the years to come—for the next civilization that lives through global warming, global cooling, superstorms, and the social upheaval that arises from not knowing what to do when the way of life that has worked for centuries suddenly no longer does so. The difference between what our ancestors wrote and what we will leave behind is a matter of whether or not we learn from the past and make the choices that allow us to survive. We're literally writing the last chapter of our world-age cycle as you read these pages. And it's unfolding as our individual choices pool together to become the collective answer to our time in history.

The Rest of the Story

When I look at the history of civilizations as it's taught today, there are portions that are clear and others that make no sense. It makes no sense, for example, that the older pyramids found in Egypt, such as the Great Pyramid and others on the Giza Plateau, are more sophisticated in their construction than the ones built in more recent times, 2,000 to 3,000 years ago. (An attempt was made in the late 1980s to construct a replica of the Great Pyramid standing next to the original one. After a year of mishaps and technical challenges, the project ended in failure.)

From the Great Sphinx on Egypt's Giza Plateau, to the excavations revealing the temple complex at Göbekli Tepe in Turkey, the scientific proof of advanced civilizations in our ancient past is undeniable. The question we must address now is not whether such ancient civilizations could have existed, but what their existence means. Embedded within the single question of meaning are deeper ones of *Who? Why?* and *What?* Who was here to build the sites? Why did they disappear? What did the builders know that we've forgotten? The answers to these questions may be the most important keys to avoiding the same mistakes in our time that led our predecessors to lose *their* civilizations.

So far, the traditional timeline of world history has failed to address these questions. But really, how could we expect it to? It's incomplete. The history that we teach our children today simply doesn't reveal the true extent of our time here on Earth, or our past accomplishments, or the lessons from previous civilizations that would apply to our challenges today. In short, the traditional way of viewing history fails to fully honor our ancient and global heritage.

During my time working in the defense industry during the Cold War years, I learned a valuable lesson that has helped me find context for the things in life that seem to make no sense: when I come across something that makes no sense, it's generally because I don't have all of the information.

For example, my job at the time was to take the output from a computer program that someone else had written and of which I had no previous knowledge, and run this output through a logic process that I had developed, before handing the results off to someone else who, in turn, had no knowledge of what I'd just done. It was a way of thinking called "compartmentalized knowledge," more commonly known as a "need-to-know" basis of working.

I was only given what I needed to know to accomplish my task alone and nothing more. The idea was that because only someone higher in the organization, with a higher security clearance, saw the big picture of our software and what the program was doing, it was a more secure system. Sometimes the need-to-know way of doing things can work well, like in a huge classified defense project during wartime. When it comes to the history of our world, however, it doesn't.

The Emerging Story

I have no doubt that new sites of antiquity and more artifacts will continue to be uncovered as the need to house and feed seven billion people leads to digging in more land once used for agriculture. With each of these new discoveries, we will undoubtedly add to what we already know of our past. The explorations described in this chapter, and others like them, are the keys to creating the framework we need to give meaning to our subsequent discoveries. Without such a framework, we risk placing the new discoveries into the category of "anomalies," and may lose the chance to peer through the powerful window they offer us into the past.

The paradigm-shattering discoveries described in this chapter, along with others, are changing our entire idea of the past in two ways: (1) they are expanding the boundary of time within which history is believed to have occurred, and (2) they are changing what we believe about the capabilities of our ancestors. A comparison of the revised versus the traditional view of history helps us see just how radical this rethinking is.

From the comparison in Figure 4.8 on the next page, it is clear that what we've come to think of as the history of world civilization is not the entire story. Rather, it's one part of a much bigger picture. What we generally accept as the beginning of civilization falls precisely at the end of a 5,000-year cycle that our ancestors knew was coming, and marks the beginning of the cycle we're living today. They knew the transition between cycles was coming, because it always does.

Every 5,125 years, the natural changes in Earth's position in space create a celestial alignment that signals the end of one cycle and the beginning of the next. Ancient and indigenous traditions commonly call the time between these alignments *suns, worlds,* or *world ages.* The changes in climate, sea level, civilization, and life that have accompanied the world ages in the past have been so great that when they occur, the existing world is said to end. The knowledge that these cycles occur, and what happens when they do, is known today as the *doctrine of world ages.*

A beautiful example of this kind of knowledge today is found with the native Hopi of America's Desert Southwest. Their traditions describe three vast cycles of time—three previous worlds—that existed before the fourth one that we live in today. They detail how each world ended in a great cataclysm: the first with earthquakes and the sinking of continents, the second with the world covered in ice, and the third with a great flood. The prophecy says that the fourth world, *our world,* is ending in our lifetime and that we will soon be living in the fifth. Although couched in terms that are nonscientific, the Hopi description of the events that ended each era is eerily similar to the history of the earth that is preserved in the geological record.

We know, for example, that there was a period of tremendous earthquakes and volcanoes that wreaked havoc upon the planet around 20,000 years ago. We know that the ice age ended about 12,000 years ago, and there was a period of melting ice and tremendous rains lasting for nearly 4,000 years. It's this period that is often associated with the biblical Flood.

TRADITIONAL THINKING ABOUT OUR PAST	REVISED THINKING ABOUT OUR PAST
1. Civilization has evolved one time in human history.	1. Civilization has developed multiple times in human history.
2. Civilization has developed in a linear way from less to more evolved.	2. Civilization has developed in a cyclic way, with each cycle generally developing from being less to more evolved.
3. The history of world civilizations is about 5,000 years old.	3. The most recent cycle of world civilizations is 5,000 years long.
4. The oldest civilization in the world is Sumer, dating back to 3500 B.C.E.	4. The oldest known civilization in the world is Göbekli Tepe, now dated at 9500 B.C.E.
5. We are living in the most advanced civilization in the history of the world.	5. Civilizations in the past were capable of technological achievements that cannot be duplicated today.

Figure 4.8. Comparison of traditional thinking regarding our past with the new interpretation based upon recent discoveries. The contrast between the two worldviews is striking and suggests that we are the latest iteration in a succession of civilizations, and experiences in our day are similar to the ones in times past.

According to the Hopi, the same cycles of time and nature that have heralded changes in the past are now bringing the present world to an end, even as the next begins. What makes the Hopi traditions so compelling to us today is their accuracy. The key here is that the Hopi knew of these cycles before the modern world could confirm them scientifically. If their knowledge of *past* cycles is so accurate, then what does that mean for their prediction of what's to come in our *future?*

World History: Revised

From the traditions of the Hopi, the Maya, and others, it becomes obvious that when we look to our past through the traditional eyes that appreciate only the last 5,000 years or so of history, it's like the experience of catching just the ending notes of a great song on the radio. While we may hear something we really love, if we tune in too late we only catch a sound bite—the last few seconds.

Since the time of Napoléon's excavations in Egypt in the late 1700s and early 1800s, we've built our understanding of civilization's rise, fall, wars, conquests, and migrations largely on historians' interpretations of only 5,000 years of our past: a snapshot of a moment in time. But as we now know, this period is actually like one small sound bite of the big song of our past. Only when we embrace the time *before* traditional history begins—events that took place more than 5,000 years ago—will we be capable of hearing the entire composition.

Without listening to the totality of the song, without viewing the entire picture of our past, the time we call the history of civilization falls short of helping us solve the mysteries of how we've come to be as we are, and how we can learn from—and hopefully avoid repeating—the mistakes of our ancestors.

Fortunately, when we marry the fact of advanced, late–ice age civilizations with the history that we commonly accept today, a new timeline of humanity begins to emerge. With this timeline, we gain a continuity of human experience and a new way of thinking about ourselves.

* * *

Figure 4.9 is a revised timeline of world history that takes into account the oldest scientifically confirmed evidence of civilization known as of this writing. I wouldn't be surprised, however, to discover additional evidence in parts of the world that have been "hidden" for much of the last 5,000 years. Antarctica, for example, could be just such a place.

The ice covering about 98 percent of this mysterious continent averages at least one mile in thickness and has been in place for about 15 million years. As global warming has reduced the thickness in some places, and melted it away altogether in others, I would expect us to soon find evidence of ancient civilizations that has been preserved for a long time underneath, meaning that it was probably there when the ice was at its minimum, during the interglacial eras of Earth's past.

Sites that are twice the age of known civilizations—such as ancient Rome, Greece, and Egypt—may help to explain the "sudden" appearance of turnkey civilizations that seem to be immediately off and running with sophisticated knowledge as soon as they show up. We may find that the knowledge of Egyptian pyramid building, Stonehenge astronomy, and Mayan timekeeping is a wisdom that was originally developed, then preserved and passed on, by even more ancient civilizations.

One of the striking patterns that we see in the revised timeline is the clustering of civilizations around the heavy vertical lines marking the world-age cycles. Everything that we have traditionally thought of as ancient history has occurred within the last 5,000 years of the current Great Cycle. With the larger perspective of the new timeline, from classical Rome and Greece; to ancient Egypt and the Mayan, Aztec, and Incan cultures, each of these civilizations seems to appear relatively recently in light of the expanded scale of history.

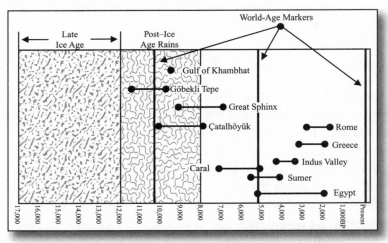

Figure 4.9. Revised timeline of world civilizations based upon new archaeological discoveries. The timeline includes an additional site, Turkey's Çatalhöyük (not described in this book), which is now scientifically dated at 8,000 to 10,000 years old. Note the relationship between the known civilizations and the cycles of world ages (the heavy vertical bars) separated by spans of 5,125 years.

Each of these ancient civilizations demonstrated sophisticated systems of art, science, mathematics, and architecture that developed mysteriously. We may discover that their high-level knowledge is the remnant of similar achievements in the previous world age, and that their predecessors' knowledge, in turn, came from an advanced civilization that was even older. Time will tell. The key to where such ancient wisdom comes from, and who knew it first, may well be found in our understanding of the world-age transitions that occur every 5,000 years or so.

Lessons from the Past

Albert Einstein once stated: "We shall require a substantially new manner of thinking if mankind is to survive."[22] In a way that is typical of a timeless insight, his words are as meaningful today as they were when he spoke them in the mid-20th century.

The message unfolding as we reveal the deep truth of our past is that the history of civilizations we are teaching in our classrooms and preserving in our textbooks is not *the* history of the world. Rather, it is one piece of a much bigger history: that of a Great Cycle, a world age that began 5,125 years ago. As good as our chronicling of the cycle may be, it is incomplete. It does not tell the story of the world age that came before ours, or of the one that came before that.

We can look at the cycles of climate change, for example, and how it altered the way we lived in the past. We can look to periods of war and interludes of peace to see which mode of dealing with change worked for our ancestors. It's these kinds of insights that give us the reasons to do what Einstein suggested: think very differently about ourselves, who we are, our relationship to the world, and the patterns of war and hate in our past.

H. G. Wells once said that human history "becomes more and more a race between education and catastrophe."[23] There is probably more truth to Wells's statement than we'd like to acknowledge. When I reflect on his words and the crises threatening our civilization right now, I cannot help but think of our ancestors in the past and how they handled their crises.

The evidence tells us that they lived through huge climate changes at the end of the ice age. They had big challenges to deal with, and big changes to make. Just as we find ourselves forced to make choices to adapt to our global challenges before we have all of the answers, they had to do the same, for in their day, as in ours, temperatures were increasing, ice was melting, sea levels were rising, and coastlines were disappearing. Without understanding why their world was changing so fast, and so much, they depended upon their choices for their very survival.

The parallel between our ancestors in their time and us in ours is unmistakable. And while the specifics of technology and population may differ, there are general themes playing out today that are remarkably similar. When we look at the huge changes ripping through our world in this way, each Great Cycle becomes an opportunity to learn from our mistakes of the past, and make new choices in the face of repeating experiences.

Like a real-life *Groundhog Day* (the 1993 motion picture where Bill Murray plays a man caught in a single day of his life that repeats dozens of times until he recognizes the moment when his choice can break the cycle and change the outcome), our understanding of how our ancestors responded to cycles of crises in the past may offer us the opportunity to choose wisely before we make the same kinds of mistakes that led to the collapse of great early civilizations.

To think this way leads to new questions that we owe it to ourselves to answer:

- What can we learn from the collapsed civilizations of the past that may help us avoid in our time the mistakes they made in theirs?

- Where are we in H. G. Wells's "race" between learning about the past and catastrophe?

- How do the discoveries of advanced civilizations, dating to a time before traditional history begins, fit into our story of the past?

- Is it a coincidence that the beginning of recorded history happens to coincide with the end of the last world age and the beginning of the present one?

It's in our nature to share stories. Each day of our lives we continue to do what people in this world have always done: We talk about ourselves. We record our discoveries, and describe our experiences. We share our hurt and our joy, our surprises and our disappointments. We preserve our experiences of the things that have left a deep and lasting impression upon us for those whom we will never know, who will live in lifetimes that we will never see.

When we merge thousands of years of oral traditions describing our past with the physical evidence being recovered precisely in the places that the stories describe, we must acknowledge what for some people is an uncomfortable truth. A growing body of scientific evidence is leading to two inescapable conclusions:

1. We've been in this world for much longer than our traditional history acknowledges.

2. Something happened to our world in the past, something that brought an end to all that our ancestors had built and cherished. From the biblical Flood and native wisdom traditions to the Epic of Gilgamesh and the Mahabharata, we have the stories to remind us.

If what they shared is even partially correct, it's important for us to recognize and embrace these stories of our past today. Our ancestors tried desperately to tell us their stories. And they did so because they believed that whatever they experienced in their time would occur again in ours. Now the evidence is clear, and their message is beginning to make sense.

From Göbekli Tepe and the Great Sphinx, to ancient Caral and the Maya, a story links the modern world of today with our past: the story of us, where we come from, and how long we've been here. Ancient legends and myths contain the history of our species. Just like an orphan yearning to know who his or her parents are, we long to know the truth of our origins. And when we acknowledge the evidence of our true antiquity, we begin to understand how we can use the experience of our collective past to steer us into the choices today that might have helped our ancestors. This is precisely why sharing the deep truth of our history is so vital to us.

If great civilizations have appeared in the past, lasted thousands of years longer than ours, and then disappeared so suddenly that their memory has been reduced to a fairy tale in our memory, we must ask: Could the same thing happen again? Is it happening *now?*

In the discoveries themselves, we may find the clues to solve the deepest mysteries of our past, as well as the answer to these two questions.

> **Deep Truth 4:** New discoveries of advanced civilizations dating to near the end of the last ice age provide insights into solving the crises in *our* time that our ancestors also faced in theirs.

CHAPTER FIVE

BY CHANCE OR DESIGN: NEW EVIDENCE OF HUMAN ORIGINS

"The mystery of life isn't a problem to solve, but a reality to experience."

— FRANK HERBERT (1920–1986), NOVELIST

Imagine that you're walking with a friend through an open field and you both suddenly look to the ground in the same instant. As you do so, you see a watch lying at your feet, and your friend sees a rock at his or hers. Glancing up, if you ask one another how the watch got there, the chances are good that you'll each have a very different answer than if you ask the same thing about the rock. For all either of you knows, natural processes deposited the rock in the place where you and your friend have found it. And it's quite possible that the rock has remained in that place, undisturbed, for thousands of years. But both of you know that the same thing can't be true for the watch. It's made of finely tuned components that were not randomly deposited on the ground by natural processes. Each part of the timepiece was designed, fabricated, and assembled by someone, or something, in more recent times (certainly more recently than the rock). With this simple analogy (which I've paraphrased) in his book *Natural Theology,* early-19th-century theologian William Paley initiated the argument for an intelligence underlying nature's patterns.[1]

Paley drew two conclusions from his analogy:

— The **first** is that just as the existence of the watch implies that there was a designer who built it and set it into motion, the existence of complex systems in nature and living things implies the existence of a cosmic "watchmaker": an intelligent force that guided the formation of the universe and set the sequence of life into motion.

— Paley's **second** conclusion has to do with the likelihood that complex systems, and living things that depend upon one another to exist, can just "happen" by chance. In the watch example, it's only when each piece is already crafted, finely tuned, and assembled precisely in the way we find it that the watch can do what it was designed to do: keep track of time. The key here is that if any of the parts were not already made when the watch was put together, or if any piece were to fall away and be lost afterward, the watch could not do what it was designed to do.

"If the different parts had been differently shaped from what they are," Paley said, "or if a different size from what they are, or placed after any other manner, or in any order than that in which they are placed, either no motion at all would have been carried on in the machine, or none which would have answered the use that is now served by it."[2]

Paley studied the universe and the world around him in his day and concluded that they work in much the same way the watch does: "Every indication of contrivance, every manifestation of design, which existed in the watch, exists in the works of nature; with the difference, on the side of nature, of being greater or more, and that in a degree which exceeds all computation."[3]

One hundred and eighty-two years after Paley's analogy, evolutionary biologist Richard Dawkins discounted the possibility of such intelligence in his book *The Blind Watchmaker* (W. W. Norton & Company, 1986):

> The only watchmaker is the blind force of physics, albeit deployed in a very special way. A true watchmaker has foresight: He designs his cogs and springs, and plans their interconnections, with a future purpose in his mind's eye. Natural selection, the blind unconscious, automatic process that Darwin discovered which we now know is the explanation for the existence and apparently purposeful form of all life, has no purpose in mind. It has no mind's eye. It does not plan for the future. It has no vision, no foresight, no sight at all. If it can be said to play the role of watchmaker in nature, it is the blind watchmaker.[4]

While the idea behind the watchmaker argument is simple, the implications are nothing short of paradigm shattering! Here's why:

The way we think of our beginnings on Earth forms the foundation for everything we think about ourselves. Either there is an intentional design at the foundation of life or there is not. We are either the product of a random series of natural events or the result of an intentional and intelligent design. There appears to be little room for a middle ground. Knowing the truth has never been more important. The stakes have never been higher.

This question is something that our ancestors resolved to the satisfaction of their time in history. Now it's a belief that *we* are struggling with, and must resolve in *our* time. And we must do so in the language that we've come to trust and rely upon in describing our relationship to the world: that of science. The belief is all about human life. Precisely when does it begin? When does it end? Who has the right to end it?

A very different question—and maybe the biggest question of all, the one with the greatest implications—is: *Where did human life come from? What are our origins?*

> The way we think about our origins is the foundation for the way we think about ourselves, our relationship to the earth, our relationships to one another, our capabilities, and our destiny.

These are huge questions, and the answer to each one has huge ramifications. When we combine the answers, they hold a power rarely found in the answer to any single question: the power to unite us as friends, families, and societies—or to do just the opposite. Any answer that doesn't support what we've been led to believe has the potential to rip us apart by challenging the very core of the convictions upon which we base our society today.

The controversy surrounding the practice of abortion has led to the bombing of clinics, elicited threats against women looking to terminate their pregnancies, prompted murders of doctors who perform these procedures, and become a focus in the elections of powerful leaders throughout the U.S. year after year. From this, and the firestorm of protests that have erupted over legal rulings in different states regarding what we can teach our children about our origins in classrooms and textbooks, it's very clear that we must come to terms with the facts of our existence in a way that meets the needs of our 21st-century world. The sooner we do so, the sooner we will begin to heal the hate and suffering that has been tearing at the fabric of our society for the last century or so.

It's all about the way we think, what we believe, and how we answer the ultimate questions of life.

Asking the Right Questions

When John Ciardi, the acclaimed translator of Dante's *Divine Comedy*, wrote: "A good question is never answered,"[5] I wonder if he had in mind the question of human origins. Ciardi went on to clarify just what he meant, saying, "It [the question] is not a bolt to be tightened into place but a seed to be planted to bear more seed toward the hope of greening the landscape of idea."[6] Could he have been asking himself the question that lies at the core of the most heated legal, political, and scientific debate in human history today: *Where do we come from?*

Danish philosopher Søren Kierkegaard once said that human life "is a mystery to be lived, not a problem to be solved."[7] As much as we may like the poetic sensibility of Kierkegaard's words, this is certainly one mystery that we *do* need to solve. Along with its religious/spiritual implications, it plays a role in our most basic beliefs—the keys to creating a lasting civilization. Clearly, we must come to terms with life's origins if we hope to advance as a peaceful, cooperative, and compassionate society.

But this means that we must ask the right questions, and in such a way that they can be answered. The key lies in unlocking two seemingly timeless mysteries:

1. How did human life begin on Earth?

2. When does a human life begin in the womb?

First things first. Before we can even think about probing this pair of mysteries, there's another, even more basic question that we must answer.

In the first years of the 21st century, a time when our microscopes are so sensitive that we can witness the instant that a sperm penetrates an egg and the "marriage" of DNA begins a new life, we have yet to agree on precisely *what* it is we've just witnessed.

As obvious as it sounds, and as much as we may assume that we've already done so, the scientific community still hasn't agreed on a clear definition of life. Just what is it?

What Is Life?

August 20, 1975, marked a pivotal turning point in our understanding of just where and how we fit into the big picture of the cosmos. At 5:22 P.M. on that day, a powerful Titan Centaur III rocket blasted away from Complex 41 at Cape Canaveral, Florida, with an unprecedented cargo. It was carrying the *Viking I* spacecraft, the first human-made device that would land on the surface of Mars, our planetary neighbor.

One month later, *Viking II* followed, and began the same nearly 500-million-mile journey as its twin. It left from the same place in Cape Canaveral, using the same kind of rocket booster to launch it on its way to the same destination as *Viking I*. The two *Viking* probes were our best hope for capturing the first close-up photographs and physical samples of the mysterious red planet. At the end of their flights, they would go down in history as the most successful planetary explorations ever. Although the final signals from the last *Viking* were received in November 1982, the success of the missions continues to be the buzz of the scientific community to this day.

In the mid-1980s I found myself working in Denver, Colorado, for the Martin Marietta Corporation, which had built both of the *Viking* spacecrafts. While I was hired as a software developer on the defense side of the company, suddenly I was collaborating with the team of scientists, engineers, and project managers on the aerospace side that had made the missions to Mars possible.

In the course of our conversations, and taking advantage of the opportunity to sift through volumes of data sheets describing the ambitious Mars program, I found there was something specific about the *Viking* missions that made them stand out from every other one that NASA had launched. It was the single objective that, for me personally, made the risk and expense of the entire project worthwhile.

Buried within a project folder, at the end of a list of routine bullet points that summarized all of the *Viking* program's objectives, was a brief statement. Following technical jargon about the climate of Mars and the surface characteristics and composition of the Martian soil, I found a few words that touched upon the question that had lingered within me, unanswered, since the day I'd watched the world's first manned space missions on our family's tiny black-and-white TV in the 1960s. Objective number 5 simply stated that goal of the mission was to determine "whether life is, or ever has been, present."[8]

Scientists were initially surprised in 1976 that no organic materials whatsoever were found in the Martian soil samples taken by both *Viking* craft. At the time it was commonly believed that some form of simple life would be discovered in what was assumed to be iron-rich soil. For 30 years, the data from *Viking I* and *Viking II* has been the subject of controversy, question, analysis, and reanalysis. A September 5, 2010, report published in *Science Daily* describes how a new theory may now explain why no signs of life were found 30 years ago. It suggests that the process of detection itself may have killed any microbes present, and that what is called the "smoking gun" for the building blocks of life on Mars may have actually been there all along.[9]

The search for life on Mars—or anywhere else in the universe, for that matter—is a beautiful example of the dilemma that scientists face professionally today, and that we ourselves face as a society. Whether we ever find life or not hinges upon the way we define what it is we're looking for. *Precisely what is life to begin with?*

What I discovered as I worked in the defense industry in the 1980s was an amazing fact that remains true today three decades later: different scientists, from different disciplines, answer the question in different ways. They do so using specific terms that reflect their unique expertise. So even the experts haven't agreed on a universal definition of our very existence.

In the college textbook *Chemistry, Matter, and the Universe* (Benjamin Cummings Publishing, 1976), for example, the definition of life seems to be rather sterile: "Life is a behavior pattern that chemical systems exhibit when they reach a certain kind and level of complexity."[10] This seems pretty cut-and-dried, doesn't it? Or does it? I'm sharing this definition here because it comes directly from a book published in the same year the two *Viking* spacecraft landed on Mars, and reflects the thinking that was considered leading-edge back then.

In 1944, Erwin Schrödinger, a theoretical biologist and renowned physicist (creator of the famous "Schrödinger's cat" thought experiment), suggested that something is alive if it "avoids the decay into equilibrium."[11] While Schrödinger definitely uses fewer words in his definition, this is probably not a meaningful way for the average person looking for signs of life to know if they've found it. His definition is a reference to the law of physics stating that stuff is always moving from a state of chaos to a state of balance. As long as something is alive and can do all of the things that living things do—such as metabolize, repair itself, and reproduce—it is in chaos. When living things can no longer do these things, they decay into the balance of simple elements through decomposition. In other words, they die.

In the March 22, 2002, edition of *Science,* molecular biologist Daniel E. Koshland, Jr., elaborated on a possible definition of life.[12] He identified seven conditions that can be used as guidelines to determine whether or not something is living. Briefly, living things:

1. Must have a program to make copies of themselves

2. Adapt and evolve to reflect changes in their environment

3. Tend to be complex, highly organized, and have compartmentalized structures

4. Have a metabolism that allows them to convert energy from one form to another

5. Can regenerate parts of themselves, or their entire forms

6. Can respond to their environment through feedback mechanisms

7. Can maintain multiple metabolic reactions at the
    same time[13]

Although all of these defining features are no doubt accurate
from the perspective of the scientists who crafted them, when I
read them I find myself feeling a little empty, as if something is
missing. Are we simply the product of "chemical systems" that
have attained some degree of complexity, or systems that are moving from chaos to balance? Can the beauty and symmetry of life
really be reduced to something that sounds so routine and, well,
lifeless? Or are we something more? Is there a mystical element to
life that science has yet to measure or even acknowledge?

If there is something more to life than the previous definitions
suggest, maybe that's why the jury is still out as to whether or not
the *Viking* probes found evidence of it in the soil of our planetary
neighbor. Maybe we were looking in the right places, and looking
at the right stuff, but doing so in the wrong *way.* While newer definitions have attempted to put "life" back into *life,* they still sound
like pale echoes of the 1976 way of thinking.

One of the reasons why a clear definition of life remains elusive is that it implies yet another, even deeper understanding of
how life originated in the first place. The questions of what life is
and how it began are so interrelated that it's hard to answer one
without addressing the other. In other words, we must know what
life is to know when it begins, for how could we know when it
starts if we don't know what it even *is?* This apparent quandary,
however, may also be good news. Because it implies that if we can
answer one of the questions, we may well be on the track to answering both.

Our origins have been a question mark for as long as we've
been here. The rock art preserved on the cave walls of Australia
and Northern Europe, dated to between 20,000 and 35,000 years
old, confirms that we've been wondering where we come from,
and how we got here, for a very long time. Of course, we're still
asking the same question because it hasn't been answered in a way
that makes sense in our modern world.

So let's take a closer look. When it comes to the deep truth of life, and specifically of *human* life, precisely what *is* it? When does it begin? Where do we fit in?

When Does a Human Life Begin?

It's been said that it's best to avoid three topics in conversations with people we don't know, in the workplace, and at family celebrations and on special occasions: *politics, religion,* and *abortion.* But while it may not be acceptable to bring these topics up at social gatherings, abortion is an issue that has become hard to avoid. From featured articles between the glossy covers of magazines, to the televised debates between men and women competing to lead the most powerful nations in the world, and guidelines issued by the Vatican in Rome, the subject of abortion has found its way right into the heart of the very topics that we've been encouraged to avoid speaking about in the past: politics and religion.

It becomes clear from history that the moral issues of when, how, and if a pregnancy should be ended have been resolved based upon the values and beliefs of different societies of the time. Beliefs are deeply personal and come from culture, conditioning, religion, and family. So when we think about abortion from these perspectives, it's probably not surprising that the issues have lingered for so long and largely gone unresolved in our multicultural society today.

The highest court in the United States tried to bring resolution to the subject of abortion from a legal perspective in 1973. On January 22 of that year, in the case of *Roe v. Wade,* the Supreme Court made a landmark decision regarding a woman's right to choose to end her pregnancy. In a 7-to-2 majority vote in favor of Roe, the court ruled that the right to privacy outlined in the 14th Amendment to the United States Constitution includes a woman's decision, made along with her doctor, to have an abortion. Justice Harry A. Blackmun summarized the decision: "The right of personal privacy includes the abortion decision, but this right is not unqualified and must be considered against important state interests in regulation."[14] The court added a caveat with respect to the way the choice is carried out. It stated that a woman's right to terminate her pregnancy must be balanced against the laws of the individual state where the woman lives, as she is making a life-or-death decision.

Laws vary within the 50 states. So while the court made its official ruling, taking into account the opinions of both scientists and advocates for personal choice, the ultimate decision was left to the discretion of local governments. Whether or not abortion is legal would still be based largely upon the values and beliefs of the individual communities.

Nineteen years later, in 1992, the Supreme Court's original decision was modified during a court challenge to reflect a change in the language describing the different stages of pregnancy. Before the 1992 ruling, the nine-month average time of a full-term pregnancy was described in legal documents in increments known as *trimesters,* each of which represents a third of the gestation period. So, for example, the first trimester is the first three months of pregnancy, the second trimester the next three months, and so on. The revised legal language focuses less on what stage the pregnancy is in, and more on the state of development of the fetus itself.

Specifically, it focuses upon whether or not the unborn fetus is "viable," meaning it could survive if it were removed from the womb. Rather than helping resolve the confusion, the revised guidelines seem to have only sparked a deeper resentment surrounding the basic question. There is a strong feeling among many people in the world that, viable or not, a fetus is a human life at any time after conception, and therefore deserves the rights and protection that come with being human.

Clearly abortion continues to be among the most controversial and hotly debated issues in our society. With a number of local and national elections in the U.S. on the horizon, each candidate's views on this topic will undoubtedly have some influence to tip the voting scales one way or another. According to Kenneth T. Walsh, the chief White House correspondent for *U.S. News &*

World Report, "The 'wedge issues' are coming back. . . . These are the social questions that have divided Americans for many years, such as gay rights, abortion, and family values."[15]

While science is making inroads to help us understand the process and origins of life, to some people these discoveries miss the point altogether. They have strong feelings and strong beliefs about what life is and when it begins, regardless of what science may reveal. For others, though, the argument is open-ended and without resolution. The core issue for both camps, however, revolves around the same theme, the unknown factor that is the subject of this chapter: When does an individual human life actually begin?

While we may never know precisely where we've come from or how we happen to be here on Earth, we do know with a degree of certainty when different stages of life occur in the womb. So you may be thinking, *If we know about these stages and when they begin, then what's the problem?* This is where the controversy comes into play. *Because* there are different stages of life, there are different definitions of life that pertain to each. This fact forces us to be very specific when we ask the question of precisely when life begins. We must be knowledgeable enough to be clear about what stage we're discussing. I'm sharing this information here because there is a new discovery that may help.

Scientists have identified a mysterious point in the development of an embryo when the characteristics that make us who we are (the DNA that defines our human traits) awaken and "kick in." While this discovery cannot tell us what's right or wrong when it comes to the choices we make about life and death, at the very least it helps us to know what kind of life we're talking about, and what kind of choice we're making.

From Conception to Birth: It's All Life

Historically, the branch of science that studies life itself—biology—generally relies upon four criteria to define life: *metabolism, growth, reaction to stimuli,* and *reproduction.*[16] When something displays these four characteristics, biologists consider it to be a living being.

> Biologists generally define life as something that meets four criteria: *metabolism, growth, reaction to stimuli,* and *reproduction.*

We will use this accepted definition of life as a place to begin, and build from it to add to our understanding of when an individual human life, as we think of it, begins in the womb.

Ultimately, no matter how we define it, it's clear that for humans, life starts with the union of two cells: a sperm and an egg. For the vast majority of people in the world, that union occurs in the womb. The study of life in the womb has got to be one of the most fascinating and mysterious areas of science today. While we have the technology now that allows us to witness the instant when a sperm and an egg unite and marry the genetic "stuff" of DNA that becomes us, and we can document the nuts and bolts of the mechanisms that make human life possible, there are still things that happen before we are born that science cannot explain.

A summary of the stages of human development in the womb will give us a framework for our ongoing discussion. It will allow us to pinpoint the specific places in development where the various changes that define us as "us" occur, and where stages of life emerge from conception until birth. Because the same process has occurred for almost everyone reading this book, I will make this summary a personal one. I will address it to you and me. This is what happened to *us* in the wombs of *our* mothers, to make *us* as we are in this moment. So let's begin. . . .

— **Our beginning.** Later in this chapter, we'll explore the topic of the origin of life from the perspectives of Charles Darwin's theory of evolution and the competing theory of intelligent design. When it comes to scientific proof of how life begins, one thing is absolutely certain: the stuff of life begins with living stuff. And although there have been experiments to explore other ways that life can emerge, there are no scientifically documented cases in the peer-reviewed literature of it originating from anything that's not already living.

> Life in general, and human life in particular, is only known to result from biological material that is already living.

When it comes to what happens in the wombs of our mothers, one fact is important to bear in mind: *Life begins with life*. We begin from living essence. The sperm and the egg that merge as our "beginning" are alive and serve as the *living* conduits of the *living* essence from which we emerge.

— **Fertilization.** Although the moment that a human sperm and an egg unite is often called the "instant of conception," it's more accurate to say that this is when the *process* of conception begins. It actually takes about 24 hours for the nuclei of the sperm and the egg to fuse, sharing the genetic information from each parent, and fertilization to occur.

— **Our zygote.** I think it's fascinating to note that although the sperm and the egg that merge as our early beginning are already two complete, separate, living cells—and already fulfilling all of the biological requirements for life—when they join together to form a new entity, that is a single new cell. In other words, the biological math here is that 1 cell + 1 cell = 1 cell, rather than 1 + 1 = 2. But even though we are talking about a single-celled organism, the new cell is *more* than either of the two that merged to create it. It is packed with a greater potential than the sperm or the egg could have had alone. This union of greater potential is "us" at the first stage of our lives. From this stage onward, it's our first cell that holds the possibilities for all that we may become.

There's an important distinction that I'd like to emphasize here, which is that the genetic code that holds the *potential* to determine who and what we will become exists at this stage as precisely that: potential only. *The genetic information that is the blueprint of life is not fully active at this point.* I'd also like to note that the new science of epigenetics shows that the potential we inherit from our parents is not "set in stone," as previously believed, and may be altered in our bodies through changes in our physical, chemical, and emotional environments.[17]

The scientific term for this point in development is the *zygote* stage. A zygote begins after fertilization when the sperm and egg have merged into a single cell. This stage lasts until the first cell division, when our single cell splits into two identical cells (see Figure 5.1). The length of time that a zygote exists as one cell before it divides into two does not appear to be part of the precise clockwork of the universe.

Initial cell division does not happen within the same time frame for every conception. Instead, it seems that nature gives us some leeway in our early development in terms of when this process, which will continue until we take our last breath in this world, is set in motion. Our first cell division generally begins somewhere between 12 and 20 hours after our zygote forms.

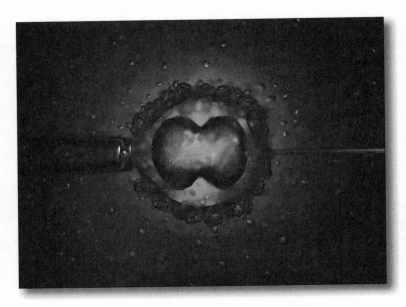

Figure 5.1. The length of time from fertilization until our first cell division varies from individual to individual. In the image above, the division process has started and the single cell of the zygote is seen splitting into two identical cells. The dimples visible on each of the cells are the nuclei containing genetic information. (Credit: iStockphoto: © Pete Draper.)

— **Our two-cell stage.** At the two-cell stage, our cells begin to respond to nature's unseen clock and start to divide on a rhythmic basis. Each cell division falls into a window of time that can be predicted and calculated by the one before it. This process—called *binary cell division*—continues every 12 to 20 hours. So, to summarize from the time of fertilization: our first division from one cell to two generally happens between hours 47 and 55; the next division, from two to four cells, then takes place 12 to 20 hours later; and the third division, when each of our four cells divides and we become eight cells, occurs another 12 to 20 hours after that.

Something mysterious and wonderful occurs at the eight-cell stage in our lives, approximately 95 hours (3.9 days) after fertilization. This mysterious event plays a key role in the person we will become, and therefore adds a new dimension to the difficult choices we occasionally must make in regard to the stages of a human life.

— Our eight-cell stage. A pivotal moment in our lives, this stage initiates a mysterious process within our earliest cells, one scientists are just beginning to understand and therefore cannot fully explain. At the eight-cell stage of life, the genetic blueprint of our DNA "kicks in" and the characteristics that make us who and what we are become activated.[18]

A study published in *Nature* in 2010 stated: "After fertilization the embryonic genome is inactive until transcription is initiated during the maternal-zygotic transition."[19] While scientists are able to document that this change, called *embryonic gene activation* (EGA), has definitely occurred, traditional methods of research still can't explain precisely *why* it does.

> At the eight-cell stage of life, a mysterious process that is still not fully understood awakens the code of life. The DNA, with the traits that make us who and what we become, is activated.

In other words, it's at this stage that the characteristics we think of as human go to work to make us . . . *us*. As mentioned earlier, our genetic code can be thought of as the settings from the cosmic factory of life that get us started in this world. They're with us at birth, but they're not set in stone and can change, given enough time and the right conditions.

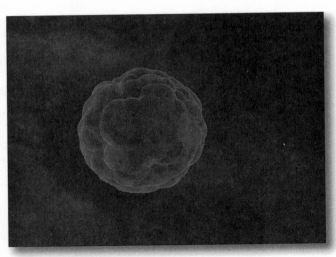

Figure 5.2. *Top:* An embryo at the eight-cell stage, which occurs approximately 95 hours after fertilization. Here a mysterious process begins, and the genetic information in our early development "kicks in." (Credit: iStockphoto: © alxpin.) *Bottom:* The blastocyst stage when our cells first begin to take on different roles. Some move inward to become the fetus, and others migrate outward to create what will become the placenta. It is at this stage that our first stem cells are formed. (Credit: iStockphoto: © geopaul.)

— **Our morula.** Somewhere between 12 and 20 hours after our 8-cell stage has occurred, each cell divides again, creating the 16 new cells that form the next stage in our development. At this point, the arrangement of the cells resembles a sphere-like mulberry. (*Morula* is Latin for "mulberry.") Up until this point, the cells have been dividing as identical cells *within the membrane* that keeps them from growing outward, the *zona pelucida*. At the 16-cell stage, the cells begin to change their shape and "pack" together tightly, in a process that is actually called *compaction*.

— **Our blastocyst.** Following the morula stage, which occurs about five days after fertilization, the *blastocyst* stage begins. At this point the embryo is a tiny, hollow ball about the size of the eye on a Roosevelt dime. Differences develop between the dividing cells for the first time, with the inner cells becoming the inner mass that forms the fetus. It is this inner mass that contains our first stem cells. The outer cells flatten to form the thin outer surface that creates a fluid-filled cavity. It's the outer surface that will become the placenta. The blastocyst is the "vehicle" that travels through the fallopian tubes, enters the uterus, and implants into the lining of the uterus to become the fetus.

— **Our fetus.** Generally during the eighth week after fertilization, our time as an embryo ends, and we become a *fetus*. At this point, the organs are physically present, but only at the beginning stages of functioning. Although we can sense changes in our environment, for reasons detailed later in this chapter, it's believed that we cannot feel the sensation of pain. This is the last stage of development until our birth into the world as a newborn baby.

The Deep Truth of Human Life

When we talk about the beginning of human life, the stages of development described in the previous section make it easy to see why there are so many different opinions and perspectives. *The deep truth is that the beginning of a human life is a process, rather than an event.* Life begins as life. As I'll discuss later on, humankind has yet to create living stuff from something that is not already alive. From this understanding of what happens in the womb, it becomes clear that at every stage of development our cells are "alive" in a different way.

The living essence of a father's sperm and a mother's egg each holds half of the living material needed to form a new being. When the sperm and egg merge to form "one" of us, the first cell that's created through their union meets the biological definition of life in general. So we are definitely alive from the first cell of our existence. But the root of the controversy is less about living cells, and more about when we assume the qualities that we consider to be human. And this is where a clear understanding of what happens in the womb, and when it happens, may be useful.

While scientists are working hard to unlock the mystery of what turns on our genetic code, there is no doubt that our DNA activates at the eight-cell stage. As mentioned previously, during this phase of development (the embryonic gene activation stage), we acquire the characteristics that we have inherited from our parents—the traits that hold the potential for what our lives can become. This is one of those places where a unified way of thinking about our world may give us an understanding that an isolated view from a single field of science cannot. It's one of those places, as well, where we can only benefit from crossing the traditional boundaries that have kept the sciences separate in the past.

Recent discoveries in the study of quantum physics show beyond any reasonable doubt that we are surrounded by a sea of living energy. This means that we can't separate life from the energy that surrounds it. They exist together. They interact together. And it's through this interaction that we experience life as we do. Embracing a holistic way of thinking may be the key to understanding what happens to activate our DNA's map of life at the EGA stage . . . and here's the reason why:

The field we are bathed in—known by names ranging from the Divine Matrix and the Mind of God, to simply the Field— is what fills the "empty space" between things. Modern biology also calls this field part of the "environment" surrounding living things. This is an important concept when we think about where human life begins and what happens at the eight-cell stage. The study of epigenetics has shown that while the code of DNA within our cells definitely tells our bodies how to function, the signal activating the code appears to come from outside of the cell.[20] In other words, it comes from the field itself!

We know this through the process of cell rejection, common after organ transplants. When an organ from one person is placed inside the body of another, the recipient's body doesn't recognize the new tissue as being "self." And because it doesn't, it treats the new tissue as a foreign object by rejecting it. A breakthrough came when scientists discovered how to suppress the rejection mechanism so transplanted organs could grow and thrive in new bodies.

Often I co-present seminars with cell biologist Bruce Lipton (whom I mentioned in the last chapter). During one of our programs, I had the opportunity to slip into the back of the audience and listen in. As we all know, there are no accidents in the world, so it's not surprising that I came into the room just as he was describing a phenomenon I had struggled to understand. It involved organ transplants and the problems I had heard of from friends who had received them.

On the screen at the front of the room, I watched as my friend Bruce skillfully explained that when the inside of a cell (the nucleus containing its DNA) is removed from its original membrane and placed into the membrane of a different cell that has different receptors (antennae) on its surface, different portions of the transplanted DNA are activated. The key point here is that it's the same DNA in both cells, but the different receptors are picking up different kinds of information from the field that surrounds them. In other words, it's the same blueprint in either cell, but different antennae are tuned to the field of the environment. Suddenly the whole problem of organ rejection, along with a number of other mysteries, became less mysterious.

The reason why I'm sharing this information here is because it's only at the eight-cell stage that this gene activation is known to occur. This fact implies that it's only at this stage—the EGA stage, about four days after fertilization—that our cell receptors "wake up" and acquire the signal from the field that tunes them to produce the characteristics that make us human, and unique.

✳ ✳ ✳

In Figure 5.3, I've developed a high-level summary of the key characteristics leading up to our birth, and the average stage at which we develop these characteristics under typical conditions in the womb. The purpose of sharing them here is for a scientific point of reference only: to give us something more than an emotional reaction upon which to base our opinions on life and its beginnings; something to reference when we find ourselves without an informed opinion.

During my search to obtain the latest research describing the stages of human life, it became clear that the differences among individuals make it difficult to precisely time what happens in each stage. For this reason, the information that follows is meant as a synthesis of general opinion, and not as a table of absolute timing for events in the womb.

STAGE	NUMBER OF CELLS	ELAPSED TIME	CHARACTERISTICS
Fertilization: Embryo stage begins	2 cells become 1	About 24 hours after sperm cell and egg cell unite	23 chromosomes from mother and 23 from father merge into the 46 chromosomes that define a human.
Zygote	1 cell	About 11 hours after fertilization ends	Cell division (cleavage) begins, and each cell divides about every 12 to 20 hours.
	2 cells	About 12–20 hours after last cell division	
	4 cells	About 12–20 hours after last cell division	
	8 cells	About 12–20 hours after last cell division	Genes are activated. Blueprint for human traits is set into motion ~71 to 95 hours, or 2.9 to 3.9 days, after fertilization begins.
Morula	10–30 cells	About 4 days	Last stage before fluid-filled cavity of blastocyst forms.
Blastocyst	40–150 cells	About 5 days	Cells start to differentiate.
		18th day	First heartbeat is detected.
		22nd day	Heart is functioning and pumping blood.
Fetus		6 weeks	Brain waves are detectable.
		8 weeks	Embryo stage ends, and fetal stage begins. All organs are in place, and hearing is present.
		10 weeks	All organ systems functioning; skeletal system, nerves, and circulation function.
		12 weeks	Reflexes develop. End of first trimester of pregnancy.

Figure 5.3. The stages of human life from fertilization through 12 weeks, often called the "first trimester."

What Does It Mean?

By this point it's apparent that to answer the question of when human life begins, we must be clear what form of human life we're asking about.

- If we define human life as the single, new cell created at the stage of conception, then we think of human life as beginning within the first 24 hours of fertilization of the egg by the sperm.

- If we believe that human life begins at the stage when the DNA awakens to give us the human characteristics inherited from our parents, then it begins at the eight-cell stage, between 2.9 and 3.9 days after fertilization.

- If, as some indigenous cultures believe, life is defined by the presence of a heartbeat, then the human heart becomes viable and begins pumping blood on or about the 22nd day after fertilization.

Some people feel that the presence of brain waves, occurring at about 6 weeks, is a clear sign of human life, although the studies show that consciousness is not present until much later, around the 28th week.

Following the Supreme Court's decision that gave authority to individual states as to when and how an abortion can be performed, some doctors were required to inform a woman seeking an abortion that a 20-week-old fetus has the ability to feel pain. This is one of the places where new technology has changed that opinion. A study published in the lay science journal *Discover* (December 1, 2005) indicates that the nervous system that's needed to experience sensation becomes active at approximately the 28th week.

Mark Rosen, an obstetrical anesthesiologist at the University of California–San Francisco, and his colleagues have found that the "wiring at the point where you feel pain, such as the skin, doesn't reach the emotional part where you feel pain, in the brain" until about 20 weeks later than was believed to be the case in 1973 when the Supreme Court handed down its *Roe v. Wade* decision.[21] This interconnected system of nerves and brain function that Rosen describes must be in place before we can have what has been called our "magical journey of consciousness."

A September 2009 *Scientific American* report exploring whether or not our conscious experience begins within the womb, during birth itself, or after birth states that the "physical substrate" of tissue needed to relay and interpret electrical signals in the body, the "thalamocortical complex that provides consciousness with its highly elaborate content, begins to be in place between the 24th and 28th week of gestation."[22] This is an example of how technology has shed new light on when and how we develop through the different stages of life.

Advances in technology in years to come will give us deeper insights into precisely what it means to be alive. And just as the science of the early 21st century offers us information that was simply not available 40 years ago when the legal decision of *Roe v. Wade* was made, we will undoubtedly know more 40 years from now to help us to refine our choices.

What we can say with certainty is this: The deep truth of our existence is that life itself begins wherever the two living cells of a sperm and an egg join to create the stuff that *life* is made of. It's only after the first eight cells have formed that we activate the DNA giving us the characteristics that can be recognized as *human.*

Developing a deeper understanding of when life in the womb begins will undoubtedly lead to a deeper knowledge of that which, for some people, is the even bigger question: how life *itself* began, and how it began here on Earth.

Darwin's Conclusion: Evolution

On one of TV's most popular science-fiction series, *The Outer Limits,* each installment seemed to play into some facet of the world as we knew it at the time the program aired, between 1963 and 1965. This was especially true for the final episode of the series, entitled "Origin of Species."[23]

We lived in a very different world in 1963 than we do today. We were just emerging from the Cuban Missile Crisis; and the images from the nightly news reminded Americans of how vulnerable they were to atomic attack, and what to do if one happened. (In all honesty, turning school desks on their sides to hide behind, as the announcements showed, would probably do little to protect students if an atomic blast actually occurred in their neighborhoods.) It was during this time as well that some of the earliest fossil remains believed to be human ancestors were discovered at Olduvai Gorge in Tanzania.

Since the mid-19th century, scientists had been on a search to find fossilized evidence of the succession of human ancestors linking us today with our earliest beginnings, a succession believed to exist based on the "theory of evolution." Because of the ideas that Charles Darwin proposed a century earlier, the fossils of ancient humanlike creatures found in Africa and elsewhere throughout the world were being linked with *us*. While the theories of Darwin were mentioned briefly earlier in the book, I promised a more in-depth description of his ideas and their implications, which I am glad to offer now.

Since 1859, the scientific discussion of human origins has centered around a notion known best as the *theory of biological evolution*. While countless versions of evolutionary theory have been described in countless classrooms, journals, and textbooks over the past 150 years, the general idea of evolution has remained essentially the same. In a nutshell, the theory proposes that all life, including human life, is related, and began with a common ancestor. Since that ancestor, life-forms have changed over long periods of time to become those we see today. And while Darwin's theories do not describe precisely how the common ancestor of all life came into existence, assumptions drawn from his theories imply the answer.

Darwin first shared his ideas with the general public through the book most widely known by its popular title, *On the Origin of Species by Means of Natural Selection*. A closer look at the 1859 publication, however, shows that the book was initially published with a longer, two-part title that gives a very different sense of what it intended and what it might address. Before being shortened to the familiar one we see today, the original title of Darwin's book was *On the Origin of Species by Means of Natural Selection, or the Preservation of Favoured Races in the Struggle for Life.*[24]

With this book, Darwin planted the seeds in his time of the controversy that continues to rage throughout the modern world today. It's the depth of the emotional response triggered by what his book implies, and the way that his ideas are interpreted, that is the root of some of the most divisive beliefs between peoples and the justification for some of the greatest human suffering in recorded history.

Darwin formed his evolutionary theory from firsthand observations that he made over the course of his now-famous ocean voyage that began in 1835. During this voyage, he observed a greater variety of plants and animals than had any other European scientist of his day. An excerpt from the Introduction to his book gives us a clue as to what the journey meant to him personally:

> When on board H.M.S. 'Beagle' as a naturalist, I was much struck with certain facts in the distribution of the inhabitants of South America, and in the geological relations of the present to the past inhabitants of that continent. These facts seemed to me to throw some light on the origin of species—that mystery of mysteries, as it has been called by one of our greatest philosophers.[25]

Much of Darwin's theory is based upon observations that he made while studying fossils and wildlife, especially species of birds, on the Galapagos Islands. It wasn't until his return to London that he realized that what he originally thought were specimens collected from *different* families of finches, for example, were actually variations of the *same* family.

The question Darwin faced was how to explain the differences, such as beak size and shape, among finches that had developed isolated from one another on separate islands. The additional discovery of fossilized remains of creatures resembling modern-day animals, although much larger in size, added to the mystery Darwin confronted.

Using sound scientific methods of observation, hypothesis, experiment, and analysis, Darwin applied the best methods of his day to explain what he had discovered during his historic journey. The result of his work led to his theory of evolution by natural selection.

In essence, Darwin's theory of evolution by natural selection simply states that:

- Changes occur in a species (random mutations from the environment or reproductive errors). The members of a population that have life-supporting changes, like stronger beaks for cracking harder nuts, or camouflage-like coloring for protection, have an advantage over other members of the same species that don't share these characteristics. This portion of the theory is summarized in the term *microevolution.*

- Over time and under changing conditions, traits possessed by individuals that ensure their survival will win out over other traits possessed by members of the same species that don't ensure survival. Because they will survive longer, individuals with beneficial traits will produce more offspring that will also have the desirable traits. This part of Darwin's theory is described as *natural selection.*

- Eventually, the members of a species with the new changes mutate to the point that they can no longer breed with members of the original group. These members become a new species separate from their original ancestors. This process is called *speciation.*

When I look at the essence of the argument that Darwin published more than a century and a half ago, along with the data that he and others have accumulated since that time, the observations themselves make perfect sense. There can be little doubt on the part of anyone with an honest and open mind that the process of evolution, in and of itself, is very real. It is a fact that we see confirmed in the fossil record of species living in the past. We see it in nature today.

But while the process of evolution is a fact in the plant and animal kingdoms, the big question is, what does it mean for us? In other words, does the evolution that we see around us apply to human life as well? Does it explain how we've come to "be" as we "are" today? Is what Darwin observed as the "struggle for life" in the natural world the root of the human struggle that we see throughout the world today? These kinds of questions cut right to the core of the deepest controversies raging over the ideas about human development, the seeds of which were planted a century and a half ago.

Objections to Darwin's Ideas

Many of the objections to Darwin's work appear to be less about the idea of evolution itself, and more about what the theory implies and the assumptions that are drawn from it. In other words, Darwin was speculating about life processes that neither he nor anyone else had witnessed. He dispelled any doubt as to whether he personally believed that his theories applied to life beyond the plant and animal kingdom in general, and to us specifically.

In *On the Origin of Species,* he describes his sense that we, like other forms of life on Earth, are the result of evolutionary selection occurring over very long periods of time. In a single statement in the Conclusion of the book, he clearly summarizes his ideas about how that would have occurred: "We must likewise admit that all the organic beings which have ever lived on this earth have descended from some, one primordial form."[26]

Some of the objections to Darwin's theories are based on a purely emotional aversion to the idea that we could have evolved from less sophisticated forms of life. Some are based in religious doctrine stating that humankind is special, created directly by the hand of God. And while the theory of evolution is largely embraced by the scientific community today, the emergence of new technology has enabled discoveries in areas ranging from cell biology to genetics, leading a growing number of scientists to question whether Darwin's theory is the complete explanation for why life—and more specifically, human life—is the way it is.

The main concerns regarding evolution stem from three assumptions that are the keys to the theory:

- *Evolution Assumption 1:* Life may arise spontaneously from nonliving material.

- *Evolution Assumption 2:* Nature doesn't endow a species beyond what it needs to live.

- *Evolution Assumption 3:* Existing species may evolve into entirely new species slowly, over long periods of time.

A closer look at these assumptions shows, based upon what is known and validated as scientific fact today, that accepting them in their entirety presents serious problems. Let's look at each in turn.

Evolution Assumption 1:
Life May Arise Spontaneously from Nonliving Material

This first assumption is the key to the title of this chapter, "By Chance or Design." Rarely have I found it possible to use the word *never* when talking about a scientific theory. But this is one of those opportunities. It's a scientific fact that life has *never* been documented to form from any combination of stuff that's not already living. For mysterious reasons that scientists have struggled to understand for at least 300 years, it simply has not occurred.

Evolutionists often address this contradiction by suggesting that although we don't see the spontaneous creation of life *today,* the conditions for such processes may have been present at some time in the past, and then been destroyed by the development of life itself. The fact is that they don't know with certainty that this has ever happened. No one does. And that's the problem with the assumption.

The scientific attempt to create organic stuff from a "soup" of inorganic stuff in modern times inevitably brings to mind the landmark experiment of chemist and biologist Stanley Miller and Nobel Prize–winning physical chemist Harold Urey at the University of Chicago in 1952.[27] The initial experiment was conducted using the elements and compounds that scientists in the mid-20th century believed made up Earth's early atmosphere (water vapor, ammonia, hydrogen, and methane) and various forms of catalysts, like simulated lightning, to trigger the simplest beginnings of life.

While no living material resulted from the experiment, the study reported that five amino acids were present at the end. When scientists evaluated the earlier experiments in 2008, however, it was shown that there were actually 22 amino acids produced. While this sounds like encouraging support for Darwin's ideas, the analysis also discovered that the early models of Earth's atmosphere were not accurate.

New discoveries have revised the scientific thinking regarding Earth's early atmosphere. When the Miller-Urey experiment was repeated with a new chemical composition (water vapor, carbon dioxide, and nitrogen), *none* of the building blocks of life were produced. The absence of even a single amino acid has pretty much led to the end of this kind of thinking.

From this experiment, and others that have been performed since, there appears to be something that science simply has yet to account for—some missing ingredient in the recipe of life that has never been present in the laboratory experiments. Even when the conditions of temperature, moisture, and chemistry seem favorable for the spontaneous genesis of life, it also seems that there's *some force beyond the properties of chemistry* that's needed to breathe life into the elements of creation.

This force does not appear to be accounted for in the theories of Darwin or his disciples, or in the conventional wisdom of modern scientists. Of the three assumptions of evolutionary theory, this one appears to be the weakest, and I would not be surprised to see this part of the argument disappear from the conversation in the 21st century.

Evolution Assumption 2:
Nature Doesn't Endow a Species Beyond What It Needs to Live

In essence, this assumption is that living things only develop the traits that give them an edge in life when they need them, and not before. These new traits provide individuals with a greater opportunity to survive and live longer and will be passed on to new generations slowly, over periods of time, through the process of natural selection. The language for this assumption is commonly that "nature never over-endows a species beyond what is needed for everyday existence."

While this assumption is based upon Darwin's observations and may explain the change in the beak size of finches that enables them to better crack nuts (adding to their food supply), or in the coloring of moths to match the tree bark used for camouflage (protecting them against predators), the assumption breaks down when we try to apply it to humans—and specifically to the size of our brains. Here's why.

The increase in the brain capacity of modern humans is one of the anomalies that don't fit well into the template of evolutionary theory. Simply put, our brains became larger than they needed to be. The increase in size gave early humans capabilities believed to have been beyond what would have been required by the first of our kind *(Homo sapiens)*, who lived on Earth 200,000 or so years ago.

This may be best illustrated through a simple table showing the proposed lineage leading to the modern humans of today. Because this sample of our supposed ancestors is based upon the tree of relationships that evolutionists generally accept, I'll use it to show why evolutionary theory doesn't seem to apply when it comes to the size of our brains.

The list that follows shows the most recent branches of the evolutionary tree that are believed to lead to us, and the approximate brain size for each ancestor along the way. The capacity is measured in cubic centimeters (cm³).[28]

Name	Approximate Age	Approximate Brain Capacity
Homo sapiens (modern human)	200,000 YBP	1,450 cm³
Homo heidelbergensis	600,000 YBP	1,348 cm³
Homo habilis	2,500,000 YBP	700 cm³

YBP = Years Before Present

Figure 5.4. The brain capacities for the latest members of the commonly accepted human lineage. Modern humans appeared about 200,000 years ago, with a brain capacity about 100 cm³ larger than our ancestors had 400,000 years earlier. Contrary to the idea of evolutionary theory, this was more than is believed to have been needed at the time, and has not changed since.

While the brain sizes are approximate, they tell a story that has direct bearing on one of the basic assumptions of evolutionary theory. It took nearly 2 million years (approximately 1.9 million years) for the brain capacity to increase from 700 cm³ to 1,348 cm³ (between *H. habilis* and *H. heidelbergensis*), a growth of 648 cm³. But it took only 400,000 years for the next increase of 102 cm³ (between our nearest known ancestor, *H. heidelbergensis,* and modern humans). In evolutionary terms, this most recent gain happened in the blink of an eye, and maybe more important, occurred before it is believed that we needed it.

The same brain that makes us capable of abstract thinking—which gives us the power to formulate complex mathematical equations and simulate possibilities in our minds before we choose them, as well as to create the values and beliefs currently driving the most advanced civilization in the history of the world—possesses abilities far in excess of what the first of our kind needed to survive day by day when they appeared 200,000 years ago. According to the ideas of evolutionary theory, it shouldn't happen this way. As Darwin himself stated in his theory, "Natural selection acts only by taking advantage of slight successive variations;

she can never take a great and sudden leap, but must advance by short and sure, though slow steps."[29]

While the size of our brains is one fact of human existence that presents a big problem for evolutionary theorists, it's also only an aspect of a larger problem: the anatomical form of the modern human itself. Our brains haven't changed much for the last 200,000 years, and our bodies haven't either. We have essentially the same bodies today as fossils show that our ancestors had 200 millennia ago. The question is: *Why?* If evolution really applies to *us* as much as it does to other forms of life, then why have we remained unchanged over this period of time?

When we think of the enigma of how our brains developed, it underlines even more the powerful observation of evolutionary biologist Stephen Jay Gould regarding fossil evidence in the geological record and the "awesome improbability of human evolution."[30]

Evolution Assumption 3:
Existing Species May Evolve into Entirely New Species Slowly, Over Long Periods of Time

This third assumption of evolutionary theory states that the mutations within a group can go so far as to create an entirely new species: a form of life with DNA so different from the previous ones they've evolved from that they can no longer mate with the original population. The biggest problem with this theory is that it is based upon speculation, not fact. To the best of my knowledge, there is no documented evidence of a new species emerging from an existing one. When it comes to humans, it may be that what we see as the ability to *adapt* better describes what has been observed, and possibly been mistaken for evolution, than the process of evolution itself.

The indigenous tribes of the Arctic and Siberia, for example, have developed extra flesh around their eyes, allowing them protection from the perpetual glare of sunlight reflected off the snow and ice that greet them outside their homes each day. While this characteristic *is* believed to be a direct response to their environment, *it's a change in their appearance only.*

The members of these tribes have lived in, and adapted to, the harsh environment of the polar regions for at least 10,000 years. During that time, however, they have not evolved into a new species of human, and there appears to be no evidence that they will. Genetically, these people still belong to the species *Homo sapiens.* Their bodies have simply adjusted to the conditions of the environment that their world presents to them.

If species do, in fact, truly *evolve* with new DNA, rather than adapt over time, it's reasonable to expect that somewhere in the ongoing search that began in 1859, at least one transitional form would be discovered in the fossil record. Instead, as the case of modern humans and Neanderthals illustrates, species thought to have evolved *from* one another over time have instead been found to have lived and died alongside one another, during the same time. The fact that Neanderthals' DNA is so different from ours has placed them on a separate branch of the human evolutionary tree and left us where we were to begin with. As of this writing, there is no physical evidence of transitional species to support this assumption of evolution. This makes our descent from Neanderthal, for example, impossible.

Speaking in specific and technical terms, paleontologist and evolutionary biologist Steven M. Stanley leaves no room to doubt the fact of this lack of transitional evidence in the fossil record. "The known fossil record," he states, "fails to document a single example of phyletic evolution accomplishing a major morphologic transition and hence offers no evidence that the gradualistic model can be valid."[31] While Stanley and other evolutionary biologists, such as Gould, offer new insights into why this lack of evidence may exist, the fact is that it does.

The geological record itself shows that the vast majority of species that have lived on Earth appeared during the *Cambrian explosion,* a period that is to biology what the big bang is to astrophysics. It was during the Cambrian explosion, about 540 million years ago, that "all of the eight major animal body plans in existence today, along with 27 minor ones, had emerged. And no new body plans have developed since."[32] The key idea here is that the basic elements of life on Earth appear to have emerged in a relatively brief span of time—not as the result of a slow evolutionary process over a long period.

Evolution: Does the Theory Fit the Evidence?

With problems in the three basic assumptions of Darwin's theories, where does that leave us? In *On the Origin of Species,* Darwin himself acknowledged the lack of evidence showing one species transitioning into another:

> . . . the number of intermediate varieties, which have formerly existed on the earth, [must] truly be enormous. Why then is not every geological formation and every stratum full of such intermediate links? Geology assuredly does not reveal any such finely graduated organic chain; and this, perhaps, is the most obvious and serious objection which can be urged against my theory.[33]

It's clear that there are big problems with Darwin's evolutionary theory, especially when it's applied to humans. After 150 years of direct questioning by some of the best minds of our time, and serious investigations conducted under the auspices of the most prestigious universities in the world, the problems haven't gone away. These troublesome facts have led a growing number of scientists to approach the question of life's origins from a different direction.

What they now suggest offers a completely fresh perspective based upon a scientific question that goes directly to the heart of our existence: Do we exist because of a cosmic plan that forms the foundation of life's complexity? In other words, are we here *by design?* If so—if life does reflect a design just like the presence of a watch implies a watchmaker—then who, or what, is the designer?

Some of the best minds of our time now suspect that in addition to the recognized process of nature, life appears to be as it is by design. This book began by asking the question: *Who are we?* For now, we can say with reasonable certainty that we are more than we have ever dared to imagine, and perhaps capable of all that we have ever dreamed. To even the most skeptical scientist, a growing body of evidence suggests that the force of some kind of pattern—a design of unknown origin—underlies our existence and implies the presence of an even greater intelligence.

Life: By Design?

In the same way that Darwin's theory is represented by a term summarizing its content—*evolution by natural selection*—the alternative explanation of a cosmic blueprint reflected in life also has a name: the theory of *intelligent design,* often simply shortened to *ID.*

According to the Center for Science and Culture, a program that supports scientists and scholars exploring the evidence of ID, the theory "holds that certain features of the universe and of living things are best explained by an intelligent cause, not an undirected process such as natural selection."[34] Although the name itself was actually used even before Darwin published his first book in 1859—in publications such as *Scientific American* (1847), for example—it has come into general usage in the late 20th century and now in the 21st century.

While some members of the scientific community continue to question whether the new approach and studies related to it are truly scientific, the fact is that the investigations are being conducted by professionals from accepted scientific disciplines, using accepted scientific methods to answer the questions that traditional mainstream scientists have failed to address.

Before the term *intelligent design* became popular in 1989, another alternative theory to Darwin's evolution was present as a movement: *creationism.* And just as Darwin's supporters are called Darwinists, the supporters of creation theory are called creationists. Although there are several viewpoints within the creationism camp (the old Earth, the young Earth, and the progressive), the general theme for all of them is based upon the same principle: that one or more supernatural beings—a god or gods—created life, humans, and the natural world. I'm mentioning this theory here to draw a distinction between it and intelligent design.

While intelligent design is often associated with creation theory, in its purest form, it's not. ID does not attempt to identify an intelligence responsible for the patterns in nature and life. It doesn't even state that such an intelligence exists. It simply proposes that life, and more specifically, human life, is the result of a design based upon complex processes that did not evolve naturally. While some supporters of ID may have strong beliefs that God is, in fact, the designer, the actual science of ID does not go that far.

In the previous section, we summarized the key assumptions for evolutionary theory. I'd like to do the same for intelligent design, and then address each one in more detail. Intelligent design is based upon two key assumptions:

- *Intelligent-Design Assumption 1:* There is an order in the universe.

- *Intelligent-Design Assumption 2:* The complexities of living systems can best be explained by directed, rather than random, processes.

In layman's terms, the bottom line to ID is that the intricate and entangled systems forming the basis of the universe are so finely "tuned" for life that they could not have happened by chance. The theory says, in the same vein, that the complexities of life, in general, and human life, specifically, cannot be an accident of biology resulting from random mutations over long periods of time.

Is a Watch Still a Watch Without the Parts?

One of the key arguments of ID theory cites the complexity of life itself, and the astronomical odds against the intricate machinery of the cell or the information system of the DNA molecule having formed spontaneously as the result of an undirected process over a long period of time. In *On the Origin of Species,* even Darwin himself remarked on how unlikely it is that natural selection was solely responsible for the degree of specialization that we see in organs and tissues. As an example, he singled out the complexity of an eye, stating, "To suppose the eye, with all its inimitable contrivances for adjusting the focus to different distances . . . could have been formed by natural selection, seems, I freely confess, absurd in the highest degree."[35] Following this and similar observations, Darwin left us to our own conclusions with regard to precisely what additional force or forces may be responsible for the complex nature of life.

In a similar way, when Francis Crick, the Nobel Prize–winning co-discoverer of the DNA molecule, was asked about the possibility that life has arisen from a chance series of events, he remarked, "An honest man, armed with all the knowledge available to us now, could only state that in some sense, the origin of life appears at the moment to be almost a miracle, so many are the conditions that would have had to have been satisfied to get it going."[36]

Charles Darwin made his observations in 1859. Nearly 100 years later, with the benefit of tremendous advances in science and experimental methods, Crick arrived at similar conclusions. The theme of these statements by Darwin, Crick, and today's supporters of ID is the complex nature of life itself. Darwin had no way of knowing what we do today about cells and DNA. Acknowledging this, I. L. Cohen, a mathematician and member of the New York Academy of Sciences, summed it up better than I possibly could: "At that moment, when the DNA/RNA system became understood, the debate between Evolutionists and Creationists should have come to a screeching halt. . . . The implications of the DNA/RNA were obvious and clear."[37]

Irreducible Complexity

Cohen's statement identifies a key to the role of evolutionary theory in our worldview today. When he formed his theory, Darwin had no way of knowing that even the simplest bacterium, the single-celled *E. coli,* requires 2,000 different proteins to exist, and that each of those proteins has an average of 300 amino acids that make it what it is. He simply could not have known just how complex the basic units of life really are. One of the strongest arguments in support of ID is precisely this complexity, and the fact that many of the systems of life exhibit what is called *irreducible complexity.*

Irreducible complexity is a technical-sounding term for what is actually a very simple idea. It essentially means that if any portion of a system stops working, the entire system stops working. A watch, as described previously, is often used to illustrate this point. So is a common mousetrap. When all of the parts of a mousetrap are in place, it does what it was designed to do: it traps a mouse, or any other small animal, that has taken the bait of cheese or peanut butter and tripped a lever that delivers a deadly blow.

To work the way it was designed, the trap is based upon a system of parts, with each one performing a specific task to accomplish the ultimate goal. There is the delicate lever that holds the bait, for example, and the powerful spring that comes down with a lethal force so quickly when the bait is disturbed that the mouse doesn't even know what hit it. While the trap sounds like a simple gadget, and it is, if even one part is missing, it simply won't work. Without the spring, the lever will never snap. Without the lever, the spring will have nothing to trigger it. Because all the pieces of the trap are needed for the system to work, it can be said that the mousetrap cannot be reduced by taking away any parts and still be functional. It is an example of irreducible complexity.

The advanced technology of our time has shown us numerous examples of life's irreducible complexity. We all know that when we cut a finger or scrape a knee, our bodies will bleed briefly, and then the bleeding stops. The reason it does so is that our blood clots at the site of the injury. While we take that clotting for granted, it is a perfect example of irreducible complexity.

Twenty separate proteins must be present for our blood to clot and bleeding to stop. What makes this so interesting is that if even one of the proteins is absent, the clotting mechanism won't work. If it doesn't, bleeding will continue until there's no more blood in our bodies to be bled out. All 20 of the proteins must work together at the same time for them to do what they do.

In terms of evolution, this means that all 20 of the necessary proteins had to have been already formed, and all in the same place, before the blood that gives our bodies life could form. This is an example of a life function that could not have happened through evolution. And it's only one example. The little waving arms (cilia) that allow cells to travel in fluid have more than 40 moving parts that must all be present for the cell to swim. If any part is missing, the cell can't move.

The human cell has been called the single most complex piece of machinery ever known to exist. Until the mid-20th century or so, cells were essentially thought of as tiny bags of chemicals. We now know that nothing could be further from the truth. In fact, if we could enlarge a single cell to the size of a small city, its complexity would surpass the infrastructure that it takes to keep a municipality going. A sample of a cell's important structures includes:

- Ribosomes that manufacture proteins

- Endoplasmic reticulum that makes and transports important chemicals used by the cell

- A nucleus that carries the instructions for the cell on how to function

- Microtubules that allow the cell to move and change shape

- Cilia (little waving arms) that allow some cells to move in fluid

- Mitochondria that generate energy for the cell

- A membrane that communicates with the environment and determines what gets into, and leaves, the cell

These are a sampling of some of the functional parts involved in processes that are happening at any given moment in time—for instance, right now as you're reading these words—in each of the approximately 50 trillion cells of your body. As we discover what each process does, it becomes obvious that all of the cellular machinery had to be already created and in place for our first cells to do what they do. From clotting blood to swimming cilia, these are all beautiful examples of irreducible complexity.

By Choice or by Chance?

In the classic textbook *Molecular Biology of the Gene*, Nobel Prize winner James D. Watson, co-discoverer of the DNA molecule, describes the uniqueness and mystery of living cells: "We must immediately admit that the structure of the cell will never be understood in the same way as that of water or glucose molecules. Not only will the exact structure of most macromolecules within the cell remain unsolved, but their relative locations within cells can only be vaguely known."[38]

There appears to be *something* about the process within the miracle factory of each cell of our bodies that defies explanation through conventional wisdom and traditional thinking. From such observations, we begin to sense just how unlikely it is that we're the result of a "fluke" of creation. Thus, the message encoded within each of our cells takes on even greater meaning.

In nature, *order* is often seen as a sign of intelligence. The existence of predictable and repeatable patterns that can be described by universal formulas is an example of what is meant by this word. In candid interviews late in his life, Albert Einstein shared his belief that such an underlying order exists in the universe, as well as his sense of where such order comes from. During one of those conversations, he confided, "I see a pattern but my imagination cannot picture the maker of the pattern . . . we all dance to a mysterious tune, intoned in the distance by an invisible piper."[39] In our search for meaning in life, the very presence of order is often viewed as a sign that Einstein's "invisible piper" exists.

To even the most skeptical scientist, it's obvious that the DNA of life resembles a complex and intricate sequence of information, a program that tells our cells what to do and when to do it. While both intelligent design and evolution offer useful insights into the nature of our origins, *we may discover that the merging of key concepts from both theories* offers the best explanation of the evidence observed so far.

Such a *hybrid theory of creation* takes into account the observations of evolution by affirming that our world is ancient and that certain processes do, in fact, occur over long periods of time. Additionally, it incorporates the view of ID that a special force, beyond that which is known or acknowledged by conventional scientists today, is responsible for setting into motion the conditions from which life on Earth began in the first place, as well as for activating the genetic code that kicks in precisely three cell divisions after fertilization, when we're eight-celled creatures.

The key to moving beyond the stalemate of the evolution-versus-ID controversy is to define what it is that we are looking for. Is it evidence, or is it proof?

> When it comes to evolution versus intelligent design, are we searching for evidence or proof?

If we're looking for proof to lock in either theory, then we must be honest with ourselves: we'll probably never find it. The only way we could actually *prove* either theory is to witness the process directly. Barring a quantum advance in the technology of time travel, however, in plain terms . . . that simply "ain't gonna happen." It can't, because whatever happened to begin life in general, and human life specifically, occurred a long time ago—and we weren't here to see it. Clearly the best we can hope for is *evidence*. The evidence that we find for both theories, and our willingness to accept whatever we discover, will ultimately lead us to the truth of our origins.

We've done this before with ideas that didn't fit new evidence, and it led to some of the greatest revolutions in the history of human understanding. When Newton's concept of an atom being a "thing" gave way to the quantum discoveries demonstrating that the atom is energy, the world of physics changed forever. Newton's ideas worked well enough to allow science to progress to the place where the new advancements opened the doors to deeper understanding. We are witnessing precisely the same thing happening in the search to understand our origins.

For now, a combined theory incorporating elements from both ID and evolution appears to be our best explanation for the mystery and miracle of life. While acknowledging the physical evidence discovered to date, it also allows for the intuitive sense, held by the vast majority of people in our world, that we are part of something greater.

Clearly the question of life's origins has big consequences. For some people, exploring these topics means opening the door to uncomfortable possibilities. To penetrate some of our most ancient and enduring mysteries means that we must think very differently about ourselves, our relationships to one another, and even life itself. Thinking differently means that we must change everything—from the way we use war to resolve our conflicts . . . to when and how we choose to take a human life at any time, whether it is through abortion, euthanasia, or genocide.

It is precisely these answers that are necessary to move us away from the deeply entrenched emotions permeating every area of our society, from our school systems to our medical systems. While we still may not all agree on exactly what course of action to take regarding the treatment of life, now, in the presence of the facts, we have more than heated emotions upon which to base our beliefs. Clearly, what we *don't* know, and the meaning we attach to what we don't know, signals the direction for the next great frontier of discovery.

Deep Truth 5: A growing body of scientific data from multiple disciplines, gathered using new technology, provides evidence beyond any reasonable doubt that humankind reflects a design put into place at once, rather than a life-form emerging randomly through an evolutionary process over a long period of time.

CHAPTER SIX

WAR DOESN'T
WORK ANYMORE:
WHY WE'RE
"WIRED" FOR PEACE

*"Ours is a world of nuclear giants and ethical infants.
We know more about war than we know about peace,
more about killing than we know about living."*

— GENERAL OMAR N. BRADLEY (1893–1981),
FORMER CHAIRMAN OF THE JOINT CHIEFS OF STAFF

Before his death in 1984, filmmaker Sam Peckinpah said,
"There is a great streak of violence in every human being. If it
is not channeled and understood, it will break out in war or in
madness."[1]

Peckinpah's words echo mainstream thinking when it comes to violence and humans. In classrooms and textbooks throughout the world, we've been led to believe that war among people is as natural as night and day, and that it's been with us from the time of our earliest ancestors. Whether it's the depiction of cavemen and cavewomen who lived 10,000 years in the past, or the fictional image of scientists walking through a "star gate" that takes them across the universe 100 years into our future, we're so accustomed to thinking of ourselves as a warlike species that we almost expect to see scenes of armies and combat in any drama involving humans.

Contributing to this "warlike" way of thinking about ourselves are the interpretations of myriad studies from experts such as University of Illinois archaeologist Lawrence H. Keeley, author of *War Before Civilization* (Oxford University Press, 1977). Based on his scholarly exploration of our past and his interpretation of what he's found, Keeley's opinion is that war is a natural state of human affairs. "War is something like trade or exchange," he says. "It's something that all humans do."[2]

While it's easy to buy into this kind of sweeping generalization, there's a big problem: The facts simply don't support it. New discoveries have led to a startling conclusion regarding the origins of war and the role it plays in our lives. The bottom line is that recent archaeological evidence of the oldest civilizations known to have existed on Earth (Göbekli Tepe, the Gulf of Khambhat, and Caral) suggests that war may in fact be a habit that has developed only during the present 5,000-year cycle of civilization, rather than a natural way of life. And this is a beautiful example of where false assumptions, drawn from limited information, lead to justifications of violence as a viable option for us.

The discovery of the world's oldest civilizations is pushing our history, and our history of war and peace, back to near the end of the last ice age. With earlier dating, the emerging view of our ancient ancestors is painting a radical new picture of our past. A growing body of scientific evidence suggests that the large-scale wars, like those fought in the last 1,000 years or so, are not the common practice we've been led to believe. Instead, the lack of weapons, armaments, and defenses such as protective walls implies that wars happen on a basis that is linked to extreme conditions such as climate change, rather than being an ongoing way of life throughout history.

R. Brian Ferguson, a professor of anthropology at Rutgers University, is among a growing number of scientists who disagree with the conventional take on war in society. "In my view the global archaeological record contradicts the idea that war was always a feature of human existence," he says. Ferguson summarizes the essence of the new evidence: "Instead, the record shows that warfare is largely a development of the past 10,000 years."[3]

I find the time frame that Ferguson describes fascinating, as it corresponds to two of the 5,000-year-long climate cycles described by indigenous traditions as "great world ages." In other words, the present world age that began about 5,000 years ago (which is the generally accepted length of the history of civilization) is the period in which the wars that Keeley has explored took place. And while war may, in fact, be commonplace during the present cycle of civilization, it's not the whole of human experience. Somewhere along the way we learned to solve our problems through warfare. The latest evidence suggests, however, that it's not our natural tendency to do so.

From America's Desert Southwest to the mountains of Peru and the deserts of Turkey, new discoveries showing the rarity of conflict seem to support Ferguson's view. Cycles of war seem to ebb and flow, and it may be no coincidence that much of the ebb and flow correlates to big changes in Earth's climate, like those we're seeing in the world today. In light of the new discoveries, the questions about our past now are less about what caused the wars in the ancient world, and more about why they're absent in the earliest evidence of civilization.

Acknowledging the new discoveries, Harvard University psychology professor Steven Pinker thinks it might be good to rethink the traditional assumptions about what causes war, and focus upon the concept of peace. Instead of asking, "Why is there war?" Pinker says we may want to think about the question differently, or even ask an entirely new one. We might ask, for example, "Why is there peace?"[4]

His reasoning is clear. If we can learn what causes the ebb and flow of large-scale violence, we may also find the key to heading off the greatest threat to humankind today. Recognizing the current trend toward less violence and the fact that we must be doing *something* right, Pinker reflects, "It would be nice to know what, exactly, it is."

Mystery at Chaco Canyon

"Once you've heard the sound, you'll never forget it."

The voice of the ancient-looking man who shared those words with me echoed in my mind. And he was right. The high quartz content of the sand that crunched under my feet lent it an eerie sound—a high-pitched crackle that bounced off the sandstone walls of the canyon towering above me. With each step, the ring of the last tone was just fading as the next one reached my ears, blending with the wind into a continuous chorus as I walked.

I remember thinking how ironic it was that every grain of quartz-sand now crunching beneath my feet had once been locked into the hardened sandstone of the cliffs bordering the trail. Through countless windstorms, innumerable floods, and thousands of years of icing and thawing, tiny grains had been freed from the walls, only to become even smaller fragments as they cracked under my weight.

It was a late-August morning years ago in the high desert of the Four Corners area of northern New Mexico. I had happened upon the Native American elder on the trail earlier that morning. For reasons that neither of us questioned, we had both been drawn to the same ancient ceremonial site, on the same day, at the same time. Together we made our way along the dusty, packed-sand trail that paralleled the pink-and-yellow cliffs rising from the valley floor. We had both come to learn from the past—he from his ancestors through their voices in the caves; and me from the temples, drawings, and clues they had left behind.

"There were no wars here," the man said to me as we stopped along a small rise to catch our breath. "The people who lived here had no need for war."

"Really?" I asked. "How do we know that?"

"This is one of the great mysteries that scientists see when they dig here," he replied. "This place looks huge to us today, but it's only a piece of the community that lived here before.

"Over 4,000 people lived in this valley, in these buildings," he continued, as he swept his open arms across the valley that lay behind and in front of us. "But they lived peacefully. There were no weapons found here. Not one. There are no signs of war. None. There are no mass graves, no ashes, no burial sites." He concluded: *"Our ancestors did not need them, because they had learned another way."*

I listened carefully to what my Native American friend was telling me. What he did not know, and could not have known, was that the information he was sharing with me that morning was precisely why I'd come to this place.

The site was Chaco Canyon, New Mexico, a place unlike any other in the world. Chaco Canyon is a mystery for a number of reasons. While there are a multitude of theories that attempt to make sense of what remains there, the truth is that no one knows much about the Chacoans. No one really knows where they went or why they disappeared. And we can't know for certain, because they left no written records . . . at least none written in a form we recognize today.

What we do know is that in one of the most isolated and hostile places in North America, a mysterious people arrived seemingly from nowhere and built homes, communities, and ceremonial centers on a scale unseen before that time—or since—for reasons that are unclear to this day. Their technology seems to have arrived intact. In other words, they did not begin with a primitive way of living and slowly advance in stages over a long period of time to the level of sophistication that sets their site apart from other ancient settlements in the area. Almost "overnight" they had the architectural know-how to construct four-story buildings, and to create reservoirs and diversion structures to capture precious water. As a result, they had the agriculture to support large populations, estimated to have peaked in the early 12th century C.E.

While they appear to have had no wheels, they built perfectly straight roads that extend for hundreds of miles in all directions— roads that were only recognized as such in images made from space during NASA's *Apollo* missions of the 1970s. And just as suddenly as they appeared, they were gone. While there are theories that chalk up their disappearance to an extended drought and other extremes in weather, the truth is that no one knows for certain who the Chacoans were, where they came from, or why they left.

The elder was right—from a century of tedious surveys, painstaking excavations, and intense study of the oral traditions of the Chacoan descendants themselves, no evidence of war has been found at Chaco Canyon. There are none of the protective walls that would be expected for such huge complexes, no signs of weapons, no mass graves, and no mutilated skeletons.

As if he could read my mind, my Native American friend answered my next question before I could even ask it. I was wondering why anyone would choose this location to build such a vast complex. *Why here of all places?*

"They built here because of what lies beneath this site," he said. "Chaco is not the first place to exist here. It's only the most recent. It's built on top of what was here before, which is built on top of what was here before that . . ."

It's not that I didn't believe him, but I had to ask anyway: "How do we know that for certain? How do we really know that something was here before this ancient temple came into existence?"

For my friend, the answer was easy. "The ancestors tell us," he said.

In their stories, they keep the memory of their ancestors alive. And their ancestors tell of the ancient ones, those who lived in Chaco Canyon before the "Chacoans."

＊ ＊ ＊

It wasn't until 1993 that modern science caught up with the stories of the Chacoans' ancient ancestors. During that time I was leading a group through the area when we saw a university research team near one of the main Chaco Canyon sites. The researchers were in the area with remote-sensing equipment to search for evidence of a previous civilization, one that was in Chaco Canyon *before* the Chacoans built what stands there today. Using sophisticated earth-penetrating radar, the researchers were able to "see" below the existing buildings in one of the best-preserved portions of the site. When I asked to see what they had found so far, the operator of the radar was happy to show me.

While it's impossible to know for certain what the radar was showing without actually excavating the site—a process that would mean destroying the existing temple that was exposed at the surface—there were definitely the signs of ancient buildings beneath the surface. Once again, my native friend was right. Someone *had* been there before. I was standing on the remains of the ancient and undocumented civilization that proved it.

As the rays of the late-summer sun cast their long shadows across the valley, the question that kept coming to me was why there was no evidence of mass burials, weapons, or struggle. With the exception of a few skeletons of a later age found in storage rooms, there were no bodies recovered in this valley that had once housed up to 4,000 people. Did the inhabitants know something then that we've forgotten today? Did they find a way to live and work together, like the later Chacoans apparently had, that did not require the warfare that we take for granted in our civilization? Time, and the continued excavation of Chaco Canyon, will tell.

No Walls, No Wars

One of the anomalies characterizing both ancient Caral and Chaco Canyon is that there is no evidence, no telltale sign, of war. In a once highly populated site like Chaco Canyon, this is an unusual revelation. In other sites of large populations and ancient warfare, the bodies of massive armies are found buried in mass graves with heads and limbs severed, ax gashes in the skulls, and other injuries that we would typically expect to see from an ancient battlefield. We find none of that in either of these sites. We also find no evidence that the people of the time needed to protect themselves from anything.

In both Chaco Canyon and Caral, there are no high protective walls or signs of moats surrounding the complexes, as we'd expect from a place where people felt they needed to defend themselves. In fact, looking beyond the Americas to places like Göbekli Tepe, the oldest known civilization on Earth, it appears that it's only in the more "recent" examples of the last 5,000 years or so that civilizations like those in Egypt, Rome, and Greece thought of war as a way of life. It's clear that we've not always been the warlike species that we seem to be today. The question is: *Why not?*

Did our ancestors find a way to solve their problems without war that we've forgotten? And if so, then can we unlearn our violent habits, as we do any bad habit? With the sophistication of the modern weapons and the magnitude of the destructive power they hold, it's now more important than ever to address such unanswered questions.

Wars of Necessity

"Gasps echoed through the Nobel Hall in Oslo yesterday as Barack Obama was unveiled as the winner of the 2009 Peace Prize, sparking a global outpouring of incredulity and praise in unequal measure."[5] The theme of this line from an article in the October 10, 2009, edition of England's *Sunday Times* was echoed in newspapers, television commentary, and living rooms throughout the world. The newly elected President of the United States had been in office for only 11 days and was fast asleep in the White House when the announcement was made half a world away.

While Obama is only the third U.S. President to receive the Nobel Peace Prize while in office (Theodore Roosevelt won in 1906, Woodrow Wilson in 1919), it wasn't his stint in the White House that stirred the controversy. It was perceptions of what he had, and had not yet, achieved during his brief time in office that set off the debate. Former political prisoner, 1983 Nobel Prize winner, and president of Poland (1990–1995) Lech Walesa summed up publicly what many people felt privately when he was asked by reporters for his comments on the announcement: "Who? What? So fast? There hasn't been any contribution to peace yet. He's proposing things, he's initiating things, but he is yet to deliver."[6]

As Obama stood at the podium to accept his award only nine months after his inauguration, the media surprise that greeted his win was transformed into gasps from the live audience. But this time, they were heard for a different reason. The President, who had just received the highest award of peace in the world, started off his speech by taking a very unpopular position on war.

He began by stating the obvious: "I am the Commander-in-Chief of the military of a nation in the midst of two wars." He continued, "I'm responsible for the deployment of thousands of young Americans to battle in a distant land. Some will kill, and some will be killed. And so I come here with an acute sense of the cost of armed conflict—filled with difficult questions about the relationship between war and peace, and our effort to replace one with the other."[7]

Although many people criticized Obama for the words that introduced his acceptance, it's what he said next that has sparked the question of whether he was, in fact, the best nominee for the award. Obama addressed the idea of war head-on: "We must begin by acknowledging the hard truth: we will not eradicate violent conflict in our lifetimes."[8] But then he took a leap beyond simply stating the conditions of the world as it is.

Suddenly he was telling us not to be surprised to see more war, stating that there will be conditions where it will not only be inevitable, but it will be warranted. "There will be times when nations—acting individually or in concert," he said, "will find the use of force not only necessary but morally justified."[9] It was this comment that touched off the controversy, the outrage, and questioning of Obama's merit as a nominee. Are there really times when war is the only solution? As necessary as it may appear, is there ever a time that war can be "morally justified"?

Within the memory of many people reading this book there were two wars that the United States chose to enter with precisely these ideas in mind:

1. The first, declared by President Woodrow Wilson in 1917 to be the "war to end war" (building on a term first used by British author H. G. Wells after the war first broke out in Europe in 1914), was **World War I**. In his war declaration to Congress, Wilson stated that the scales of civilization hung in the balance, and without America's aid he feared that all would be lost.

2. The second war many consider "morally justified" was **World War II**, which America entered on December 8, 1941, a day after the U.S. naval base in Pearl Harbor was attacked. Because the enemy was obvious, the goals were clear, and the mission was achievable, World War II has been called the "Good War."

Wars to End All Wars

Before he died at the age of 96, my grandfather would talk to me for hours about the world and the way it was in his "time." He was born in Central Europe at the beginning of the last century, and he always began his stories by telling me that we live in a world today that is very different from in his day. While I knew what he was saying was certainly true, each time I listened to his stories, I knew even more just what he *meant*. My grandfather would tell me of a world where horse-drawn wagons shared the road with the new invention of automobiles . . . where many homes had no electricity and telephones were rare. It was a world where there was no network of superhighways, and indoor toilets were a luxury.

Whenever he would tell me about the people he'd known and the jobs he'd held, there was always a point where the tone of the story would shift. The smile would disappear from his face, and his voice would change as he allowed himself to recall three times in his life when the world and everything in it was transformed: the Great Depression and the two world wars. And although these were definitely different experiences, they were also definitely related.

While he was too young to actively serve in World War I himself, the scale of the war and the toll it took on his friends, neighbors, and everyday life in Europe left the memories that became scars by the time of the next "Great War." Based upon the information that the average person, including my grandfather, had access to, World War II was a conflict that made sense. At least it made sense to the people of the time.

Throughout the course of the war, the largest armies in the world faced off against one another: the United States, Great Britain, and Russia . . . against Germany, Japan, and, for a time, Italy. Officially the entire war lasted for four years. (I say "officially" because there is a school of thought suggesting that World War II never really ended. While the treaties were signed and the troops returned home, the way the world was carved up at the end of it continues to be a key factor in the antagonism stirring the wars we're fighting today.)

The term "Good War" became hugely popular in 1984, familiar as the title of a book that won a Pulitzer Prize for its author, Studs Terkel: *The Good War: An Oral History of World War Two*. But how good can any war really be? In Terkel's book, and from my grandfather's stories, the immense cost of World War II, in terms of loss of human life and the complete destruction of cities that had stood for centuries, seems to be about as justified as any war can ever be. Most historians agree that the death toll for World War II stands at about 50,000,000 people—*that's 50 million human lives!*

When we think of each human life lost in terms of what our own lives mean to us, the toll is unimaginable. For perspective, the number of lives lost in World War II by the time it ended in 1945 was about 2.5 percent of the population of the entire world. There are two key reasons why World War II was justified, and they can be summarized in three words: *Hitler* and *Pearl Harbor*.

When America entered World War II, it was obvious why. In the minds of those among the Allied Powers who supported the war effort, the United States was drawn into the conflict and responded defensively. It was clear who the enemy was. It was clear what the objective was, and it would be clear when that objective was met. When all of the factors were weighed, there appeared to be little gray area when it came to rationalizing America's involvement in World War II. It was a defensive war expressing the classic and age-old fight between good and evil, a fight to end the horrors of Hitler's Germany and a response to Japan's attempt to impose Japanese rule on the world. And while bad things happen in any war, the Allies saw the ideas and methods of Germany, and later Japan, as an unacceptable threat to the principles of freedom and the world's democracies.

Although the world was certainly different in the mid-20th century than it is today, the reasons used to justify the war of that time are still invoked more than a half century later to argue for the ones of today. While there are certainly similarities between the way World War II and the present-day War on Terror began, any similarities end quickly and the differences become obvious upon closer examination.

In the following table I've highlighted some of the parallels and the differences. In the first great war of the 21st century—the War on Terror—there is no clearly defined "enemy," at least not one in the conventional sense of the word. Whether it's the gray and blue uniforms of the armies facing off in America's Civil War of the mid-1800s; the uniqueness of the combatants' helmets seen in World War I; or the insignias of swastikas, Stars and Stripes, and Japan's Rising Sun seen on flags during World War II, each side has always been clearly identified by their clothing, weapons, and so on. There is no consistent uniform or identifying symbol in the War on Terror to show who is who.

The belief regarding both the First and Second World Wars was that war was inevitable. In both cases, avoiding it was thought to be impossible, and the cause was believed "just." And a good case can be made for both wars at the time in history when they ensued. In light of the differences between then and now, and in light of the capabilities of modern weapons and existing technology, we must ask ourselves the same question once again: *Is war still the best way to solve our problems today?*

WORLD WAR II	THE WAR ON TERROR
1. U.S. involvement began with a surprise attack on American soil and the loss of 2,400 lives.	1. U.S. involvement began with a surprise attack on American soil and the loss of 2,752 lives.
2. The reason for the war could be identified and stated clearly.	2. The reason for the war is stated differently by different parties.
3. The enemy was clearly defined.	3. The enemy is nebulous.
4. The borders of conflict were clearly identified as physical locations within countries.	4. The borders of conflict are nebulous and not limited to countries.
5. The engagement of force was generally between military powers trained and prepared for battle.	5. The engagement of force is viewed by one side as a military conflict that accepts civilian casualties as part of the cost of war; the other treats military and civilian targets equally and makes little or no distinction between the two.
6. The war ended in four years with agreements on the terms.	6. The War on Terror is now completing its first decade of fighting, with no end in sight.

Figure 6.1. Comparison between the last global war, World War II, and the present global War on Terror.

Did the deaths of 2,400 people at Pearl Harbor justify the 405,000 American soldiers who lost their lives over the course of four years of the ensuing war? I don't know the answer to this question. Does the loss of 2,752 lives in the World Trade Center attacks justify the deaths of many more thousands of American and British troops and those of 139 other countries now engaged in the ten-year-long War on Terror? Is warfare really as inevitable as Barack Obama stated in his prize-acceptance speech? I don't know the answer to these questions either, but my sense is that it's less about an answer and more about a feeling.

Depending upon whom you ask, it seems that the feelings are mixed and divided, to say the least. But these are precisely the kinds of questions that need to be posed as we move forward in a time in history with the form of war that defines our world today. And it all comes down to the way we think and what we believe about war itself.

As mentioned previously in this chapter, there is a common belief that war, and its precursors of violence and hate in our societies, is a natural part of being human. If our point of reference is only the snapshot of human history that begins with the last 5,000 years, it's easy to see why.

The World's First Wars

During my book tour in France in the late 1990s, I had the opportunity to fulfill a lifelong dream in a single afternoon. There was only one day noted as a "day off" in the hectic schedule for the week to come. I took a taxi with several other authors and friends to make a visit I'd waited most of my adult life to experience. On that day I found myself in the Louvre Museum in Paris.

Throughout the pilgrimages and tours to Egypt I had led over the last decade or so, time and again I would find that the artifacts I'd traveled halfway around the world to see were no longer in Egypt. Some, such as select pieces of the King Tut exhibit, were on tour to cities like London, San Francisco, and Chicago. Others were stored in one of two places: the British Museum in London or the Louvre in Paris.

On this day, I would see in person the actual zodiac calendar from the Temple of Dendera, the massive obelisks that were no longer in Karnak. As much as I had looked forward to seeing *these* artifacts, however, there was another that had drawn me to the museum as well . . . and it wasn't from Egypt: it was the oldest documentation of large-scale war in the history of the world.

After working in the defense industry during the Cold War years of the 1980s, and having witnessed firsthand how close the world came to entering World War III, I wanted to see for myself how long we humans have been waging wars on such an epic scale. I thought that somehow, the ancient records would answer some of our most ancient questions. For example: Are we really "wired" for war? Is it natural to us, as Lawrence Keeley suggests, or is it a deeply ingrained habit that could be *un*learned just as it was learned?

My hope was that by understanding the origins of war, I would open a window of insight into the conflicts threatening our world today. What better place to begin than with the oldest records of the world's first known wars?

The fragments of the stone slab in the case in front of me at the museum were clues to the answer. They depicted a war between two armies about 4,700 years ago in ancient Sumer.

These portions of a limestone stele, discovered in 1881, record the specifics of the war between Lagash and Umma, two countries that no longer exist. This ancient record, named the "Stele of the Vultures," was only inches from where I stood in Room 1A of the Louvre's Department of Mesopotamian Antiquities (see Figure 6.2). Although only fragments of the stele remain, what they show is clear: images of the warriors themselves, in full regalia of armor and helmets, holding spears and marching in formation to war. There are also images of war's grisly aftermath: vultures eating corpses that lay exposed on the battlefield.

The Stele of the Vultures is a rare artifact showing that the Sumerians were organized and well versed in the techniques of large-scale warfare as long ago as the last world-age transition, during the biblical era.

Figure 6.2. Fragments of the "Stele of the Vultures" from the Louvre Museum in Paris. This stele is the most complete record of the world's earliest large-scale war and commemorates the victory of Lagash over Umma. *Top:* This fragment shows the earliest known images of troops marching in formation. (Credit: Eric Gaba/GNU Free Documentation License.) *Bottom:* This portion of the same stele depicts the artifact's namesake: vultures devouring the corpses left on the battlefield after the carnage of the war. (Credit: Eric Gaba/GNU Free Documentation License.)

While the Stele of the Vultures is the most complete record, it is not alone in recording the use of ancient warfare in Sumer. It was during this time as well that King Mebaragesi, the first name inscribed on the historic Sumerian "king list," declared war against his neighbors, the Elamites. When he did, he began what may be thought of as the very first Iran-Iraq conflict, fought in the area that is now Basra, Iraq—a stronghold that has played a key role in the Iraq War of the 21st century.

It may be no coincidence that such early records of the first wars date to the same time in our past when traditional historians tell us that civilization, and writing, began. The implication is that the evolution of communities and societies was actually a double-edged sword. Alongside the benefits of having security and a reliable supply of food and domestic resources were the inevitable disagreements that eventually led to wars.

While this may well be true for the examples of civilization that we see for the last 5,000 years, what about the older ones? From Göbekli Tepe and Çatalhöyük (a Neolithic settlement in Turkey) to whoever built the Great Sphinx and Caral, was war a part of the pre-5,000-year-old civilizations as well? It's impossible to answer this question without taking into consideration other factors that provide the historical context. Climate change and the competition for disappearing land and resources seem to be part of that context.

A desert burial near the Nile River in Sudan is an example of the behavior that dramatic changes in the environment can trigger. The find, known simply as "Site 117," was first excavated in the 1960s by Southern Methodist University archaeologist Fred Wendorf. Modern dating techniques have now placed it into the late ice age, at between 12,000 and 14,000 years old. We can't say for certain what happened at Site 117, except that there was definitely a war of some kind, although of nowhere near the magnitude of those fought in Sumer. While there are no documents that recorded the conflict, the discovery of this ancient site may well be evidence of the *first* war in human history.

Fifty-nine human skeletons were discovered in the desert graves, and 24 of them appear to have died in ways associated with war; many of the bodies had warlike projectiles found with them. R. Brian Ferguson, the Rutgers professor of anthropology mentioned earlier, makes an important link between the evidence at Site 117 and the abrupt climate change known to have occurred in the area at that time. "Notably, the people of Site 117," he says, "were living in a time of ecological crisis. Due to increased rainfall and the deep gorge that the Nile River had carved into the area, the adjacent floodplain was left high and dry, depriving the inhabitants of the catfish and other marshland staples of their diet."[10]

Of all human skeletons known to date to 10,000 years or older, only a handful show clear signs of personal violence, he notes.[11] This is important, because it suggests that the conflict seen at Site 117 was not necessarily a way of life, but a response to a specific condition that pitted people against one another for survival—perhaps, in this case, climate change.

The antiquity of the bodies at Site 117 may be a key in understanding the roots of war in civilization. In the earlier discussion of the dating for the Sphinx, I noted that the end of the last ice age brought a big change in climate throughout the Northern Hemisphere. This was then, as it is today, where the bulk of Earth's exposed lands existed and the greatest number of people lived. It was about the same time, 10,000 years ago, that evidence of the earliest wars is seen in the area that is now northern Iraq. The remains of what appear to be three farms include defensive walls and weapons, such as maces and arrowheads, along with human skeletons. It may be no coincidence that once learned, the habit of war has continued in this site until modern times—an irony that Ferguson notes as the "true 'mother of all battles.'"

Before the traditional "beginning" of history, now accepted to be about 5,000 years ago, the evidence clearly suggests that war was not the norm. It appears to have been rare, and when it did break out, the evidence of battles seems to coincide with changes in the climate. It's only during the time of Sumer at the beginning of the current world-age cycle that war appears to have become commonplace.

Humans have been engaged in one kind of warfare or another almost continuously since that time. So the question now appears to be: *Do the reasons for war still apply, or have we reached a time in our cycle of history when the cost outweighs the benefits?*

In other words, has war become obsolete?

The World's First Unwinnable War

After World War II, Russia and the United States had two very different ways of thinking about the world. The differences in their worldviews and political perspectives emerged from two distinct philosophies, one based in Communism and one based in capitalism. And although they had fought together as allies against a common enemy during the war, after the treaties were signed and the borders were drawn between nations throughout Europe and Asia, it was clear that two very separate spheres of influence were competing on the world stage.

It was upon this stage that the two superpowers began the 44-year-long "Cold War," as it became known. And while it's true that when it began in 1947, the Cold War was at the end of a long list of wars that the world had experienced, it was also obvious that this was no ordinary one. The technology that produced the first atomic bombs at the end of World War II assured that it could not be.

This was the first war in recorded history where the effects of one country's weapons against another had the power to devastate the entire world. The atomic by-products of radiation and nuclear fallout, and the ability of each detonation on the ground to toss tons of debris into the atmosphere, had never been a factor in any war of the past. For the first time, the fate of every life on Earth was in the hands of a few people running the war machine between two superpowers.

At the height of the conflict during the mid-1980s, the number of weapons—and countries that had them—had grown to proportions that seem unthinkable to any rationally minded person.

Declassified documents show that in 1985 the stockpiles of nuclear missiles, built and ready for use, between America and the Soviet Union alone was in the neighborhood of 65,000.

Today, after 20 years of negotiations and arms reductions, at least 22,000 of those weapons remain, 8,000 of which are considered "active." It was the threat of what using such an immense stockpile of weapons would mean for the world that led to the strategy believed to have prevented their deployment during the Cold War.

The strategy was called *mutually assured destruction* (MAD), an apt description of the probable outcome of the weapons' use by the superpowers of the time. The term, which was originated by members of the Kennedy Administration, acknowledges that in the event of an all-out war, both the attacker and the attacked will be destroyed; there will be no treaty, no armistice, few survivors, and no spoils to the victor . . . in short, only total destruction.

Any doubts as to the effects of such a war were put to rest during an unprecedented conference that took place in Washington, D.C., on Halloween in 1983. The Conference on the Long-Term Worldwide Biological Consequences of Nuclear War was led by three personalities, each highly respected in his field. Together, Paul Ehrlich, biologist and author of *The Population Bomb* (Sierra Club/Ballantine Books, 1968); Carl Sagan, cosmologist and author of *Cosmos* (Ballantine Books, 1980); and Donald Kennedy, former president of Stanford University, presented a powerful argument for the unwinnable nature of nuclear war.[12]

Articulated for the first time in such a public way, the consequence of the nuclear exchange that the Cold War implied was presented to the world in clear and graphic terms. The probable result, a phenomenon called *nuclear winter,* was described by a group of researchers known as TTAPS (the acronym of their last names: Truco, Toon, Ackerman, Pollack, and Sagan). Based on computer models that combined weather patterns with the smoke, soot, and fallout from the burning of major cities after an atomic war, the simulations predicted that tremendously less sunlight would reach Earth. Among the effects the models showed was a large drop in global temperatures from the lack of sunlight—a *nuclear winter*—that would last for anywhere from a few months to a few years, depending upon the duration of the attack. The scientists based their models on actual data documenting similar kinds of effects from ancient asteroid impacts and massive volcanoes erupting in modern times.

The conference highlighted various scenarios that took into account weather patterns, who attacked whom first, what cities were involved, and how many weapons were used by each side. None of the outcomes looked good. Not only was this the first highly publicized conference on nuclear winter, the environmental implications of the choices of war made it the first political debate over climate.

One thing became very obvious very quickly from the simulations: The world was dealing with a new kind of war, one whose purpose no longer made sense because the simulated result indicated that no one would win. The Cold War was a "lose/lose" proposition. For the first time, the idea of attacks carried out through the most advanced weapons of the time had made the prospect of war incompatible with its goal.

Shortly after the TTAPS reports of the Cold War years, and just before his death in 1983, futurist Buckminster Fuller made a prophetic observation regarding the role of war in the modern world. "Either war is obsolete," he said, "or men are."[13] Einstein had a similar theme in mind when he responded to a question about how he thought the next world war would be fought. "I know not with what weapons World War Three will be fought," he said, "but World War Four will be fought with sticks and stones."[14]

Both Einstein and Fuller were on the same track and alluding to the fact that, seemingly overnight, nuclear weapons had nullified the usefulness of war. Before 1945 the thinking that had justified wars in the past was generally based upon the following two ideas:

1. The war being fought is winnable.

2. That which remains after the war is usable.

The oversized nuclear arsenals amassed during the Cold War made it obvious that the wars of the past had become meaningless—they were no longer winnable in the traditional sense of the word. Between the sheer magnitude of the initial destruction and the aftermath of radioactive contamination, which would make any remaining land barren for a very long time, the usefulness of war for the reasons cited in the past was invalidated forever. Almost overnight, our thinking about war as it had been known for the previous 5,000 years became obsolete.

Where Did We Learn War?

The best science of our time suggests that the first large-scale wars were fought during the transition from the last world age into the climate that we see in modern times. Although the last world age certainly sounds like a long time ago, in the overall scheme of our history on this planet, it isn't—5,000 years out of our 200,000-year existence leaves 195,000 years (or 97.5 percent of our time on Earth) where we have no evidence of large-scale war among humankind.

This fact seems to suggest that war is a phenomenon that is relatively recent in our experience. There are two possible perspectives on the role of war in our past: (1) there actually were large-scale wars in ancient times, and we simply haven't found evidence of them yet; or (2) we *have* found the earliest evidence of wars, and it tells us that they are an anomaly.

As I began to understand these possibilities, I had to ask an even deeper question: *Regardless of <u>when</u> the great wars happened, <u>where</u> did we learn war in the first place?* With no violent movies to mimic, no previous experience to draw from, and no weapons or defenses to model ourselves after, who would have even thought of making the weapons of our past? Who would have thought, for example, to use a sharpened steel blade or a heavy ball with spikes coming out of it to take the life of another human?

While we may never know the full answer to this question, we can gain clues in the oldest accounts of our early experiences here on Earth. And one of those accounts has recently been reintroduced after having been banned by the early Christian church in the 2nd century C.E. It is the biblical Book of Enoch, the prophet.

It's clear that early church historians held the Book of Enoch in high regard. It's referenced in Christian commentaries by respected scholars such as Irenaeus of Lyons and Clement of Alexandria. Tertullian, the 2nd-century Carthaginian historian, for example, describes the Book of Enoch as sacred literature, acknowledging that this man's words were divinely inspired and should be given the same credibility as other scriptural documents such as the books of Isaiah and Psalms.[15] Specifically, Tertullian states, "As Enoch has spoken in the same scripture as the Lord, and 'every scripture suitable for edification is divinely inspired,' let us reject nothing which belongs to us."[16]

The biblical Book of Enoch was lost for nearly 1,500 years until a single copy was presented to the Bodleian Library at Oxford, where it was rediscovered and subsequently translated by Richard Lawrence in 1821.

The Book of Enoch begins with an account of the prophet dictating the hidden history of the human race to his son, Methuselah. Methuselah records that his father's words were spoken as the older man saw a "vision in the heavens . . . with his eyes wide open."[17] While in his awakened yet altered state, Enoch describes the reasons for humanity's decline and the source of suffering, *including warfare,* which they witnessed in their time. And this is where we find some of the earliest written clues to the origin of war. Going beyond the vague and general references that often seem to accompany the revelations of ancient prophets, Enoch shares his visions with precision.

He describes how certain "angels of the heavens" divulged the secrets of creation to humankind long ago, before the earliest members of our species had lived here long enough to gain the wisdom to use such power responsibly. He details how the secrets of plants and herbs, language, writing, and alchemy were revealed to the people of the earth. But without the maturity to apply what they learned wisely, the knowledge was misused. In his desperate quest to understand the nature of our world, Enoch asks to be shown "all that was concealed." And in response, he tells his son that he is given the actual names of the "angels who have descended from heaven to earth, and have revealed secrets to the sons of men, and have seduced the sons of men to the commission of sin."[18]

Singling out specific angels and the secrets that each one reveals, Enoch describes in the text how the angel Azazyel, for example, has "taught every species of iniquity upon the earth, and has disclosed to the world all the secret things which are done in the heavens."[19] The portion of Enoch's experience that applies to the origin of war is his description of what the angel Gadrel introduced to the people of Earth. It's this angel that *discovered to the children of men the instruments of death, the coat of mail, the shield and the sword for slaughter.*[20] (My italics.)

Making a distinction between knowledge and the wisdom that comes from applying it in our lives, Enoch describes how the secrets of heaven were eventually lost in the realm of man: "Wisdom went forth to dwell among the sons of men, but she obtained not habitation."[21] He concludes this portion of his vision: "Wisdom found not a place on earth where she could inhabit; her dwelling therefore is in heaven."[22]

✹ ✹ ✹

While Enoch's story of the tools of war being introduced from another realm was shared in the early Christian traditions, it's not the only story of otherworldly beings bringing the idea of wars, and the instruments to fight them, to Earth.

In the literature there are no fewer than 36 different traditions—spanning Sumer and ancient Egypt, all the way to modern times—that describe more than 80 "gods" of war and their relationship to humans. In addition to the familiar Christian theology of angels described by Enoch, examples include gods from the Tibetan *(Begtse),* Hindu *(Karttikeya),* Japanese *(Bishamon),* Celtic *(Teutates),* Greek

(Ares), Persian *(Dev)*, Mayan *(Buluc Chabtan)*, Aztec *(Mixcoatl)*, Poly-nesian/Maori *(Maru)*, Babylonian *(Ninurta)*, Germanic *(Tyr)*, Hittite *(Wurukatte)*, Akkadian *(Zababa)*, Finnish *(Turris)*, and Native Ameri-can *(Ictinike)* traditions as well.

When so many diverse traditions share a story with such a simi-lar theme, it's not uncommon to find that each one is a unique take on a factual event that occurred in times past. An example of this is the nearly universal account of a great flood that inundated the earth long ago (now believed to be the result of melting ice and changes in sea level at the end of the last ice age) and how each respective group telling the story played a role in repopulating the new world. I have personally heard these accounts from indigenous peoples that include the Quechua of the Andes and the Uros, na-tives of the Lake Titicaca region, in Peru; the Bedouin of Egypt's Sinai Desert; as well as the Hopi, Navajo, and Pueblo throughout America's Desert Southwest.

Just as the flood story appears to be nearly universal, the fact that so many traditions attribute the origin and techniques of war to something happening in higher realms of existence sheds new light on an ancient and seemingly senseless source of human suf-fering. While we fight our wars skillfully, believe in what we fight for passionately, and have justified our beliefs for the last 5,000 years or so, is it possible that what we fight about is not really *our* war at all? In other words, could it be that a long time ago we be-came naïve followers of an ancient belief (warfare) that originated in another realm of existence, and we began to think that the belief and subsequent wars were ours?

While this may sound like a remote possibility to some people at first, when we combine the scientific evidence of the lack of war-fare in ancient civilizations with the almost-universal theme for the origin of war from so many diverse traditions, we gain a powerful insight to help make sense of the senselessness of war. With such insight comes a new perspective allowing us to find our way out of the habit of killing one another to resolve our differences.

If we, in fact, learned from a greater intelligence "every spe-cies of iniquity upon the Earth," as Enoch suggests, and this intelligence "discovered to the children of men the instruments of death, the coat of mail, the shield and the sword for slaughter," then what would it mean to realize that the wars we fight are over someone else's ideas? Is it possible that we could wake up one day, look one another in the eyes after 5,000 years of violence, and say to ourselves, "What were we thinking?"

I'm offering this perspective because it's real. It is the secret that's shared around the campfires under the stars in the Sinai Desert of Egypt. It's the key to finding compassion, as described in the depths of conversation in the Buddhist monasteries of the Himalayas. It's the Andean perspective for a peaceful transition from the suffering that exists today to the new world being birthed as we end our most recent world-age cycle. If we need reasons to believe that we're more than the worst acts of hatred that punctuate our past, we need look no further than the countless acts of kindness and benevolence that occur around the world every day, and to the entertainment we embrace that reminds us of our truest nature.

We're Good to the Core!

My sense is that there's a desire linking most humans in the world: our deepest aspiration of kindness. We want to believe that we're good people living in a good world. Yet we're strangely drawn to books and movie plots where human goodness is pitted against the darkest aspects of our nature, and we cheer when goodness triumphs. We love it when the innocence of someone like Forrest Gump (played by Tom Hanks in the 1994 movie of the same name) reminds us of something innocent inside of ourselves.

The sense of our innate benevolence was expressed clearly and simply by the 13th-century scholar Saint Thomas Aquinas. Sounding like a wise guru we'd expect to hear on a mountaintop in a faraway place, he stated, "The goodness of the species transcends the goodness of the individual, as form transcends matter."[23] Nearly four hundred years later, scientist and philosopher Sir Francis

Bacon echoed this sentiment when he wrote: "The inclination to goodness is imprinted deeply in the nature of man . . ."[24] *It is our uniqueness as a species, coupled with our fundamental character of goodness, that opens the door for lasting change in our lives.*

In my experience of traveling to every continent of the world (with the exception of Antarctica), I've found a common theme among the people with whom I've had the privilege of sharing meals, nature, and daily life. From the villagers and monks in the remote mountains of Tibet, Bolivia, and Peru . . . to the street vendors in the bazaars of Egypt, India, Nepal, and Thailand, as well as throughout Europe, and in the rural towns and cafés of Australia and North America, people appear to be basically "good" by nature.

If I'm lost, they're willing to help. If I'm hungry, they're glad to share what little food they have. If I'm hurt, they have taken me in as a total stranger. And these are not isolated incidents from my life only. Ask anyone who has traveled across the United States or left the familiar borders of his or her home country; for each person you ask, you'll have another story of our global family and our deep sense of goodness. And it is our goodness that shows us beyond any reasonable doubt that we're "wired" for peace, not conflict.

If we look closely at the issues and hot spots of unrest in the world today, we see that the conflict is generally not with the people of the farms and villages themselves. Rather, it's the organizations attempting to change the lives of people—the governments, corporations, and political movements—which trigger the hurt and strife. As individuals and families, we seem to find ways to be happy in whatever circumstances we find ourselves.

From homeless beggars and salt-of-the-earth people who work the land, to brilliant minds in positions of technical and political power, in general, all appear to be searching for the same things in their lives: peace, food, shelter, health, the opportunity to make a good life for their families, and a better understanding of their place in creation.

Abraham Maslow, one of the great psychologists of the 20th century, first distinguished himself through his work on the social behavior of primates. In his later years, however, he dedicated himself exclusively to the study of human nature, noting the "wonderful possibilities and inscrutable depths" of our existence. Even in the presence of colleagues such as Sigmund Freud, who proposed lust, selfishness, and aggression as our basic nature, Maslow's studies led him to believe that "people are all decent underneath."[25] His unwavering faith in our goodness remained through the last days of his life, when he wrote that humankind "has a higher nature" as part of our essence, and our species can be "wonderful out of their own human and biological nature."[26]

Beyond wishful thinking, our fundamental "goodness" is borne out by innumerable examples that demonstrate the power of this quality in our lives. More than simply a modern phenomenon, from battlefield heroics to recent tragedies of floods, hurricanes, and terrorism, it's not uncommon to see one human lay down his or her life for the benefit of another.

In the face of circumstances that threaten one of our kind, more often than not a basic instinct to preserve life proves stronger than the fears and concerns we have for ourselves—and we act. This instinct appears to be so deeply ingrained into the fabric of our nature that we even extend it beyond our species to the animal kingdom as well.

Proof of Our Goodness

On a dusty road halfway around the world, the clearest possible expression of human compassion and our essential goodness was demonstrated when the lives of four American servicemen were saved in 2008.

On that day, Private First Class Ross McGinnis was manning a machine gun over the hatch covering the inside of the armored personnel carrier where he and four other soldiers were on duty. Suddenly an Iraqi fighter tossed a live hand grenade into the opening. It landed inside of the vehicle where McGinnis's fellow soldiers and friends were trapped.

McGinnis was trained to survive. He could have applied his training and taken the opportunity to jump to the ground from the turret opening to save his own life, and it would have made perfect sense for him to do so. But he didn't. And that is why this account is so powerful.

Instead, he dropped down the opening to the inside of the vehicle and offered himself as a human shield against the blast that was only seconds away. Ross McGinnis died instantly, as his body absorbed the impact and the shrapnel to save his comrades. "If [McGinnis] wouldn't have blocked it with his body, there's no doubt that nobody would have escaped it," said the driver of the vehicle, who was injured by fragments of the blast.[27]

At a White House ceremony, Ross McGinnis became the fourth soldier of the Iraq War to receive the U.S. Medal of Honor, which was presented to his parents by President George W. Bush.

"America will always honor the name of this brave soldier who gave all for his country and was taken to rest at age 19," Bush said. What Ross McGinnis gave for his country reminds us all of the fullest expression of our truest nature—we care about one another in extraordinary ways, and our care shows itself as a reflex when life is at stake. And it's not only human life that triggers our response of goodness.

✳ ✳ ✳

On November 8, 2007, the unthinkable happened to Vern Newell. But it wasn't the fact that his home was on fire that made him risk his life not once, but two times. It was what was still in the house: Newell's ten dogs. After successfully making it into the house the first time to bring some of his animals to safety, he knew that the others would die without his help. The firefighters at the scene knew it as well, but they still tried to keep him from going in again. "He [the fireman] tried to hold me back," Newell said. "He had his hands full. I kicked him in the chin, almost."[28]

Newell saved all ten of his dogs, and together, they watched as their uninsured house became engulfed in flames and burned to the ground. When he was asked why he risked his life for the animals, the answer was simple enough. "They're my family," he said.

People recognize goodness in others, and they want to be a part of it. The small town where Newell and his dogs live is no exception. Immediately the townspeople began drawing up the blueprints and making the plans to build Newell and his dogs a new home.

We've all heard stories like these before of people risking their lives to save other people, and people risking their lives to save animals. Vern Newell was lucky. He survived his risky rescue, and his story had a happy ending. But not all of them do.

On Christmas Day 2010, a 62-year-old Texas man lost his life while trying to save his family, including the family's Labrador retriever, from their burning home. In the early-morning hours, Frank Kruse pulled his wife and niece from the smoke and flames. While the family was safe, their 13-year-old Lab, named Sugar, could not be found. Frank ran back into the burning house to find the dog, and neither he nor Sugar was ever seen again. That Christmas Day, the fire from which he saved his family claimed his life and Sugar's, too.[29]

It's in moments like the ones described in these accounts that something inside of us "kicks in" and our truest nature beams through with an awesome brilliance. And it's in precisely such moments that we see just what it is that sets us apart from many other forms of life. It would have been much easier—and certainly acceptable, in light of the life-threatening situations—for the men in the previous accounts to think about saving their own lives. Faced with the choice, however, something within them transcended the logic of their minds, and they acted on behalf of another living being.

And even when we fail, as in the case of Frank and Sugar, the key is that we try—something inside of us chooses to risk our lives and even die, if necessary, to save another being. In recent years, similar stories have aired across the news networks—stories involving horses in flooded canyons of the American West, as well as dogs, cats, and even hamsters being saved from burning homes, all at the risk of their rescuers' lives.

After September 11, a little-publicized project focused on going door-to-door in Lower Manhattan's crumbling apartment buildings, collapsed hotels, and burned-out homes in search of people's pets that had been abandoned in the chaos. The reward of those who risked their lives in unstable buildings and toxic smoke brought tears to the eyes of the reporters covering the story.

One by one, family pets were retrieved—hungry, dehydrated, and *alive*—wagging their tails or softly whimpering in response to human touch. Once again, in the hours and days following September 11, to concede the loss of animal life as an unavoidable consequence of such catastrophe would have certainly been justified by the magnitude of the tragedy. The point is that we did not.

In these moments, we glimpse an example of what I believe is the truest essence of human nature. In our most basic state—free from the encumbrances and false assumptions that lead us to believe that we are needy, greedy, taken advantage of, or engaged in competition for survival—we are fundamentally a kind, compassionate, and giving species: *a species of goodness*. At the most basic level of our existence, in moments of crisis we prove to ourselves again and again the truth of our nature. The stories I've shared in this section, and thousands more, tell us so beyond any reasonable doubt.

At the same time, however, we're also a species of survivors. When we're driven to extremes, the necessity of the moment can trigger within us the power and the capacity to override our basic nature and become warriors. We *can* become violent when we need to. We *can* lash out and take the life of another to protect ourselves and our families. We *can* betray our truest instincts of goodness in order to survive. And it's the conditions we find ourselves in that can become the catalyst.

Our violence can be triggered by circumstances that we believe threaten us as individuals, families, communities, or nations. These circumstances can be either real or perceived. The point is that we sense they're present and feel threatened by them. Alone, or in any combination, we will betray our peaceful nature when:

- We feel personally threatened.
- We feel that our families are threatened.
- We feel that our way of life is threatened.

When we do betray what has been called our fundamental "goodness," it's in such moments that we witness the very worst and most frightening aspects of ourselves. It may be precisely because of these conditions that our earliest ancestors chose war 10,000 years ago. In the face of a changing climate and a limited supply of the things necessary for life—food, water, resources, mates to perpetuate their families—the perceived need for competition outweighed the benefit of cooperation. Either those fighting felt threatened personally, or felt a threat toward their families or the way of life to which they had grown accustomed. In the presence of the perceived threat, they betrayed their truest nature.

As with any sweeping generalizations concerning people, there are always exceptions. In every society, there are statistics that seem to refute our goodness, as individuals gravitate toward the darkest traits that most of us shun and abhor. Living the worst nightmares as the reality of their lives, nearly every generation has experienced the terror that may be best described as "evil incarnate," such as serial killers Jack the Ripper or Ted Bundy, wreaking havoc within otherwise-life-honoring communities and neighborhoods.

On rare occasions, such individuals have risen to places of tremendous power. Using charisma to seduce entire armies into carrying out their schemes, they commit atrocities against other races, other nations, and even their own people—acts that are unthinkable to healthy, rational people. Such moments of darkness for our species, however, may illustrate more of what we *do* under extreme circumstances, rather than what we *are* by nature. Fortunately, the Pol Pots (whose real name was Saloth Sar), Adolf Hitlers, Saddam Husseins, and organizations of terror are the exception rather than the rule; and they are few and far between.

Cooperation Is the Key

Historians describe the 20th century as the single bloodiest century in all of recorded history.[30] When I first heard this assertion, I thought it must be a mistake. Surely the Christian Crusades, for example, or the ancient Roman conquests of Europe and the Middle East would have claimed more lives in their times than the First and Second World Wars claimed in ours. But when we work out the math, the historians are right. And the numbers are truly mind-boggling.

In World War II alone, for instance, approximately *50 million* people died in combat and from war-related atrocities.[31] And the number of deaths due to human atrocities continued even after the war was over, through the end of the century. By 1999, *80 million* men, women, and children of all ages were lost to violence based in ethnic, religious, and philosophical conflicts—five times as many as were lost due to all of the natural disasters and the AIDS epidemic *combined* during the same period. It's for this reason that the last century has earned the title of the "century that murdered peace."[32]

In addition to the wars over disputed borders and disappearing resources, a new kind of atrocity saw a sharp rise in the last century: the effort to "cleanse" societies based upon ideas beyond those of traditional war. In 1948, the United Nations adopted the term *genocide* to describe this kind of killing, as well as make it possible to clearly define and outlaw it in terms of global policies. The reason why I share these frightening statistics here is because the thinking that made them possible is a poignant example of where perpetuating false scientific assumptions and carrying them to extremes can lead.

The thinking underlying all forms of genocide, and directly spelled out in some, is linked to Darwin's observations of nature, the way he portrayed them in his writings, and how they were interpreted by others. This thinking is mirrored in the ideas of philosophical works such as the infamous "Little Red Book," officially titled *Quotations from Chairman Mao Tse-Tung;* and *Mein Kampf,* the book that detailed Adolf Hitler's worldview. Both were used as justification for the brutal killings that took the combined toll of at least 40 million people: 30 million in China, and 10.8 million in the Polish and Jewish genocides of World War II.

In *On the Origin of Species,* Darwin stated clearly his belief that the "weeding out" of the weakest members of the species he observed in nature applies to us humans as well:

> It may not be a logical deduction but to my imagination it is far more satisfactory to look at such instincts as the young cuckoo ejecting his foster brothers, ants making slaves . . . as small consequences of one general law leading to the advancement of all organic beings—namely multiply, vary, let the strongest live and the weakest die.[33]

In *Mein Kampf,* Hitler clearly paraphrased this idea:

> In the struggle for daily bread all those who are weak and sickly or less determined succumb, while the struggle of the males for the female grants the right of opportunity to propagate only to the healthiest. And struggle is always a means for improving a species' health and power of resistance and, therefore, a cause of higher development.[34]

While Hitler's work seemed to echo Darwin's, Chairman Mao's own words leave no doubt as to how much his thinking was inspired by *On the Origin of Species.* He thought of his enemies as "nonpeople" who did not deserve to be treated as human. One of the slogans used during his time was: "The foundation of Chinese socialism rests upon Darwin and the theory of evolution."[35]

Later in life, Darwin seemed to backpedal with respect to some of the harsh statements in *On the Origin of Species*. Contrary to his early conclusions regarding superior strength of individuals, his later works described survival strategies in nature based on unity and cooperation, rather than "survival of the fittest." In his next book, *The Descent of Man*, he summarized his observations: "Those communities which included the greatest number of the most sympathetic members would flourish best and rear the greatest number of offspring."[36]

Although Darwin may have seen the light of his false assumptions, it might have been too late. *On the Origin of Species* was a classic text, and continues today as the foundation of a way of thinking that clearly steers us away from our natural instincts of cooperation and goodness.

Early in the 20th century, Russian naturalist Peter Kropotkin reinforced Darwin's later work with his own observations. Just as Darwin had observed the effects of evolution firsthand among species of birds during his voyage of discovery in the 1830s, Kropotkin published his own observations based on scientific expeditions to one of the harshest environments in the world: northern Siberia. He described how he'd found that cooperation and unity, rather than survival of the fittest, are the keys to the success of a species.

In his classic book *Mutual Aid: A Factor of Evolution* (1902), Kropotkin illustrated the benefits experienced in the insect kingdom through the instinctual ability of ants to live as cooperative, rather than competitive, societies:

> Their wonderful nests, their buildings, superior in relative size to those of man; their paved roads and over-ground vaulted galleries; their spacious halls and granaries; their cornfields; harvesting and 'malting' of grain; their rational methods of nursing their eggs and larvae and of building special nests for rearing the aphids—the cows of the ant—and, finally, their courage, pluck, and superior intelligence—all of these are the natural outcome of the mutual aid which they practice at every stage of their busy and laborious lives.[37]

John Swomley, a professor emeritus of social ethics at the St. Paul School of Theology in Kansas City, Missouri, leaves little doubt that it is to our advantage to find peaceful and cooperative ways to build the global societies of our future. Citing the evidence presented by Kropotkin and others, Swomley states that the case for cooperation rather than competition rests on more than just its benefit to a successful society. In a simple and straightforward fashion, he explains that cooperation is the "key factor in evolution and survival."[38] In a paper published in February 2000, Swomley quotes Kropotkin, stating that competition within or between species "is always injurious to the species. Better conditions are created by the elimination of competition by means of mutual aid and mutual support."[39]

In the opening address at the 1993 Symposium on the Humanistic Aspects of Regional Development, held in Birobidzhan, Russia, co-chair Ronald Logan offered a context for the participants to view nature as a model for successful societies. In a direct reference to Kropotkin, he stated:

> If we ask Nature: "who are the fittest: those who are continually at war with each other, or those who support one another?" we at once see that those animals which acquire habits of mutual aid are undoubtedly the fittest. They have more chances to survive, and they attain, in their respective classes, the highest development of intelligence and bodily organization.[40]

At a later point in the same address, Logan cited the work of Alfie Kohn, author of *No Contest: The Case Against Competition* (Houghton Mifflin, 1992), describing in no uncertain terms what his research had revealed regarding a beneficial amount of competition in groups. After reviewing more than 400 studies documenting cooperation and competition, Kohn concluded: "The ideal amount of competition . . . in any environment, the classroom, the workplace, the family, the playing field, is none. . . . [Competition] is always destructive."[41]

The natural world is widely recognized as a proving ground for experiments in unity, cooperation, and survival among insects and animals. From nature's lessons we are shown, without question, that unity and cooperation are advantageous to living beings. Such time-tested strategies from the world around us may ultimately lead to a blueprint for our own survival. To apply such a strategy, however, an additional factor must be accounted for in our world that does not appear in the animal kingdom. As individuals, and as a species, we generally must know "where we are going" and what we can expect when we get there, before we change the way we live. We need to know that the result is worthwhile and something to look forward to.

A growing body of ancient, scholarly, and scientific evidence suggests that in the absence of conditions that drive us to be animal-like in our actions, when given the opportunity, we prefer to live peaceful and compassionate lives that honor the benevolent aspects of our species. In other words, the conditions of life seem to bear out what the science has discovered. And when the three conditions we value in life are met—that is, we feel safe, we feel that our families are safe, and we feel that our way of life is safe—we allow our truest nature to shine through in everything we do. How can we know with certainty when these conditions are met? Pulitzer Prize–winning poet Carl Sandburg offered a brief answer to this question: "Sometime they'll give a war, and nobody will come."[42]

I believe Sandburg is right, because in our natural state, we are truly wired for peace.

> **Deep Truth 6:** A growing body of scientific evidence, gathered from more than 400 peer-reviewed studies, is leading to an undeniable truth: violent competition and war directly contradict our deepest instincts of cooperation and nurturing.

CHAPTER SEVEN

THE END GAME: REWRITING OUR HISTORY, DESTINY, AND FATE

"Destiny is not a matter of chance; it is a matter of choice."

— **WILLIAM JENNINGS BRYAN** (1860–1925),
AMERICAN LAWYER AND POLITICIAN

The 2007 release of the movie *The Bucket List* got a lot of people thinking about their lives and the things they'd like to accomplish while they're still healthy enough to do them. Without revealing the details to those who have not yet seen the movie, the general premise is that two men (played by Morgan Freeman and Jack Nicholson) find themselves facing their respective end-of-life issues knowing that there are things they always wanted to do, but for varying reasons never got around to doing. When one last chance to realize their dreams presents itself, they each create a list of lifelong ambitions: a "bucket list." The rest of the movie is about how their lives change and their emotional wounds are healed as they work together to realize their dreams.

During a conversation with my mom not long after *The Bucket List* was released, I asked her about her own bucket list: what places did she want to visit and what things did she want to do that she had simply not gotten around to in her lifetime?

She answered my question by explaining that she was the product of another time in history, another way of thinking; and she wasn't used to considering herself in that way. Born just after the Great Depression, she'd been raised to always take care of other people and tend to their needs first before she could even think about her dreams and what *she* wanted.

From the time she was a little girl, my mother had cared for those around her, which as an adult meant caring for those whose lives were crumbling through illness and divorce. She had cared for her parents until they died (her father at the age of 96); the people she worked with during more than a quarter century of service with the U.S. government; and my brother and me, her two sons she raised as a single parent in the 1960s following a painful divorce. Through all of these experiences of giving to others and putting other people's needs ahead of her own, Mom had placed her greatest dreams on the backburner of her life. It was with these things in mind that I asked Mom to prioritize her dreams.

I encouraged my mother to note her biggest ambitions first, and then continue down the list by dreaming with no limits. I reminded her that I would help her go *anywhere* on Earth she had ever wanted to go, see *anyone* (living) she wanted to see, and do absolutely *anything* that she had ever wanted to do. While I fully believed that my mom would be around for many years to come, I also wanted her to have the opportunity to leave this world without any regrets of, "If only I had done . . ."

Mom began to share her list out loud. I wasn't surprised by its contents because I know my mom well. It wasn't a collection of exotic journeys to faraway destinations, or a glamorous cruise on a luxurious ocean liner. Not even close. Her bucket list was modest and simple.

At the top was one last visit to see her oldest friends. They had remained in Missouri when she had moved to be closer to me in the Southwest. Next, she began to describe the things that she felt would benefit other people, like keeping her house in "tip-top" shape with a new paint job so its next owners wouldn't have to do this, landscaping the yard so that my brother and I wouldn't have to do so when she is gone at some point down the road, and putting a beautiful garden in the yard. That was it.

When I asked Mom if she'd like to begin doing the things on her list immediately—on that very day—she looked back across the table at me, shaking her head . . . a gesture that left no doubt as to what she meant. "No," she said, "not now. Things are just too hectic. Let's wait until the world settles down a little bit."

"When would that be?" I asked, thinking she was talking about the edgy feeling she'd expressed about the economy, banks closing their doors, and so much unrest in so much of the globe.

"Oh, I don't know," she said. "Let's just catch our breath. We can look at my list again when things get back to normal."

"'Normal'?" I asked. "What do you mean by 'normal'?"

Mom's answer to my question is the reason why I'm sharing her story here. It's a feeling shared by people of all ages throughout the nations of the world.

"You know," she replied, "when things get back to the way they used to be."

I looked across the table, into the eyes of my little 4'8" mother. I knew that the world she wanted to see before she allowed herself to explore her dreams no longer exists. In all probability the "normal" that she remembers, longs for, and awaits will never appear. The reason is simple: it's a world of the past.

Our world and the way we live our lives is definitely on its way out; and, if history is any indication, once our world begins to move in a new direction, as it is doing today, it's as if it were following some mystical "law" of the universe that keeps things moving forward. It can't return to where it's been. Just the way we rarely find ourselves moving backward in our lives to the relationships, marriages, jobs, and places of our past, it's unlikely that the world of 2008 or 2006 . . . or before . . . will ever be present again. And it's unlikely for one simple yet powerful reason: *that world is gone.*

What Worked Then Doesn't Work Now

My mom and I have always talked about the state of the world and where it's headed. In recent years, her optimism about people, governments, and our future has given way to a dismal picture of what looks to her like a broken planet of missed opportunities and unsolvable problems. After she listens to my optimism and patiently hears me out on my views of the beautiful world that awaits us on our very doorstep, and acknowledging the tough choices we must make to get to that world, she often ends the conversation by summing everything up in one statement.

In the direct, precise, and eloquent way that can only come from my mom, she simply says, "I give up—the world's a mess. It's all going to hell in a handbasket!" As she senses my disbelief each time she says the words, with a little twinkle in her eyes and a smile that tells me she loves me no matter what I think, she adds, "And you can quote me on that."

When we consider the systems of our way of life that seem to be stretched to the limits today, it's easy to see why many people share Mom's perspective of a broken world. So many of the things we've relied upon for generations (for example, the way money works, the way wars work, the way we used to get a job with a good company and could feel secure for the rest of our lives) don't seem to apply anymore. They just don't work. If we look honestly at what doesn't work, however, we begin to see a pattern: the only things that are "breaking" are the systems that are no longer sustainable under the stress of a changing world.

Things like the economy, decades-old dictatorships, the military force used to keep the peace in 15 war zones in the world, and abject poverty in countries that are wealthy with natural resources are all examples of unsustainable ways of life that have reached their breaking points. All are happening under the umbrella of civilization powered by the unsustainable resource of fossil fuels.

So while the world economy that has relied on markets that must get bigger and bigger, and a profit system where someone benefits at someone else's expense, may have worked for a century or so, it's not sustainable for another 100 years. And while creating electricity for a world power grid that burns through a finite source of oil, gas, and coal, destroying the very air we cherish, has worked for the last century or so, it can't go on for another 100 years either.

These are examples of our civilization's learning curve. If we can get beyond judging them as good, bad, right, or wrong, then they simply become a part of our past. They worked, and accomplished what they were designed to accomplish, at the time they were devised. They got us to where we find ourselves today and allowed us to build a global civilization that didn't exist before; provide heat, light, and a way to cook food in places that have never had such luxuries in the past; and travel from one side of the earth to the other in a day.

They also created a huge rift in the economies of the world and exploited the labor of indigenous peoples and much of the global resources to benefit relatively few people. Our choices have served us in some ways, and hurt us in others. Now the fact that so many of the systems we've chosen are collapsing all at the same time opens the door to a rare opportunity to choose again. We must *choose* where we go from here and how we shape the new world that's already emerging.

This is precisely why it's so important for us to know the truth of our origins, heritage, and existence. When we know who we are, how long we've been on this planet, and that we're no accident of nature and biology—when we have all of this information at our fingertips—we can make the informed choices that allow us to adapt to our changing world.

✳ ✳ ✳

Throughout this book you've had the opportunity to explore the way all of us have traditionally thought of ourselves through the eyes of science . . . and in light of new scientific discoveries. If you've felt torn about the huge questions of existence—such as when a human life begins, where our species comes from, how long we've been here, and whether or not we're doomed to a world of perpetual war and suffering—then you've seen new facts that may go a long way toward helping ease some of that conflict.

Although my corporate careers in the energy, defense, and communication industries were very different from one another in terms of goals and direction, a common theme wove its way through each and brought them all together. Just as so many of our experiences from one part of life apply to others, that theme spills over into my everyday life as well.

That theme is this: Each of my careers encompassed a job that I accepted during a time of crisis. From the energy crisis of the 1970s; to the nuclear crisis of the Cold War in the 1980s, and the military's information crisis involving incompatibility between different computer systems, which hampered their efforts at co-ordination during the Persian Gulf War in 1990 . . . each job was behind schedule and overbudget when I was brought on board. In a similar way, we all now find ourselves living in a world of crisis, and the solutions to our crises are behind schedule and overbudget. My sense is that the parallels I've seen in other areas of life apply here, too.

A single principle true in the corporations where I worked is also valid for us and our world: when we know the truth of the situation, the choices become clear and the decisions obvious. And while this was one of the great lessons that came to me through the corporate world, the same principle applies to what's happening on a global scale today.

A Global Community: There's No Turning Back

It's no secret that we've become a global society. Whether we give it an official name and report it on the evening news, or talk about it as a quiet conspiracy on late-night talk radio, the fact is that it has already happened. The stock markets driving the world economy are already global and trade continually 24/7. The food that keeps summertime produce in our supermarkets in the dead of winter is grown on farms half a world away and is flown, shipped, and trucked in on a daily basis. The voice that answers the number we dial at 3 A.M. for help with a travel reservation or technical assistance with our computer is very probably speaking to us from a call center located somewhere on the other side of the globe.

Clearly we live in a time when the line separating "them" from "us" in terms of trade, money, technology, and even government has become a fuzzy one. Because we're already a global society, the personal choices we make in our homes, families, and communities have worldwide implications. But globalization itself began long before any of these things were even possible. A National Bureau of Economic Research working paper entitled "When Did Globalization Begin?" was published in 2002 by the *European Review of Economic History*. This study shows that the ability to trade, and influence markets, demands for labor, and consumer prices has been going on for nearly 500 years. It describes three degrees of globalization and the impact they've had, or are having, on modern civilization.[1]

— The **first** era of globalization was defined by the trade that was happening over long distances before the 18th century. During that time, the items imported into Europe from other parts of the world included spices, sugar, silk, and other things not found in local markets. Because these items didn't compete with existing markets, they didn't create any economic ripples. Thus, early globalization essentially resulted in some people having beautiful and special things from exotic places in their homes, while their neighbors did not. The impact of globalization changed in the second era, however.

— The **second** era of globalization began in the early 19th century when Europe began importing items such as grains and textiles. These were things that were already being produced in the European markets, and the imports created the pressure of market competition on goods already being produced domestically. During this time the formation of new trading companies resulted in new partnerships, and regulation of prices was a result of the competition.

— Today, we're living in the **third** era of globalization. While we're still trading products that compete with others produced within a given country or region, another force is changing how globalization impacts our lives. Technologies and skills are competing across borders, oceans, and time zones. This kind of globalization is putting a different kind of pressure on global markets and economies. And because it's so very different from the trading of "things" and "stuff" that has happened over the past three centuries, it doesn't fit well into the existing models of trends and cycles. For this reason, the experts are challenged to tell us what kind of impact we can expect the current levels of globalization to have in the long term.

While we may not know exactly what the future of globalization holds, there is no shortage of opinions about what it has meant to the world so far. In a brief essay for *Newsweek*, journalist Thomas Friedman described how the bloody riots during the 2001 European G8 Conference in Italy and the 2009 U.S. G20 Conference held in Pittsburgh reflected people's fears that globalization is good for businesses only, and not so good for people. "But globalization didn't ruin the world—it just flattened it," Friedman says. "And on balance that can benefit everyone, especially the poor."[2]

German Chancellor Angela Merkel seems to agree. During the opening ceremonies of Germany's Hannover Fair, she stated,

"There is always a worry that globalization will hurt our affluence. I don't agree with this. We can be winners in globalization, but we have to be willing to invest and have a strong commitment."[3] Critics of globalization see something very different.

Although the views opposing Friedman's and Merkel's vary in their specifics, in general they argue that it's not the change in the standard of living for the world that the protesters fear. It's more about the feeling that huge corporations are gaining increasing control over everyday people and the way we live. Perhaps even more relevant is the fear of the average person being powerless to stop these corporations from doing the things that are good for the bottom line of business, but bad for the human race and the sustainability of life on the planet.

Clearly globalization, in the form that we see it today, is a double-edged sword. It's not a democratic process, and it's paid for by those who stand to benefit the most. Just as clearly, it is a fact of life. We've definitely gone global, and there's no turning back. So while there's no doubt that business, banking, and industry now work as global entities, what about governments? Are we headed for some form of global governance? Or, as some people suggest, do we have one already?

Moving Toward Global Government?

At nearly every summit, conference, and media interview I take part in, there's one question I can count on being asked, either on or off the record: Do I believe that we will be living under some form of global government soon; and, if so, when? I'll begin this section of the book with the same words I use to respond to questions of that kind.

First, I don't have an "inside track" or a telephone hotline to the White House or leaders of the world. I can't read their minds, I don't know what they're thinking, and I don't know why they make the decisions they do. I have access to the same resources and information that the people asking the questions do. It's the way I use those resources, coupled with my background in systems thinking, that helps me make sense of what sometimes looks like a senseless world.

When I worked as a software designer in the energy and defense industries, for example, part of my job was to write computer programs that search for patterns. As I described in my book *Fractal Time*, it was the perfect opportunity for me to do formally and professionally something that I had done casually since I was a child: search for patterns in people, life, and nature. As a professional, I was simply using the technology of high-speed computers to sift through huge amounts of data to find them faster. During my time in the industry, I was searching for geological patterns of oil-bearing rock, or patterns of errors in sophisticated software systems.

Now I still look at patterns in the world. But today the ones I'm looking for are those of our past. The cyclic patterns of Earth's history, war and peace, the collapse of economies, and the rise and fall of civilizations—and our ability to calculate those patterns—form the basis for much of the way I answer questions about our future.

I don't know precisely what the future holds. What I do know is that the cycles of the past carry patterns that tell us what we can reasonably expect in times to come. If we have the wisdom to recognize the patterns, then we can give ourselves an edge, and a fair idea of what today and tomorrow will bring. We can also know the moments in our future—the *choice points*—where our choices for change have the greatest opportunity of success.[4]

When it comes to cyclic changes in history, the patterns that I point out are no secret to the leaders who have created the world as we see it today. From the public descriptions of what happened during the last world-age shift offered by indigenous elders, and the oral traditions of the Tibetan nomads who described cyclic changes of climate to me over their campfires in the late 1990s; to the probabilities and trajectories of time described to me by the shamans high in the Andes Mountains of southern Peru after September 11, 2001, and the ancient Mayan glyphs that calculate those cycles as sophisticated calendars . . . clearly it's no secret that we're living a time of change that has been predicted, anticipated, welcomed, and feared since it last occurred about 5,000 years ago.

Today's changes include the greatest shifting of power, wealth, technology, and information in recorded history. So it's not surprising to me that we would see a globalization of governments along with that of business, industry, and finance during the same time of change. Global governance is already here. And if the post–World War II years of the 20th century are an indication of how it will be implemented, this will be an unfolding process, rather than an event marked by one moment in time.

The foundations for global government, as well as a higher level of global cooperation, have been forming since the world was carved up into new nations and economies following World War II. The consolidation of business into trading blocs, such as the European Union (EU), created in 1993; the African Union (AU), founded in 2001; and the Association of Southeast Asian Nations (ASEAN), established in 1967, is how separate nations with common interests form higher-level organizations that benefit them individually as well as collectively.

Additionally, the consolidation of currencies, such as we've seen with the *euro* in Europe; the proposed currency known as the *eco* for West Africa, which is expected to go into use in 2015; the *Eastern Caribbean dollar;* and a proposed shared currency for United Arab Emirates, Bahrain, Saudi Arabia, Kuwait, Oman, and Qatar are all elements of cooperation that signal a higher form of governance.

So my answer to the question of whether we are moving in the direction of some form of global governance is *yes,* because it's already here and happening on increasingly deeper scales. Will we ever go back to the world of the past? Probably not. Is global governance a good thing or a bad thing? I don't know. The answer depends upon how it's put into place.

The formation of the EU may provide an example in microcosm of what's possible if the same guidelines were applied on a global scale. The stated goals of the EU were clear from the beginning. It was set up with the "aim of ending the frequent and bloody wars between neighbors, which culminated in the Second World War."[5] Equally clear was the path that the EU chose to accomplish their goals—the "four freedoms" of movement:

- Movement of goods
- Movement of services
- Movement of people
- Movement of money

Today, 27 countries form the EU; and while each one has largely kept its language, culture, art, lifestyle, and the other things that make it unique, the easing of trade and travel restrictions has brought about an era that the Europeans I've met personally, living within the EU system itself, see as a positive one.

Holding the EU as an example of what can happen when different nations work together for common goals, it is evident that global governance could be a good thing. Clearly if it means lessening or eliminating the barriers preventing the basic needs of every man, woman, and child on the earth from being met, and doing so without compromising their uniqueness, then it could be a positive change. And if the necessities of life—things like food, water, medicine, electricity, and technology—were made accessible to all of the members of our global family, while at the same time we worked together to solve the crisis points threatening our future, then the world would probably benefit from such a governance.

One of the stated goals when the EU was formed was to eliminate the violent competition for resources that led to the bloodshed, suffering, and wars of the past. If such a level of cooperation were achieved on a global scale, and it included the sharing of human and natural resources, then it's entirely possible that wars over resources could become a thing of the past. The accomplishment of these goals would certainly go a long way toward addressing the three criteria identified earlier that make us violent and warlike: the perceived threats to ourselves, our families, and our ways of life.

There is obviously a dark side to global governance as well, however. If the systems and policies that make it work are based on something other than the "four freedoms" of the EU, then the benefits identified previously could never materialize. If, for example, the governing principles were based upon greed, control, and profits for the bottom line of business and corruption, people would still suffer from the same disparities of wealth, lack of life's necessities, and hopelessness of ever changing their life circumstances. Clearly if this were the case, then global governance could turn into a worst-case scenario akin to the dark and frightening future described in George Orwell's novel *1984*. It's all about how it's done.

* * *

Already a number of options have been proposed to deal with the unprecedented stress that our changing world brings to the systems we rely upon for our way of life. For any of the solutions to work, something will need to happen that has never happened before, or at least not in the recorded history of the last 5,000 years or so. Problems—such as a population of ten billion people, growing shortages of food and water, the spread of pandemic disease, and adapting to climate change—are so massive that a single nation alone, or even a union of nations, cannot solve them.

For the first time in the known history of the world, solutions need to be implemented on a global scale. To do so requires the cooperation of many of the largest and most powerful nations. It's the urgency of the crises we face that will open the door to unprecedented opportunity, and the choices that it brings. Will the solutions be implemented in the spirit of cooperation and mutual aid? Or will they be implemented through the same fears that have led to problems in the past and destroyed so much that we cherish? If the experts are right, we won't have to wait long to find out.

While we are in varying stages of designing, gathering support for, and implementing a number of different plans to meet the crises identified in Chapter 3, one project that is among the most highly developed and most public, which has also received the greatest acceptance and is furthest along in terms of funding and implementation, was actually spelled out more than a decade ago, at the turn of the millennium. In September 2000, the 55th session of the United Nations General Assembly adopted "The United Nations Millennium Declaration," a resolution for new global partnerships to achieve a series of goals addressing a number of global concerns.[6]

The goals, now known as the UN Millennium Development Goals (MDGs), are built around a set of core initiatives that 192 countries and 23 international organizations have already agreed to and signed off on.[7] The key elements of this ambitious plan are identified as the eight high-level goals listed below.

Within each goal are a number of subgoals that lead to the governance, policies, actions, and benchmarks needed to achieve that particular objective. Among the most ambitious milestones agreed to by the members is that of eliminating extreme poverty by the year 2015.

The eight stated MDGs are as follows:

- *Goal 1:* Eradicate extreme poverty and hunger

- *Goal 2:* Achieve universal primary education

- *Goal 3:* Promote gender equality and empower women

- *Goal 4:* Reduce the child mortality rate

- *Goal 5:* Improve maternal health

- *Goal 6:* Combat HIV/AIDS, malaria, and other diseases

- *Goal 7:* Ensure environmental sustainability

- *Goal 8:* Develop a global partnership for development

Clearly these are lofty goals. It's equally clear that each one requires considerable action to be undertaken before it can be met. When we put them all together, these eight goals form the core of a radical shift in the way the world has dealt with crises in the past—a never-before-seen level of cooperation on a global scale. For this kind of cooperation to be enacted, a framework must be in place for the policies and governance needed to implement the goals. But before the framework can even be considered, the way we think of the world and ourselves must also undergo a radical shift. This is where the leadership that would make such far-reaching objectives possible—a form of global governance—comes into play. And this is precisely what the UN is proposing to meet the needs of our world in crisis.

The objectives described in the MDGs appear to fall into two distinct kinds of efforts: **Goals 1–6** identify present and specific humanitarian crises, all of which are happening now; and while **Goals 7** and **8** also involve human crises, a closer look at these initiatives shows that they create the framework for deeper levels of cooperation in future projects.

One of the subheadings on the document describing the MDGs, a goal listed as "Target 8.A," states the need to "develop further an open, rule-based, predictable, non-discriminatory trading and financial system."[8] This goal uses complex-sounding language that appears to tie in with the previous discussion of new kinds of money, and consolidated monetary and trading systems. This kind of goal carries these projects well beyond the relief efforts, emergency assistance, and humanitarian aid that have often been associated with UN projects in the past.

I encourage you to become familiar with these goals for yourself by exploring them at the official United Nations website (**UN .org**). If recent changes on the world stage are any indicator, we can expect the UN to assume a greater level of visibility and responsibility; and take a new, more powerful role in addressing the great crises of our time. It's good for all of us to know the plan.

Birthing a New World

Earlier, we explored the Mayan idea of time and the cycles of time on Earth that synchronize with those of the cosmos. Through oral prophecies, the Maya left descriptions of what we could expect during the transition years from one world age to the next. They knew what to expect because they (and our mutual ancestors) had lived through such cycles in the past, and they were aware of the fractal nature of cycles. In other words, what the Mayan calendar shows as the "birth" from one age to the next in the cosmos corresponds to the familiar birth that each of us experiences coming into this world. From the Mayan point of view, it's impossible to separate the two . . . and here's why.

The average time that we spend in the wombs of our mothers (our gestation period) is about 260 days, while the average time that it takes for Earth to complete one huge wobble in our orbit (the precession of the equinoxes) is about 26,000 years. In terms of patterns, the 260 days before *our* birth is a fractal of the 26,000 years it takes Earth to "birth" a new precession cycle.

The Maya knew that for each birth, the conditions would shift to make way for the new life. In the case of world-age cycles, the shift is the breakdown of things that *don't* work in the face of the changes, in order to make way for the things that *do*. This is precisely the way our indigenous ancestors thought of our time in history: as a cosmic birth into a new cycle of life.

With any new cycle, they knew that we would have to develop a new way of being. Many people have interpreted the 2012 end date of the Mayan calendar to mean that the end of the world is just around the corner. A deeper understanding of the Mayan traditions, however, reveals that it's not about the end of the world itself; rather, it's about the end of a world age—and with it the end of a way of life.

But just as the end of anything is the beginning of what comes next, the end of our world-age cycle is the beginning of the new cycle that follows; it's the birth of a new world. Anthropologist, historian, and Mayan *Ajq'ij* (ceremonial priest and spiritual guide)

Carlos Barrios summed this up from the perspective of the present-day Maya, during a talk in Santa Fe, New Mexico, in 2002: "The world will not end. It will be transformed. The indigenous have the calendars, and know how to accurately interpret it, not others."[9]

The analogy of our birth from the womb and our birth from one world age to the next is a good one. It makes even more sense when we apply it to where we find ourselves in the world today. For both our emergence from the womb and our emergence from the fifth world age of indigenous American traditions into the sixth, once the process begins it's a one-way journey that carries us from a place to which we can never return. In both cases, we can never go back to where we've been.

While the reason we can't return to the womb is obvious, the reason we can't go back to the familiar world of our past may be less so; nonetheless we're on a one-way trip. We can't go back to the world of the past because it no longer exists. It transformed before our eyes while we were living the change—in plain sight.

Here is the key to understanding the Mayan message about time. The world we've grown up with, become comfortable with, and grown accustomed to was never meant as a destination. It could never last as a permanent way of being because it simply never was sustainable. The world of the mid-20th century was a stepping-stone, a point inaugurating a learning curve, which has led us to another way of life. If we doubt that this is true, we need only look to the ways of life in the past to see that the days of $0.57 for a dozen eggs, $0.49 for a gallon of milk, and $0.31 for a gallon of regular-grade gasoline are gone. Gone as well are the values and loyalties that defined our jobs, our families, and the independent and separate ways we used to think of ourselves and our nations in the world.

For these reasons, the world that my mom is waiting for will never arrive, and life will never get back to "normal." Life today is the new normal. And it's carrying us in one direction: forward. We can't stop the ride, but we can direct where it takes us. We can't stop the change, but we can guide it to a gentler landing.

This is where *Deep Truth* comes in. We're all better equipped to make the choices that define our future when we understand the cycles, failures, and successes of our past.

Destiny or Fate?

So where do we go from here? Where *can* we go? Whether or not we agree on *why* the world has changed, the fact is that it has. Rather than a change that runs its course, it seems that the one we're all part of now has only begun and is accelerating. It's probably happening faster than anyone could have envisioned, faster even than the visionaries could have imagined, and certainly faster than we can document in our textbooks and teach in our classrooms. This seems to be where the proverbial "rubber" meets the road. For us, it's where the spiritual and scientific "rubber" of all that we claim to be, and all that we claim to be true in our lives, meets the "road" of life and our future. It's a road that can lead to only one of two places: it will either pave the way to our destiny, or it will seal us into our fate. Very soon we'll know which route we've chosen as nations and as a world.

Our ultimate fate will be the outcome of all the major crises of our time if they are left unchecked. As illustrated previously in this book, there are five key crises:

- *Crisis Point 1:* An unsustainable world population

- *Crisis Point 2:* Climate change

- *Crisis Point 3:* Growing shortages of food and fresh water

- *Crisis Point 4:* The widening gap between poverty and wealth, health and disease, and illiteracy and education

- *Crisis Point 5:* The growing threat of war and the renewed threat of atomic war

Each crisis standing alone holds the potential to end civilization, and even life, as we know it today. Every one of the five areas of crisis identified is already present. And because each one is already happening, each crisis has established what may be thought of as the trajectory of where it will ultimately lead us over time if it is not dealt with in some way. The population explosion, for example, has established a trajectory of shorter and shorter intervals between doubling, placing our global family at somewhere around ten billion by 2050. If left unchecked, then this is what we can expect as the fate of our global family: the staggering implications of ten billion people competing for food, water, jobs, and housing, with vital resources diminishing only 40 years from now.

If we apply a similar thinking to each of the areas of crisis, it's easy to see how any one of them, if left to fate, holds the potential of leading to a frightening outcome. From this perspective, we can think of fate as what happens if we know the crisis is present and do nothing. Maybe President Ronald Reagan said this best in his 1981 inaugural address: "I do not believe in a fate that will fall on us no matter what we do. I do believe in a fate that will fall on us if we do nothing."[10] When it comes to the five crises identified by the best minds of our time, the choice to do nothing would be the choice to empower the darkest outcomes of prophecy, fear, war, and death as our fate.

There is a powerful distinction that becomes crystal clear when we think about fate and destiny. While fate may be thought of as passively dealing with the challenges that face us by doing nothing, destiny, on the other hand, is the child of action. Our destiny must be put into motion to be realized. In the case of the crises facing us, that action comes in the form of our choices. Destiny is what awaits us, as individuals and together, as we make the choices that lead to the fulfillment of our greatest potential. William Jennings Bryan summed up the nature of destiny beautifully when he said, "Destiny is no matter of chance. It is a matter of choice. It is not a thing to be waited for, it is a thing to be achieved."[11]

✳ ✳ ✳

My sense is that the crises of our time and our destiny are intimately entwined. The fact that so many pieces of our lives are being redefined and so many changes are converging during one small window of time, seemingly overnight, appears to be more than just a coincidence. We can think of this convergence as a cosmic reality check. Within the space of just a few short years, we get to see which choices we've made as a civilization work and which ones don't; we can review which systems are sustainable and which ones aren't. In full view of the broken and failed systems, we must choose: Do we work to embrace new ways of living that give us what we need in clean, sustainable ways that honor us and our world? Or do we fight among ourselves to prop up old and unsustainable ways of living that will eventually break again and leave us hanging in the abyss of the same choices again at a later time?

The ways of life that don't work are the ones crumbling at our feet right now: from debt-ridden economic systems and overburdened health care, to the growing use of our finite source of fossil fuels to provide energy for the world's expanding population. All are outward signs of the way we think about the world and our place in it. These are all parts of the language of change in the code of civilization. If we can consider how the choices we make in our lives each day fit into the bigger picture, then their role becomes clear. Our individual choices are the collective foundation of our new world age.

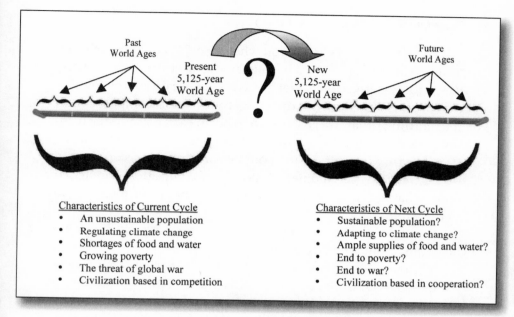

Figure 7.1. We are the generation that bridges two rare cycles of time: the end of the fifth in a series of five 5,125-year-long world ages, and the beginning of the sixth, initiating the next series. In addition to bridging one cycle to the next, ancient and indigenous traditions remind us that, as the bridging generation, our choices determine which beliefs of the last cycle we will carry as the foundation for the future.

When we look at the big scheme of things in Figure 7.1, it's clear how the conditions that end one cycle become the foundation that begins the next. It's also clear that between the cycles is a space where neither is present: *a choice point of opportunity.* This is where we find ourselves: near the end of the 36-year-long choice point between 1980 and 2016 that marks the end our 5,125-year-long cycle.[12] So, while the crises listed on the left side of Figure 7.1 are the realities of our time, the fact that they're converging at the end of the cycle opens the door of opportunity for us to change the patterns before we begin the new cycle on the right side of the figure.

Rewriting Our History: Version 2.0

We live our lives based upon what we believe. This simple fact leads to the realization that beyond anything else we may actually *do* in our lives, the beliefs that precede what we do are the foundation of all that we cherish, dream, become, and accomplish. From the morning rituals we go through to begin each day and the technology we use to make our lives better, to the technology that *destroys* life through war . . . all of our personal routines, community rituals, religious ceremonies—indeed, our civilization—are based upon what we think about ourselves and about our relationship to the world.

When we realize this fact, it makes sense to ask where our beliefs come from. The answer may surprise you.

With few exceptions, our beliefs come from what other people tell us about our world. In other words, the lens through which we see the world and ourselves and make the most important choices of our lives is the teachings of science, history, religion, culture, and our families.

When it comes to the facts of history, evolution, and life itself, for the last 300 years those "other people" have often been the scientists and organizations that preserve and teach our most cherished scientific traditions. This is where the true power of science takes on new meaning.

Beyond the satisfaction we derive from our search for "truth," the answers that science reveals about us and our role in the world are the very foundation upon which we *build* our world and define how we go about solving the problems of life.

So how does the best science of our time portray us? Historically we've been taught that we are insignificant creatures who appeared as a "fluke" of biology, arriving late in the history of the earth and having little consequence in the overall scheme of things while we're here; and when we're gone, the universe will hardly even notice our absence.

While this description may sound a little harsh, the general idea is probably close to what many of us today have been conditioned to believe. The science of the last century has led us to believe that life itself is the product of a seemingly impossible combination of elements and conditions that occurred long ago; that humankind is only one product of these chance events, and we're essentially animal-like, and thus warlike, by nature; that today's civilization is the pinnacle of 5,000 years of human ingenuity, creativity, and technology; and that we have the ability to master nature and harness the resources of the earth.

It's probably no coincidence that during the same period of time we've been asked to embrace these beliefs, humankind has also suffered the greatest losses through war, the greatest suffering through genocide, and the greatest damage to the environment we depend upon for life. It's precisely these beliefs that often leave us feeling small and helpless in the face of life's greatest challenges.

What if we're more than this? Could it be that we're really unique, very special, very powerful beings in disguise? What if we're delegates of miraculous potential, born into this world to fulfill a beautiful destiny—one that we've simply forgotten in the face of conditions that have shocked us into the dreamlike state of being powerless?

How would our lives change, for example, if we discovered that we're born with the power to reverse disease? Or what if we discovered we could *choose* the peace in our world, the abundance in our lives, and how long we live? What if we found that the universe itself is directly affected by a power that we've hidden from ourselves for so long that we've forgotten it's even ours? Such a radical paradigm shift would change everything. It would change what we believe about ourselves, the universe, and our role within it. It's also precisely what the leading-edge discoveries of our day are showing us.

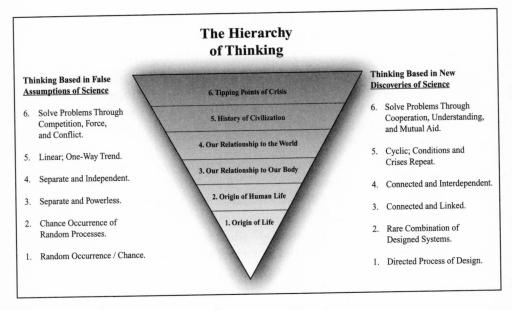

The Hierarchy
of Thinking

Thinking Based in False Assumptions of Science

6. Solve Problems Through Competition, Force, and Conflict.

5. Linear; One-Way Trend.

4. Separate and Independent.

3. Separate and Powerless.

2. Chance Occurrence of Random Processes.

1. Random Occurrence / Chance.

6. Tipping Points of Crisis

5. History of Civilization

4. Our Relationship to the World

3. Our Relationship to Our Body

2. Origin of Human Life

1. Origin of Life

Thinking Based in New Discoveries of Science

6. Solve Problems Through Cooperation, Understanding, and Mutual Aid.

5. Cyclic; Conditions and Crises Repeat.

4. Connected and Interdependent.

3. Connected and Linked.

2. Rare Combination of Designed Systems.

1. Directed Process of Design.

Figure 7.2. A difference in the core understandings of life and history revolutionizes the way we think of ourselves and solve our problems. From personal relationships to global civilizations, the choice of cooperation or competition shown in Level 6 is the result of the way we think of life in Levels 1–5. The scientific discoveries described in the previous chapters give us the reasons to think differently about ourselves as we make the choices that determine our destiny, or become our fate.

In Chapter 2, we saw how the pyramid of scientific knowledge is hierarchical. When a new discovery is made anywhere on the pyramid, the sciences above it must change in order to remain scientific. In much the same way, how we think of ourselves is hierarchical and follows this general rule.

It's easy to see that if we think of ourselves as a fluke of biology, as separate and independent from the people and the world around us, and even separate from ourselves (the false assumptions of science), solving our problems through force and conflict is a natural conclusion. When we think of ourselves as separate and powerless, conflict actually makes sense.

It's also easy to see that when science reveals we're more than we've been led to believe in terms of our origins, history, and relationship to nature and to ourselves (new discoveries), force and conflict no longer make any sense. With the revelation of such deep truths, the old ideas about solving problems immediately become obsolete. As the story that follows demonstrates, our willingness to see ourselves from a new perspective changes everything about the way we deal with life. Sometimes, such willingness even opens the door to life itself.

✳ ✳ ✳

In 2003, Aron Ralston found himself facing the defining moment of his life. As an adept climber familiar with the mountains of Colorado, he had left his engineering job with Intel to expand his climbing horizons. In May of that year, he was exploring the narrow crevices of Utah's Blue John Canyon when the unthinkable happened. As he jumped from one side of a ten-foot-deep crevasse to the other side, the rock that he had pivoted from suddenly gave way.

"I go from being out on a lark in a beautiful place and just being so happy and carefree to, like, oh shit," he said. "I fell a few feet, in slow motion, I look up and the boulder is coming and I put my hands up to try to push myself away and it collides and crushes my hand."[13]

Just like that, Ralston's life changed. His arm was pinned between the 800-pound rock and the canyon wall, and he was "captive" between the canyon walls for six days. He had no cell phone (there was no cell coverage in the remote area); no one knew where he was. In his day pack, he had two burritos, some chocolate, a video camera, and just a small amount of water. Ralston knew that the chances of anyone looking down into the crevasse to find him were slim.

On the fifth day, he resigned himself to the belief that he would die in the canyon. He scratched his epitaph on the rock wall with a small knife. He even recorded his last will and testament on the camera. And then something happened that changed everything. In the middle of the night, he had a dream of a small boy looking into his eyes and asking, "Daddy, can we play now?"

Ralston knew that he had been given a glimpse of the future and what was possible. And it's that possibility—the knowledge that he would be a father someday—that changed the way he thought of his situation, and himself. What happened next has become the subject of books, television specials, and the 2010 movie *127 Hours*.

The next morning Ralston figured out how to use his body as leverage against the canyon wall; break his pinned arm in just the right place; and use the small, dull pocketknife he was carrying to cut through his flesh, muscle, and broken bone to free himself from the rock. Following the hour that it took him to perform the procedure on himself, he climbed out of the canyon and walked until two hikers found him and called for help.

Ralston survived his ordeal, has a new prosthetic arm, and continues to climb mountains and hike canyons today. The willingness to change his thinking, the courage to follow through with his choice, and the determination to live that Aron Ralston modeled in Blue John Canyon have touched the lives of people all over the world. Ralston returns to Blue John Canyon sometimes, to the exact place of his ordeal and the rock that pinned him, for personal reasons.

"I touch it and go back to that place, remembering when I thought about what's important in life, relationships, and this quest to want to get out of there and return to love and relationships," he said, "to return to freedom instead of entrapment."[14]

✳ ✳ ✳

Aron Ralston had a profound realization that changed the way he thought of himself and his situation. And it's that change that saved his life. While we don't have to fall into a canyon in Utah to have such a realization, and hopefully no one will again, we can all learn from Ralston's experience.

Just as he chose freedom instead of entrapment, we are making the choices in every moment of our lives that lead to the same consequences. Either we choose the freedom that stems from a new and sustainable way of living; or we remain trapped in the myriad crises we're living today by clinging to the old, unsustainable ways of the past. I believe that our freedom begins with the personal commitment to know who we are in the universe. When we make such a commitment, everything from the way we think of ourselves to the way we act will change. They must, because we are changed in the presence of the deeper understanding.

It all comes back to what we believe. While it may sound too simple to be true, I am convinced that the universe works precisely this way.

The Emerging Story of Our Lives

With the hierarchy of new thinking illustrated in Figure 7.2, let's summarize the deep truths revealed in the previous chapters, and imagine the new story of human life that they tell.

— **Deep Truth 1:** Our ability to defuse the crises threatening our lives and our world hinges upon our willingness to accept what science is revealing about our origins and history.

- *Fact:* We are living at a tipping point of civilization, confronting the greatest number and magnitude of crises that humankind has faced in 5,000 years of recorded history.

- *Fact:* The global breakdown of systems ranging from world economies and the provision of health care to systems for the production and distribution of fossil fuels is a symptom of unsustainable practices based upon false scientific beliefs.

- *Fact:* To know what choices to make, what laws to pass, and what policies to enact, we must know the truth of our origins and history.

- *Fact:* The false assumptions of long-held beliefs regarding evolution and human origins now make little sense in the presence of new discoveries throughout the sciences.

— Deep Truth 2: The reluctance of mainstream educational systems to reflect new discoveries and explore new theories keeps us stuck in obsolete beliefs that fail to address the greatest crises of human history.

- *Fact:* The sound principles of the scientific method have a built-in feature for self-correction of false assumptions.

- *Fact:* For the last 300 years, we've based our choices regarding life, government, and civilization upon the way we think of ourselves and our relationship to the world—knowledge that is based in the false assumptions of an outdated science.

— Deep Truth 3: The key to addressing the crises threatening our survival lies in building partnerships based upon mutual aid and cooperation to adapt to the changes, rather than in pointing fingers and assigning blame, which makes such vital alliances difficult.

- *Fact:* We definitely need to find clean, green, and sustainable ways to provide food, electricity, and fuel for the seven billion people living on our planet.

- *Fact:* While the industrial age has certainly contributed to the greenhouse gases in the atmosphere, the climate change we see today was not induced by humans.

- *Fact:* The scientific evidence of 420,000 years of Earth's climate shows a history of warming and cooling cycles taking place at approximately 100,000-year intervals when no human industry was present.

- *Fact:* The cycles of Earth's warming over the last 420,000 years show that the rise in greenhouse gases *lags behind* the temperature increase by an average of about 800 years.

- *Fact:* It will take never-before-seen levels of alliance, synergy, and teamwork to create sustainable lifestyles that help us adapt to natural cycles of change, as well as address human-induced crises.

— **Deep Truth 4:** New discoveries of advanced civilizations dating to near the end of the last ice age provide insights into solving the crises in *our* time that our ancestors also faced in theirs.

- *Fact:* Scientific revelations of near–ice age civilizations are upsetting the traditional timeline of history.

- *Fact:* The new discoveries of science support the indigenous view of a cyclical world, with the rise and fall of civilizations, catastrophic crises, and the consequences of poor choices repeating themselves.

- *Fact:* Since early modern humans first appeared on Earth, we've been through powerful global cycles that we can learn from, including:

    - Two 100,000-year cycles of ice ages

    - Five 41,000-year cycles of changes in the angle of Earth's orbit (obliquity)

    - Forty world-age cycles of 5,125 years each

    - Eight 25,695-year-long orbital wobbles (precessions of the equinox)

— **Deep Truth 5:** A growing body of scientific data from multiple disciplines, gathered using new technology, provides evidence beyond any reasonable doubt that humankind reflects a design put into place at once, rather than a life-form emerging randomly through an evolutionary process over a long period of time.

- *Fact:* The debate over human origins must distinguish between proof and evidence.

- *Fact:* Because no one living today witnessed human beginnings, as proof of any claim, we must rely upon evidence to explain our existence.

- *Fact:* New evidence does not support the conventional wisdom of evolution by natural selection as it applies to humans.

- *Fact:* Most of the major divisions of animal life known to exist today appeared on Earth during the time of biology's "big bang": the Cambrian explosion of life into diverse forms that occurred about 154 million years ago.

- *Fact:* The organization of biological information as DNA, coupled with multiple examples of irreducible complexity, adds to the growing body of evidence that random processes cannot explain human existence.

- *Fact:* Modern humans first appeared on Earth about 200,000 years ago, and today we are virtually identical to these earliest members of our species.

- *Fact:* While science may never identify precisely what, or perhaps who, is responsible for humankind, the evidence of intelligent design is strongly present.

— **Deep Truth 6:** A growing body of scientific evidence, gathered from more than 400 peer-reviewed studies, is leading to an undeniable truth: violent competition and war directly contradict our deepest instincts of cooperation and nurturing.

- *Fact:* Scientific studies show conclusively that nature is based upon a model of cooperation and mutual aid, not violent competition and war.

- *Fact:* For 150 years we've built a civilization based on models of violent competition and the false assumption of so-called social Darwinism, aka "survival of the fittest."

- *Fact:* We are nonviolent beings by nature, but can become violent when any one of three conditions are met: we feel threatened, we feel that our families are threatened, or we feel that our way of life is threatened.

- *Fact:* Large-scale war seems to be a learned response to life challenges, not a natural human trait.

These six deep truths based on scientific facts can no longer be discounted when we think about the way we solve the problems facing us. Because we base the way we live our lives; solve our problems; and build our communities, nations, and civilizations on how we think of ourselves, it's more important than ever before to take these truths into consideration. Rather than think of the crises in the world as the barriers preventing us from getting started, we may find that they're actually the doorways we must step through to accelerate the process.

In my book *The Divine Matrix* (Hay House, 2007), I shared the story of a friend who had left everything he loved, including his career, friends, and family, to move to the wild beauty of northern New Mexico. I asked him why he had left so much behind to come to the isolation of the high desert.

He began by telling me that he had come to find his "spiritual path." In the same breath, however, he also told me that he had not been able to begin the search for his new path because too many problems seemed to be "getting in the way": he was having trouble with the family he'd left behind; his business plans for the future seemed to be hopelessly stuck; the stress of his move and his problems had created new health issues; and the contractors who were building his new, spiritual home seemed to be working on a schedule very different from what he thought he'd agreed to. His frustration was obvious.

I originally shared the story to illustrate a point, and that point may apply even more now to where we find ourselves in the world today.

From my perspective, we are incapable of anything other than a spiritual path. To put it another way, as beings of spirit we are capable *only* of spiritual experiences. Regardless of what life may look like, how many obstacles seem to be in our way, and how deeply the universe "conspires" to keep us from our spiritual journey, it's impossible to separate all the things that happen each and every day *from* our spiritual path. In fact, I believe that they *are* our spiritual path.

Just as I offered this possibility to my friend, I would like to propose that the conditions of our world as they are today are no accident. They didn't happen overnight, and they won't just "go away" on their own. As I mentioned before, the fact that so many crises are converging during such a small window of time can be no coincidence. It's now, as we cross from one world age to the next, that we must make the choices that will define the next world-age cycle. Do we unleash our destiny of greatness, or seal our fate of war and suffering?

Where Do We Go from Here?

Without a doubt, this book is about big ideas. When we think about the crises identified in the previous chapters, it's easy to feel overwhelmed and insignificant. And we've only begun to touch upon the deepest aspects of many of the topics. Throughout the world, in different languages, there is a common thinking when it comes to the crises we face: that the problems seem so big that "we can't possibly make a difference as individuals." Where would we even begin?

The answer to this question is brief. For some people, it may sound too simple. But the simple elegance of nature makes big changes possible from small experiences, because it's the choices we make in our everyday lives that merge with those of other people to become the collective answer to the crises of our time.

> Our individual choices become our
> collective answer to our time in history.

It's in the way we choose to live our lives each day that the essence of our choices—the theme of cooperation or competition, the power of love or fear—is imbued into the field that connects all things. It's these choices as well that ultimately show up in the way we deal with the crises in the world. To be very clear, this doesn't mean that we do nothing; just the opposite, in fact. This is about action. It's the kind that appears each day in the way we live our lives.

Each day we have the power in our hands to help or hinder the lives of others. Do we help the car in the adjacent lane in front of us by slowing down so the driver can safely make it to the freeway exit he or she overlooked, or do we ignore the car's blinker and risk our lives and the other person's as we whiz by in our lane because the driver is trying to "cut us off"? Do we buy into the hostility of a grocery clerk having a bad day, or do we recognize that his or her rudeness is nothing personal?

I've seen the principles of heart-based coherence work successfully in diverse venues ranging from a corporate boardroom to a theater of 5,000 people. The key is that when we change, the world changes. In a world bathed in a scientifically validated field that connects all hearts, the question is less about how to reach "them"—the CEOs of corporations and the leaders of nations—and more about what we choose to place into the quantum field, or energetic matrix, connecting us all.[15]

When the facts of *Deep Truth* give us the reasons to think differently about ourselves, that difference is expressed in everything we do throughout our daily routines. With these ideas in mind, the following broad categories are examples of everyday choices with the potential for a global impact. In fact, precisely these choices can tip the scales of balance, peace, and life in our favor in times of crisis:

— **Media.** A growing body of evidence suggests that the images and words we surround ourselves with affect the reality of our world. This leads us to ask a key question: *When we see a movie or listen to the radio with our friends and families, are we simply entertaining ourselves? Or, as the studies suggest, are we creating the building blocks for the world that we live in?* The parallels between late-20th-century end-of-the-world scenarios in movies and the unique crises of our time are striking and may illustrate precisely this point. Clearly a balance of media input is important here. For this reason, our choice to support positive, life-affirming images and outcomes sends a powerful message to the studios that produce films and other programs.

— **Food.** One of the simplest and healthiest things we can do in our lives to tip the scales of conscious commerce in our favor is to encourage and support the business of locally grown, organic produce. When we "eat local," we eliminate the huge carbon footprint left by burning fuel to fly, ship, and truck out-of-season fruits and vegetables grown on corporate farms halfway around the world to the supermarkets in our communities. Most grocery stores now sell organic produce. Each piece of fruit and vegetable should have a label on it that tells you how it was grown and where it is from. Many communities also have food co-ops and restaurants that support local and organic "farm to table" enterprises. Look for these in your area.

— **Business.** While no one wants to go back in time to the "primitive" lifestyles of our past—and there's certainly no need to—we do have options, when we supply our homes and offices with the things we need, as to what sources we support. If we're purchasing paper products, for example, we can buy paper towels and facial and toilet tissue made from recycled sources that reduce the need to cut fresh trees. Also, we can buy new molded-plastic products made from recycled materials—including bottles, yogurt containers, and even toothbrushes—without using more of the resources that are already in short supply.

— **Conscious living.** When it comes to the impact that our choices have upon the world, there is certainly no shortage of resources to guide our decision making. While this book has created a framework from which to think of ourselves in new and empowering ways, other authors have devoted their life's work to a deeper understanding of conscious living. Because different people learn in different ways, we are fortunate that there are myriad approaches we can employ to create the new, more collaborative and cooperative world that's emerging. The following are well-written books exploring specific areas of conscious living in diverse and meaningful ways:

- *Spontaneous Evolution: Our Positive Future (and a Way to Get There from Here),* by Bruce Lipton and Steve Bhaerman (Hay House, 2010)

- *Voluntary Simplicity: Toward a Way of Life That Is Outwardly Simple, Inwardly Rich,* by Duane Elgin (HarperCollins, 2010)

- *Promise Ahead: A Vision of Hope and Action for Humanity's Future,* by Duane Elgin (HarperCollins, 2001)

- *Global Shift: How a New Worldview Is Transforming Humanity,* by Edmund J. Bourne (New Harbinger/ Noetic Books, 2009)

- *Plan B 4.0: Mobilizing to Save Civilization,* by Lester R. Brown (W. W. Norton & Company, 2009)

- *The HeartMath Solution: The Institute of HeartMath's Revolutionary Program for Engaging the Power of the Heart's Intelligence,* by Doc Lew Childre and Howard Martin (HarperOne, 2000)

The Choice Is Ours

We began this book by asking a single question—the un-answered question underlying every choice we'll ever make, the one that lives within every challenge that will ever test us and that forms the foundation for every decision we'll ever face: *Who are we?*

In light of what we've discovered throughout this book, we now see why it's more than just important that this question be answered. It's *necessary.* It's *vital.* The way we do so determines how we think of ourselves and how we live in the world. It shows up in everything from the way we care for ourselves and our young-est children, to the way we treat our aging parents. It forms the foundation for principles governing how we share resources like food, water, medicine, and the necessities of life; when and why we go to war; what our economy is based upon; what we believe about our destiny and fate; when we save a human life; and when we choose to end life. In short, our answer to this question forms the core of civilization itself.

So, who are we? While we have probably sensed the answer in-tuitively throughout our lives, now the science we rely upon and trust has validated our deepest knowing.

Who Are We?

We are mysterious beings of mysterious origins.

We appeared on Earth, looking as we do today, about 200,000 years—30 world-age cycles and two ice ages—ago. Our bodies bear the unmistakable signs of an intelligent design. We come into this world "speaking" the silent language of the heart that communi-cates with the fields that give birth to and connect all things. We were the architects of advanced civilizations that date at least to the end of the last ice age, and probably before. We are peaceful beings who become violent when we fear for our lives, our fami-lies', or our ways of life.

Only during the last 5,125 years of the current world age have we developed the habit of large-scale war. The unsustainable conditions of our world have led us to the crisis points where we must either recognize the truth of our origins and history, and choose our highest destiny; or deny these truths and succumb to the depths of our darkest fate.

Now that we've answered the question of who we are, the next big question relates to our future. What is the legacy that you and I will leave to those who will call *us* their ancestors? Will our children's history books look to us and say that we valued cooperation over competition, and that we learned to love instead of fear?

Or will they look to us and say that we missed the greatest opportunity of 5,000 years of human history—the chance to replace the false beliefs of our past with the truth that empowers us to achieve our destiny? We've already answered these questions with our words. Now we must *live* what we've spoken. Will we base the emerging new world on the deep truths of our existence?

We won't have to wait long to find out.

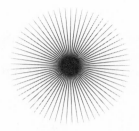

ENDNOTES

Introduction

1. The Institute for Public Policy Research in Britain, the Center for American Progress in the U.S., and the Australia Institute formed an independent task force of politicians, scientists, and businesspeople, co-chaired by Stephen Byers and U.S. Senator Olympia Snowe, to study the issue of global warming. "Report: Global Warming Near Critical Point," Associated Press (January 24, 2005). Retrieved from: **http://www.msnbc.com/id/6863557/ns/us_news-environment**.

2. Albert Einstein, as quoted in an article, "Atomic Education Urged by Einstein," *The New York Times* (May 25, 1946), and later quoted by Michael Amrine, "The Real Problem Is in the Hearts of Man," *The New York Times Magazine* (June 23, 1946).

Chapter 1

1. Michael Crichton, *Sphere* (New York: Alfred A. Knopf, 1987): pp. 348–349.

2. Jonathan Sarfati, "Archbishop's Achievement: James Ussher's Great Work *Annals of the World* Is Now Available in English," Creation Ministries International. Website: **http://creation.com/archbishops-achievement**.

3. Ibid.

4. Thomas Hunt Morgan, *Evolution and Adaptation* (New York: The Macmillan Company, 1903): p. 43.

5. Charles Darwin, *On the Origin of Species* (Seattle: Pacific Publishing Studio, 2010): p. 236.

6. *Evolution and Adaptation*: p. 43.

7. University of Glasgow, "Rare Tests on Neanderthal Infant Sheds Light on Early Human Development," *ScienceDaily* (April 4, 2000). Website: **http://www.sciencedaily.com/releases/2000/03/000331091126.htm**.

8. Ibid.

9. Hillary Mayell, "Neandertals Not Our Ancestors, DNA Study Suggests," *National Geographic News* (May 14, 2003). Website: **http://news.nationalgeographic.com**.

10. Yuxin Fan, Tera Newman, Elena Linardopoulou, and Barbara J. Trask, "Gene Content and Function of the Ancestral Chromosome Fusion Site in Human Chromosome 2q13-2q14.1 and Paralogous Regions," *Genome Research*, vol. 12 (Cold Spring Harbor Laboratory Press, 2002): pp. 1663–1672. Website: **http://genome.cshlp.org/content/12/11/1663.full**.

11. J. W. IJdo, A. Baldini, D. C. Ward, S. T. Reeders, and R. A. Wells, "Origin of Human Chromosome 2: An Ancestral Telomere-telomere Fusion," *Proceedings of the National Academy of Sciences of the United States of America*, vol. 88, no. 20 (October 15, 1991): pp. 9051–9055.

12. "Gene Content and Function of the Ancestral Chromosome Fusion Site in Human Chromosome 2q13-2q14.1 and Paralogous Regions."

13. "Origin of Human Chromosome 2: An Ancestral Telomere-telomere Fusion."

Chapter 2

1. *The Human Experience,* directed by Charles Kinnane (Grassroots Films, 2011). Website: **http://www.grassrootsfilms.com/films.html**.

2. Albert Einstein, *The Theory of Relativity & Other Essays* (New York: MJF Books, 1950): p. 53.

3. Isaac Newton, translated by Andrew Motte, *Newton's Principia: The Mathematical Principles of Natural Philosophy,* first American edition (New York: Daniel Adee, 1846). Retrieved from: **http://rack1.ul.cs.cmu.edu/is/newton**.

4. Lee Gomes, "String Theory Skeptic," *Forbes Magazine* (September 21, 2009). Website: **http://www.forbes.com/forbes/2009/0921/opinions-peter-woit-physics-ideas-opinions.html**.

5. James Le Fanu, "Science's Dead End," *Prospect,* issue 173 (July 21, 2010). Website: **http://www.prospectmagazine.co.uk/2010/07/ sciences-dead-end.**

6. Ibid.

7. Tom Abate, "Genome Discovery Shocks Scientists," *San Francisco Chronicle* (February 11, 2001). Website: **http://articles.sfgate.com/2001-02-11/news/17583040_1_chemical-letters-president-of-celera-genomics-human-genome-project.**

8. Ibid.

9. Frank L.H. Wolfs, "Appendix E: Introduction to the Scientific Method," Department of Physics and Astronomy, University of Rochester, New York. Website: **http://teacher.pas.rochester.edu/phy_labs/ appendixe/appendixe.html.**

10. Andrew Curry, "Gobekli Tepe: The World's First Temple?" *Smithsonian* magazine (November 2008). Website: **http://www.smithsonian mag.com/history-archaeology/gobekli-tepe.html.**

11. Ronald Logan, "Opening Address of the Symposium on the Humanistic Aspects of Regional Development," *Prout Journal,* vol. 6, no. 3 (September 1993).

12. Michael J. Behe, "Evidence for Intelligent Design from Biochemistry." From a speech delivered at Discovery Institute's "God & Culture Conference" (August 10, 1996). Website: **http://www.arn.org/docs/ behe/mb_idfrombiochemistry.htm.**

13. Glen Rein and Rollin McCraty, "Structural Changes in Water and DNA Associated with New Physiologically Measurable States," *Journal of Scientific Exploration,* vol. 8, no. 3 (1994): pp. 438–439.

14. E. W. Silvertooth, "Special Relativity," *Nature,* vol. 322 (August 14, 1986): p. 590.

15. Niels Bohr, "Discussion with Einstein on Epistemological Problems in Atomic Physics," in *Albert Einstein: Philosopher-Scientist,* P. A. Schilpp (ed.) (1949): p. 240.

16. A. A. Michelson and Edward W. Morley, "On the Relative Motion of the Earth and the Luminiferous Ether," *American Journal of Science,* vol. 34 (1887): pp. 333–345.

17. "Special Relativity."

18. Max Delbruck, *Mind from Matter? An Essay on Evolutionary Epistemology* (Hoboken, NJ: Blackwell Publishers, 1985): p. 167.

19. Peter Machamer, *The Cambridge Companion to Galileo* (Cambridge, U.K.: Cambridge University Press, 1998): p. 64.

20. E. O. Wilson, *Consilience: The Unity of Knowledge* (New York: Vintage Books, 1999): p. v.

21. Anastasia Lebedev, "The Man Who Saved the World Finally Recognized," **MosNews.com** (May 21, 2004). Retrieved from: **http://www.worldcitizens.org/petrov2.html.**

22. Ibid.

23. *The American Heritage College Dictionary,* third edition (Boston: Houghton Mifflin Company, 1993): p. 489.

24. Ibid: p. 1406.

25. Ibid: p. 1096.

26. Opinion voiced by Sir Martin Rees, Royal Society Research Professor at Cambridge University, and quoted by Andrew Walker, "Sir Martin Rees: Prophet of Doom?" *BBC News* (April 25, 2003). Website: **http://news.bbc.co.uk/1/hi/in_depth/uk/2000/newsmakers/2976279.stm.**

27. George Musser, "The Climax of Humanity," *Scientific American,* special edition "Crossroads for Planet Earth" (September 2005): p. 44.

28. Ibid: p. 47.

29. Ibid: p. 47.

30. Tad Williams, *To Green Angel Tower, Part 1* (New York: DAW Books, 1993): p. 771.

Chapter 3

1. *Millennium Ecosystem Assessment (MA) Synthesis Report,* United Nations Educational, Scientific and Cultural Organization. Compiled by 1,300 scientists in 95 countries, the report warns that the harmful consequences of environmental degradation could grow significantly worse in

the next 50 years. Website: **http://portal.unesco.org/en/ev.php-URL_ID=26641&URL_DO=DO_TOPIC&URL_SECTION=201.html**.

2. "The Climax of Humanity": pp. 44–47.

3. Ibid: p. 44.

4. Lindsay Patterson, "Jeffrey Sachs on Trying to Feed 9 Billion People by 2050," *EarthSky: A Clear Voice for Science* (October 26, 2009). Website: **http://earthsky.org/food/jeffrey-sachs-on-trying-to-feed-9-billion-people-by-2050**.

5. Jeffrey Sachs, "Can Extreme Poverty Be Eliminated?" *Scientific American,* special edition "Crossroads for Planet Earth" (September 2005): p. 56.

6. J. R. Petit, et al., "Climate and Atmospheric History of the Past 420,000 years from the Vostok Ice Core, Antarctica," *Nature,* vol. 399 (June 3, 1999): pp. 429–436. Website: **http://www.nature.com/nature/journal/v399/n6735/abs/399429a0.html**.

7. Craig Idso, Keith Idso, and Sherwood B. Idso, "Ice Core Studies Prove CO_2 Is Not the Powerful Climate Driver Climate Alarmists Make It Out to Be," *CO_2 Science,* vol. 6, no. 26 (June 2003). Website: **http://www.co2science.org/articles/V6/N26/EDIT.php**.

8. H. Fischer, M. Wahlen, J. Smith, D. Mastroianni, and B. Deck, "Ice Core Records of Atmospheric CO_2 Around the Last Three Glacial Terminations," *Science,* vol. 283, no. 5408 (1999): pp. 1712–1714.

9. Ibid.

10. Concluding statement by Al Gore, *An Inconvenient Truth.* Transcript at: **http://en.wikipedia.org/wiki/An_Inconvenient_Truth**.

11. A partial list of scientists opposing the mainstream scientific assessment of global warming. Website: **http://en.wikipedia.org/wiki/List_of_scientists_opposing_the_mainstream_scientific_assessment_of_global_warming**.

12. Ibid.

13. Ibid.

14. Ibid.

15. Ibid.

16. Ibid.

17. Ibid.

18. Ibid.

19. Ibid.

20. Benito Müller, "No Trust Without Respect: Adaptation Quick Start Funding at the Cross Roads," Oxford Institute for Energy Studies (March 2010). Website: **http://www.oxfordenergy.org/pdfs/ comment_01_03_10.pdf**.

21. "Lower Missouri River Ecosystem Initiative Final Report 1994–1998," version 3, USGS Columbia Environmental Research Center (December 1998). Website: **http://infolink.cr.usgs.gov/AboutInfoLINK/ lmreifinal.pdf**.

22. Ibid.

23. Emma Woollacott, "Loss of Biodiversity Could Damage World Economy, Says UN," *TG Daily* (May 11, 2010): Website: **http://www .tgdaily.com/sustainability-features/49704-loss-of-biodiversity-could- damage-world-economy-says-un**.

24. Niles Eldredge, "The Sixth Extinction," **ActionBioscience.org**, American Institute of Biological Sciences (June 2001): Website: **http:// www.actionbioscience.org/newfrontiers/eldredge2.html**.

25. Ibid.

26. "News Release: Experts Warn Ecosystem Changes Will Continue to Worsen, Putting Global Development Goals at Risk," World Resources Institute (2005). Website: **http://archive.wri.org/news.cfm?id=324**.

27. Porter Stansberry, "Time Is Running Out," *Stansberry's Investment Advisory* (January 2011).

28. "Kitty Williams Finally Tells Her Survivor Tale," Institute for Holocaust Education. Website: **http://ihene.org/nebraska-survivor-stories/ kitty-williams-finally-tells-her-survivor-tale.html**.

29. Ibid.

30. Richard C. Cook, "It's Official: The Crash of the U.S. Economy Has Begun," Center for Research on Globalization (June 14, 2007). Website: **http://www.globalresearch.ca/index.php?context=va&aid=5964.**

31. Ibid.

32. Lester R. Brown, "Is Our Civilization at a Tipping Point?" *Hunger Notes,* World Hunger Education Service. Website: **http://www.world hunger.org/articles/09/editorials/brown_tipping.htm.**

33. ———, *Plan B 3.0: Mobilizing to Save Civilization* (New York: W. W. Norton & Company, 2008).

34. United Nations Department of Economic and Social Affairs, Population Tables. Website: **http://www.un.org/esa/population/ publications/sixbillion/sixbilpart1.pdf.**

35. "Population Growth Rate," *The World Factbook,* Central Intelligence Agency. Website: **https://www.cia.gov/library/publications/the- world-factbook/rankorder/2002rank.html?countryName=Fiji& countryCode=fj&regionCode=au&rank=136.**

36. Joel E. Cohen, "Human Population Grows Up," *Scientific American,* special edition "Crossroads for Planet Earth" (September 2005): p. 48.

37. *Millennium Ecosystem Assessment (MA) Synthesis Report.*

38. Ibid.

Chapter 4

1. Robert M. Schoch, "The Great Sphinx," *The Official Website of Robert M. Schoch.* Website: **http://www.robertschoch.com/sphinxcontent. html.**

2. Ibid.

3. Ibid.

4. Ibid.

5. Ibid.

6. A description of the excavation with images of the site and an interview with lead archaeologist Klaus Schmidt. Sean Thomas, "Gobekli

Tepe: Paradise Regained?" *Fortean Times UK.* Website: http://www.forteantimes.com/features/articles/449/gobekli_tepe_paradise_regained.html.

7. Ibid.

8. Patrick Symmes, "History in the Remaking," *Newsweek* (February 19, 2010). Website: http://www.newsweek.com/2010/02/18/history-in-the-remaking.html.

9. Ibid.

10. Ibid.

11. K. Pustovoytov, K. Schmidt, and H. Parzinger, "Radiocarbon Dating of Thin Pedogenic Carbonate Laminae from Holocene Archaeological Sites," *Holocene,* vol. 19 (December 1, 2009): pp. 1153–1160.

12. Radio Carbon Context Database: Website: http://context-database.uni-koeln.de/c14.php?vonsite=389.

13. Robert M. Schoch, "Turkey," *The Official Website of Robert M. Schoch.* Website: http://www.robertschoch.com/turkey.html.

14. Ibid.

15. Tom Housden, "Lost City 'Could Rewrite History,'" *BBC News* (January 19, 2002). Website: http://news.bbc.co.uk/2/hi/south_asia/1768109.stm.

16. Ibid.

17. Ibid.

18. Ibid.

19. Description and photographic survey of Caral, Peru. Website: http://www.go2peru.com/caral.htm.

20. Michael D. Coe, *Breaking the Maya Code* (New York: Thames & Hudson, 1999): p. 61.

21. Richard L. Thompson, *Mysteries of the Sacred Universe: The Cosmology of the Bhāgavata Purāna* (Alachua, FL: Govardhan Hill Publishing, 2000): p. 225.

22. Albert Einstein, as quoted in an article, "Atomic Education Urged by Einstein," *The New York Times* (May 25, 1946), and later quoted by Michael Amrine, "The Real Problem Is in the Hearts of Man," *The New York Times Magazine* (June 23, 1946).

23. H. G. Wells, *The Outline of History: The Whole Story of Man* (New York: Garden City Books, 1949): Chapter 40.4. Website: **http://www.ibiblio .org/pub/docs/books/sherwood/Wells-Outline/Text/Part-II.htm**.

Chapter 5

1. William Paley, *Natural Theology* (New York: Oxford University Press, 2006). Online discussion of the God-watchmaker analogy: **http:// en.wikipedia.org/wiki/Watchmaker_analogy**.

2. Ibid.

3. Ibid.

4. Richard Dawkins, *The Blind Watchmaker: Why the Evidence Reveals a Universe Without Design* (New York: W. W. Norton & Company, 1986): p. 5. Website: **http://hyperphysics.phy-astr.gsu.edu/nave-html/ faithpathh/dawkins.html**.

5. Lee Thayer, *Pieces: Toward a Revisioning of Communication/Life* (Greenwich, CT: Ablex Publishing Corporation, 1997): p. 62.

6. Ibid.

7. Attributed to Søren Kierkegaard. Website: **http://www.goodreads.com/quotes/show/204183**.

8. "Viking Mission Objectives Summary," National Aeronautics and Space Administration, Planetary Data System. Website: **http://starbrite .jpl.nasa.gov/pds/viewMissionProfile.jsp?MISSION_NAME=VIKING**.

9. "Did Viking Mars Landers Find Life's Building Blocks? Missing Piece Inspires New Look at Puzzle," *Science Daily* (September 25, 2010). Website: **http://www.sciencedaily.com/releases/2010/09/ 100904081050.htm**.

10. Richard E. Dickerson and Irving Geis, *Chemistry, Matter, and the Universe* (Menlo Park, CA: Benjamin Cummings Publishing, 1976): p. 529.

11. Erwin Schrödinger, *What Is Life?: with "Mind and Matter" and "Autobiographical Sketches"* (Cambridge, U.K.: Cambridge University Press, 1992). Website: http://dieoff.org/page150.htm.

12. Daniel E. Koshland, Jr., "The Seven Pillars of Life," *Science,* vol. 295, no. 5563 (March 22, 2002): pp. 2215–2216. Website: http://www.sciencemag.org/content/295/5563/2215.full.

13. Ibid.

14. *Roe v. Wade,* U.S. Supreme Court, Case 410 U.S. 113 (1973). Website: http://www.law.cornell.edu/supct/search/display.html?terms= abortion&url=/supct/html/historics/USSC_CR_0410_0113_ZO.html.

15. Kenneth T. Walsh, "Abortion, Gay Rights Are Back Ahead of 2012 Election," *U.S. News & World Report* (March 10, 2011). Website: http:// www.usnews.com/news/articles/2011/03/10/abortion-gay-rights- are-back-ahead-of-2012-election.

16. Biological criteria for life. *Britannica Online Encyclopedia.* Website: http://www.britannica.com/EBchecked/topic/340003/life.

17. Bruce Lipton, *The Biology of Belief: Unleashing the Power of Consciousness, Matter & Miracles* (Santa Rosa, CA: Mountain of Love/Elite Books, 2005): pp. 67–69.

18. Nadine L. Vastenhouw, Yong Zhang, Ian G. Woods, Farhad Imam, Aviv Regev, X. Shirley Liu, John Rinn, and Alexander F. Schier, "Chromatin Signature of Embryonic Pluripotency Is Established During Genome Activation," *Nature,* vol. 464 (April 8, 2010): pp. 922–926.

19. Ibid.

20. *The Biology of Belief:* pp. 67–69.

21. Elise Kleeman, "When Does a Fetus Feel Pain?" *Discover* (December 2005): Website: http://discovermagazine.com/2005/ dec/fetus-feel-pain.

22. Christof Koch, "When Does Consciousness Arise in Human Babies?" *Scientific American* (September 2, 2009). Website: http://scientificamerican.com/article.cfm?id=when-does- consciousness-arise.

23. Narration for the opening of "The Origin of Species," the last episode of *The Outer Limits,* season 4. Website: **http://homepage.eircom.net/ ~odyssey/Quotes/Popular/SciFi/Outer_Limits.html.**

24. Complete works of Darwin online: **http://darwin-online.org.uk/ contents.html.**

25. *On the Origin of Species:* p. xii.

26. Ibid: p. 246.

27. Notes describing the Miller-Urey experiment. Website: **http://www .chem.duke.edu/~jds/cruise_chem/Exobiology/miller.html.**

28. Compilation of hominid characteristics, including cranial capacity. Website: **http://en.wikipedia.org/wiki/Template:Homo.**

29. *On the Origin of Species:* p. 89.

30. Stephen Jay Gould, *Wonderful Life: The Burgess Shale and the Nature of History* (New York: W. W. Norton & Company, 1989): p. 24.

31. Steven M. Stanley, *Macroevolution: Pattern and Process* (San Francisco: W.M. Freeman and Co., 1979): p. 39.

32. "Explosion of Life," *The Shape of Life,* PBS. Website: **http://www.pbs .org/kcet/shapeoflife/episodes/explosion.html.**

33. *On the Origin of Species:* p. 151.

34. Definition of intelligent design from The Discovery Institute, Center for Science and Culture. Website: **http://www.discovery.org/csc/ topQuestions.php.**

35. *On the Origin of Species:* p. 82.

36. Francis Crick, *Life Itself: Its Origin and Nature* (New York: Simon & Schuster, 1981): p. 88.

37. I. L. Cohen, *Darwin Was Wrong: A Study in Probabilities* (Greenvale, NY: New Research Publications, 1984): pp. 4–5, and 8.

38. James D. Watson, Tania Baker, Stephen P. Bell, Alexander Gann, Michael Levine, and Richard Losick, *Molecular Biology of the Gene* (Menlo Park, CA: W. A. Benjamin, 1977): p. 69.

39. Alice Caprice (ed.), *The Expanded Quotable Einstein* (Princeton, NJ: Princeton University Press, 2000): p. 220.

Chapter 6

1. Attributed to David Samuel "Sam" Peckinpah, American filmmaker and screenwriter. Website: **http://www.quotegarden.com/violence .html.**

2. R. Brian Ferguson, "The Birth of War," *Natural History,* vol. 112, no. 6 (July/August 2003): pp. 28–35.

3. Ibid.

4. Steven Pinker, "Why Is There Peace?" The Greater Good Science Center at the University of California–Berkeley (April 1, 2009). Website: **http://greatergood.berkeley.edu/article/item/why_is_there_peace.**

5. Catherine Philip, "Barack Obama's Peace Prize Starts a Fight," *The Sunday Times* (October 10, 2009): Website: **http://www.timesonline.co.uk/ tol/news/world/us_and_americas/article6868905.ece.**

6. Ibid.

7. "Full Text of Obama's Nobel Peace Prize Speech," White House on **MSNBC.com.** Website: **http://msnbc.msn.com/id/34360743/ns/ politics-white_house.**

8. Ibid.

9. Ibid.

10. "The Birth of War."

11. Ibid.

12. Andrew J. Pierre, "The Cold and the Dark: The World after Nuclear War," *Foreign Affairs* book review (fall 1984). Website: **http://www .foreignaffairs.com/articles/38893/andrew-j-pierre/the-cold-and-the- dark-the-world-after-nuclear-war.**

13. Buckminster Fuller, *The New Yorker* (January 8, 1966). Retrieved from: **http://www.quotationspage.com/quote/24952.html.**

14. Alice Caprice (ed.), *The New Quotable Einstein* (Princeton, NJ: Princeton University Press, 2005): p. 173.

15. Richard Lawrence (trans.), *The Book of Enoch the Prophet* (San Diego: Wizards Bookshelf Secret Doctrine Reference Series, 1983): p. iv.

16. Ibid: pp. iv–v.

17. Ibid: p. 1.

18. Ibid: p. 77.

19. Ibid: p. 9.

20. Ibid: p. 85.

21. Ibid: pp. 47–48.

22. Ibid: p. 47.

23. St. Thomas Aquinas (*Summa Contra Gentiles,* vol. 11), quoted by Arthur O. Lovejoy, *The Great Chain of Being: A Study of the History of an Idea* (Cambridge, MA: Harvard University Press, 1936): p. 76.

24. This quote is cited from Francis Bacon's classic text on human nature, *Of Goodness and Goodness of Nature.* This particular chapter, "Essays, Civil and Moral" (Chapter XIII), is available online as part of the Harvard Classics series (1909–1914). Website: **http://www.bartleby .com/3/1/13.html.**

25. Adapted from the Editor's Introduction, by Richard Lowry, to the third edition of Abraham H. Maslow's *Toward a Psychology of Being* (New York: Wiley, 1999).

26. Ibid.

27. "The Story of SPC Ross A. McGinnis," U.S. Army. Website: **http:// www.army.mil/medalofhonor/mcginnis/profile/index.html.**

28. "Man Risked Life Again and Again to Save His Dogs in House Fire," *For the Love of the Dog Blog* (November 8, 2007). Website: **http://forthe loveofthedogblog.com/news-updates/man-risked-life-again-and-again-to-save-his-dogs-in-house-fire.**

29. Penny Eims, "Man Dies in Fire while Trying to Save His Favorite Dog," *Examiner* (December 26, 2010). Website: **http://www.examiner .com/dogs-in-national/man-dies-fire-while-trying-to-save-his-favorite-dog.**

30. Eric Hobsbawm, "War and Peace in the 20th Century," *London Review of Books* (February 2002). Hobsbawm's statistics show that by the end of the 20th century, over 187 million people had lost their lives to war.

31. Matthew White, "Worldwide Statistics of Casualties, Massacres, Disasters and Atrocities," *The Twentieth Century Atlas*. These particular statistics were taken from a December 20, 1999, press release issued by the Munich Reinsurance Company. Website: **http://users.erols.com/ mwhite28/warstat8.htm**.

32. Jonathan Steele, "The Century that Murdered Peace," *The Guardian* (December 12, 1999). Website: **www.guardian.co.uk/world/1999/ dec/12/theobserver4**.

33. *On the Origin of Species:* p. 133.

34. Adolf Hitler, "Chapter XI: Nation and Race," *Mein Kampf, Volume One: A Reckoning* (1925). Website: **http://www.hitler.org/writings/ Mein_Kampf/mkv1ch11.html**.

35. Stéphane Courtois, Nicolas Werth, Jean-Louis Panné, Andrzej Paczkowski, Karel Bartošek, and Jean-Louis Margolin, *The Black Book of Communism*, translated by Jonathan Murphy and Mark Kramer (Cambridge, MA: Harvard University Press, 1999): p. 491.

36. Charles Darwin, *The Descent of Man* (Amherst, NY: Prometheus Books, 1998): p. 110.

37. Peter Kropotkin, *Mutual Aid: A Factor of Evolution* (1902) (Boston: Porter Sargent Publishers, 1976): p. 14.

38. Dr. John Swomley, "Violence: Competition or Cooperation," *Christian Ethics Today 26,* vol. 6, no. 1 (February 2000): p. 20.

39. Ibid.

40. Ronald Logan, "Opening Address of the Symposium on the Humanistic Aspects of Regional Development," *Prout Journal,* vol. 6, no. 3 (September 1993).

41. Ibid.

42. Attributed to Carl Sandburg, but paraphrased from a poem in German by Bertolt Brecht. Website: **http://ask.metafilter.com/56968/ What-if**.

Chapter 7

1. Kevin H. O'Rourke and Jeffrey G. Williamson, National Bureau of Economic Research Working Paper 7632, "When Did Globalization Begin?" (April 2000). *European Review of Economic History,* vol. 6, no. 1: pp. 23–50. Website: **http://www.nber.org/papers/w7632.**

2. Thomas L. Friedman, "Globalization," *Newsweek* (2010). Website: **http://2010.newsweek.com/top-10/most-overblown-fears/ globalization.html.**

3. Gregory Hale, "No Need to Fear, Globalization Is Here," *InTech* (June 2008). Website: **http://www.isa.org/InTechTemplate.cfm? Section=Talk_To_Me&template=/ContentManagement/ ContentDisplay.cfm&ContentID=69717.**

4. Gregg Braden, *Fractal Time* (Carlsbad, CA: Hay House, 2009): p. 15.

5. "1945–1959: A Peaceful Europe—The Beginnings of Cooperation," *Europa: The History of the European Union.* Website: **http://europa.eu/ abc/history/1945-1959/index_en.htm.**

6. "United Nations Millennium Declaration," adopted by the General Assembly on September 8, 2000. Website: **http://un.org/millennium/ declaration/ares552e.htm.**

7. "2015 Millennium Development Goals," United Nations. Website: **http://www.un.org/millenniumgoals/bkgd.shtml.**

8. "Millennium Development Goal 8, Target 8.A: Develop further an open, rule-based, predictable, non-discriminatory trading and financial system," United Nations. Website: **http://www.un.org/ millenniumgoals/global.shtml.**

9. Spoken by Carlos Barrios. Transcribed by Steve McFadden, "Steep Uphill Climb to 2012: Messages from the Mayan Milieu" (2002). Website: **www.redrat.net/thoughts/prophets/index.htm.**

10. President Ronald Reagan, "First Inaugural Address," Tuesday, January 20, 1981. Video and transcripts at the Miller Center of Public Affairs, University of Virginia. Website: **http://millercenter.org/scripps/ archive/speeches/detail/3407.**

11. Attributed to William Jennings Bryan. Website: **http://schipul.com/ quotes/1051.**

12. *Fractal Time:* p. 9.

13. Post on the *Singletrack* magazine forum that includes the story of Aron Ralston in his own words. Website: **http://www.singletrackworld .com/forum/topic/great-article-about-the-utah-guy-who-severed-his- own-arm-today**.

14. Ibid.

15. *Fractal Time:* pp. 193–198.

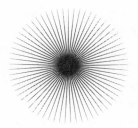

ACKNOWLEDGMENTS

Deep Truth is a synthesis of research, discoveries, and my personal journey to answer some of the deepest questions of our existence. Over the course of my adult life, and even before, many people have crossed my path and provided the bridge of experience that led to the powerful, and empowering, message of this book. While it would take an entire volume to name everyone individually, these pages are my opportunity to express my thanks to those whose efforts have directly contributed to making this book possible. I am especially grateful to:

Every one of the really great people at Hay House, Inc. I offer my sincere appreciation and many thanks to Louise Hay and Reid Tracy for your vision and dedication to the truly extraordinary way of doing business that has become the hallmark of Hay House's success. To Reid Tracy, President and CEO, I send my deepest gratitude for your support and unwavering faith in me, and my work. To Jill Kramer, Editorial Director, many, many thanks for your honest opinions and guidance, for always being there when I call, and for the years of experience that you bring to each of our conversations.

Carina Sammartino, my publicist; Alex Freemon, my project editor; Jacqui Clark, Publicity Director; John Thompson, Sales Director; Margarete Nielsen, COO; Nancy Levin, Events Director; and Rocky George, the perfect audio engineer—I could not ask for a nicer group of people to work with, or more dedicated team to support my work. Your excitement and professionalism are unsurpassed, and I'm proud to be a part of all the good things that the Hay House family brings to our world.

Ned Leavitt, my literary agent. Many thanks for the wisdom and integrity that you bring to each milestone we cross together. Through your guidance in shepherding our books through the ever-changing world of publishing, we have reached more people on Earth in more countries than ever with our empowering message of hope and possibility. While I deeply appreciate your impeccable guidance, I am especially grateful for our friendship and your trust in me.

Stephanie Gunning, my hardworking editor extraordinaire and now, my friend. Many thanks for your dedication and skill, and the energy that you embody in all that you do. Most of all, thank you for helping me to take the complexities of science and the truths of life and find the words to share them in a joyous and meaningful way. I am amazed at how you always ask just the right questions, in just the right way, to lead me to the clearest choices.

I am proud to be part of the virtual team, and the family, that has grown around the support of my work over the years, including Lauri Willmot, my favorite (and only) office manager since 1996. You have had, and continue to have, my admiration, deep respect, and countless thanks for being there always, and especially when it counts. Thank you for representing me in a way that honors the blessings we've been given. To Robin and Jerry Miner of Source Books, many thanks for your friendship, love, and support, and for sticking with us over the years through good times and others. To Rita Curtis, my business manager extraordinaire, I deeply appreciate your vision for our future, your ability to get us from here to there, and most of all, your friendship.

To my mother, Sylvia; and my brother, Eric. Thank you for your unfailing love and for believing in me. Though our family by blood is small, together we have found that our extended family of love is greater than we have ever imagined. My gratitude for all that you bring to each day of my life extends beyond any words that I could possibly write upon this page. Eric, audio/visual engineer and technical guru extraordinaire, a very special "thank-you" for your patience with the many, varied, and often challenging venues that we find ourselves working in. While I am proud to share our work together, I am especially proud to be your brother in life.

To the one person who sees me at my very best, and my very worst, my fiancée, Martha: Knowing that your deep love; your lasting friendship; and your exquisite, gentle wisdom is with me every day is the constant that I count on to get me through. You, and the furry beings that we share our lives with, Woody and Nemo, are the family that makes each journey worth coming home to. I'm in deep gratitude to you for all that you give, all that you share, and all that you bring to me and my life.

A very special thanks to everyone who has supported my work, books, recordings, and live presentations over the years. I am honored by your trust, in awe of your vision for a better world, and deeply appreciative of your passion to bring that world into existence. Through your presence, I have learned to become a better listener, and hear the words that allow me to share our empowering message of hope and possibility. To all, I remain grateful in all ways, always.

ABOUT THE AUTHOR

New York Times best-selling author **Gregg Braden** is internationally renowned as a pioneer in bridging science and spirituality. Following a successful career as a computer geologist for Phillips Petroleum during the 1970s energy crisis, he worked as a senior computer systems designer with Martin Marietta Defense Systems during the final years of the Cold War. In 1991, he became the first technical operations manager for Cisco Systems, where he led the development of the global support team that ensures the reliability of today's Internet.

For more than 25 years, Gregg has searched high mountain villages, remote monasteries, and forgotten texts to uncover their timeless secrets. His work has been featured on The History Channel, The Discovery Channel, The SyFy Channel, ABC, and NBC.

To date, Gregg's discoveries have led to such paradigm-shattering books as *The Isaiah Effect, The God Code, Secrets of the Lost Mode of Prayer, The Divine Matrix,* and *Fractal Time.* Today, his work is published in 17 languages and 33 countries, and shows us beyond any reasonable doubt that the key to our future lies in the wisdom of our past.

For further information, please contact Gregg's office at:

Wisdom Traditions
P.O. Box 3529
Taos, New Mexico 87571
(561) 799-9337
Website: **www.greggbraden.com**
E-mail: info@greggbraden.com

•NOTES•

✷NOTES✷

•NOTES•

•NOTES•

Hay House Titles of Related Interest

YOU CAN HEAL YOUR LIFE, *the movie*,
starring Louise L. Hay & Friends
(available as a 1-DVD program and an expanded 2-DVD set)
Watch the trailer at: **www.LouiseHayMovie.com**

THE SHIFT, *the movie*,
starring Dr. Wayne W. Dyer
(available as a 1-DVD program and an expanded 2-DVD set)
Watch the trailer at: **www.DyerMovie.com**

✹ ✹ ✹

CHOICE POINT: Align Your Purpose,
by Harry Massey & David R. Hamilton, Ph.D.

*GREEN MADE EASY: The Everyday Guide for
Transitioning to a Green Lifestyle*, by Chris Prelitz

*THE HIDDEN POWER OF YOUR PAST LIVES:
Revealing Your Encoded Consciousness*, by Sandra Anne Taylor

*THE MOTHER OF INVENTION: The Legacy of Barbara Marx
Hubbard and the Future of YOU*, by Neale Donald Walsch

*THE POWER OF SELF-HEALING: Unlock Your Natural
Healing Potential in 21 Days*, by Dr. Fabrizio Mancini

THE SECRET OF QUANTUM LIVING, by Dr. Frank J. Kinslow

*WHOLELINESS: Embracing the Sacred Unity That
Heals Our World*, by Carmen Harra, Ph.D.

All of the above are available at your local bookstore,
or may be ordered by contacting Hay House (see next page).

✹ ✹ ✹

We hope you enjoyed this Hay House book. If you'd like to receive our online catalog featuring additional information on Hay House books and products, or if you'd like to find out more about the Hay Foundation, please contact:

Hay House, Inc., P.O. Box 5100, Carlsbad, CA 92018-5100
(760) 431-7695 or (800) 654-5126
(760) 431-6948 (fax) or (800) 650-5115 (fax)
www.hayhouse.com® • **www.hayfoundation.org**

✹ ✹ ✹

Published and distributed in Australia by:
Hay House Australia Pty. Ltd., 18/36 Ralph St., Alexandria NSW 2015
Phone: 612-9669-4299 • *Fax:* 612-9669-4144 • www.hayhouse.com.au

Published and distributed in the United Kingdom by:
Hay House UK, Ltd., 292B Kensal Rd., London W10 5BE
Phone: 44-20-8962-1230 • *Fax:* 44-20-8962-1239 • www.hayhouse.co.uk

Published and distributed in the Republic of South Africa by:
Hay House SA (Pty), Ltd., P.O. Box 990, Witkoppen 2068
Phone/Fax: 27-11-467-8904 • www.hayhouse.co.za

Published in India by: Hay House Publishers India, Muskaan Complex,
Plot No. 3, B-2, Vasant Kunj, New Delhi 110 070
Phone: 91-11-4176-1620 • *Fax:* 91-11-4176-1630 • www.hayhouse.co.in

Distributed in Canada by:
Raincoast, 9050 Shaughnessy St., Vancouver, B.C. V6P 6E5
Phone: (604) 323-7100 • *Fax:* (604) 323-2600 • www.raincoast.com

✹ ✹ ✹

Take Your Soul on a Vacation

Visit **www.HealYourLife.com®** to regroup, recharge,
and reconnect with your own magnificence.
Featuring blogs, mind-body-spirit news, and life-changing
wisdom from Louise Hay and friends.

Visit **www.HealYourLife.com** today!